# The Servant in
# German Enlightenment Comedy

# The Servant in
# German Enlightenment Comedy

Alison Scott-Prelorentzos

 The University of Alberta Press

Published by
The University of Alberta Press
450 Athabasca Hall
Edmonton, Alberta, Canada
Canada T6G 2E8

ISBN 0–88864–026–9

**Canadian Cataloguing in Publication Data**

Scott-Prelorentzos, Alison, 1930–
    The servant in German enlightenment comedy


    Bibliography: p.
    Includes index.
    ISBN 0–88864–026–9

    1. German drama — 18th century — History and
criticism.    2. German drama (Comedy) — History
and criticism.    3. Servants in literature.
I. Title.
PT643.S38        832'.509'35264        C81-091360-7

Typesetting by The Typeworks
Mayne Island, British Columbia


Printed by D.W. Friesen & Sons Ltd.
Altona, Manitoba

For
Margie, Shirley, Joanna,
Naomi, David, and Emma

# CONTENTS

# FOREWORD

I have read this work in manuscript and can assure the reader that the treatment of the subject is thorough, fully documented, and always sensitive to questions of human values. The subject itself is clearly defined and its scope delimited in the Preface. I do not mean to suggest that this is a narrow, highly specialized study, aimed at an audience of professionals only. On the contrary, I find that the author gives abundant proof that she has developed what T.S. Eliot called "the historical sense" in his essay "Tradition and the Individual Talent":

> The historical sense involves a perception, not only of the pastness of the past, but of its presence; the historical sense compels a man to write not merely with his own generation in his bones, but with a feeling that the whole of the literature of Europe from Homer and within it the whole of the literature of his own country has a simultaneous existence and composes a simultaneous order. . . .

I believe that what Eliot says here of creative writers is also valid for scholars.

Eliot also said once of a particular study that "it will be definitive for a while." My prediction is that the present work will be definitive for a long time. That the style is lively and without jargon, which makes it pleasant reading, will help.

E. J. H. Greene

# PREFACE

There must always be a master and servants in all civilised
communities, my lady, for it is natural, and whatever is
natural is right. —James Barrie, *The Admirable Crichton*[1]

The master-servant relationship, W.H. Auden says, is the only one that
satisfies all conditions of the "inner dialogue of the human personality,"[2]
being a contractual agreement between real persons, an asymmetric
double sovereignty, with each contributing different qualities. Elisabeth
Frenzel, with an echo of Voltaire's comment on the deity, declares: "Die
Literatur hätte die Dienerrolle erfunden, wenn sie über keine reale hätte
verfügen können."[3] Auden and Frenzel are speaking of literature in
general, but in drama especially, servants have played a significant role.
In comedy, the most widespread and numerically dominant of theatrical
forms,[4] they come into their own. To the comic sphere belongs their reflection of or contrast to their masters, to the comic sphere above all the
motif of reversal of roles, which is never far from the surface, whereby
the servant becomes more than he seems, the master less. As *meneur de
jeu*, the servant is the *de facto* master, wiser and cleverer than his em-

ployer.[5] Whereas the young mistress reflects the social norm in being subordinate to parent or guardian and usually passive as compared to her suitor, in the servant pair the female generally dominates.

This study focusses mainly on the servant in German Enlightenment comedy from the 1730s to the 1760s. Paradoxically, though the writers in this period set out to forge a new literary comedy, in taste and style a marked contrast to the popular improvised theatre of the previous century, they retained willy-nilly its basic constellation of *dramatis personae,* as well as a repertoire of certain clearly delineated character types.[6] Although they are no longer purely comic, the servants are still assured a place, not so much because their existence is "natural," as butler Crichton maintains, but because it is traditional. The world of Enlightenment comedy is a world turned in on itself, a bourgeois household represented on the stage as a rule by a handful of figures, distributed according to a clear pattern. E.J.H. Greene has shown that the plots of seventy-one percent of French comedies in the century from 1660 to 1760 (including all those printed and those whose contents are known) conform to this formula: "les amours spontanées des Jeunes, contrariées par les Vieux, sont favorisées par les Valets."[7] This triadic structure is to be found also in most German literary comedies for two-thirds of the eighteenth century. The young people need someone to speak to them and for them,[8] and in this double function of confidant(e)/champion, the personal servants, now crystallized into the stock figures of valet and maid, not only have their firm place, but actually become a particular characteristic of Enlightenment comedy. One of the most striking differences between the comedy of our own day or even of the nineteenth century and that of the eighteenth may be found by looking no further than the list of *dramatis personae* between title-page and first scene: only occasionally and incidentally will a servant figure in the traditional sense be listed there today, whereas one might have difficulty in naming ten German comedies written between 1700 and 1770 in which there is no servant at all.

The servants represent the most frequently portrayed profession, which is subject to a peculiar condition—they would lose their raison d'être if they were not seen in relationship to their masters and mistresses. Studies might be done of the father figures in these comedies, for instance, or the clergymen, or the young daughters, with but peripheral attention to their servants. The servants themselves owe their existence to their connection with other figures, in support or in opposition. A master, being a bourgeois comic figure, can stand alone, but a servant without a master is a contradiction in terms. We never see servants in their own environment below stairs, in servants' hall or kitchen, but always in the realm of their betters, in antechamber, study, or sitting-room.

This, then, is the limited period and the particular context in which the servants will be viewed. Tempting as it would be to stretch the definition of servant — and of comedy — to include, for instance, Mephistopheles (as Auden can), such figures lie outside our range of vision. Originally undertaken to fill a gap in *Aufklärung* studies, this book first took shape in 1972 when I was a member of the examining committee for an excellent French literature thesis that showed how the change in the aims and tone of comedy in mid-eighteenth-century France is reflected in the evolution of the valet. At the same time, I was reading a book on J.E. Schlegel that hardly mentions his servants.[9] Until comparatively recently, German Enlightenment comedy was a rather neglected field, but in the last two decades several interesting studies have appeared. Some of these devote space to the servants, particularly those by Diethelm Brüggemann and Michael M. Metzger, which focus on the language of the plays.[10] In Walter Hinck's detailed account of the influence of the Italian popular theatre on the German comedy,[11] there is enough discussion of the servants to make a fair-sized book in itself and any study of the subject must be indebted to Hinck for insights into both general historical development and individual plays; however, his is, by the nature of his topic, a particular perspective. Before 1979 there was no book-length account of the servants themselves, not even of Lessing's (though early in that year Robert Rentschler's lively article on the maid-servant in Lessing's early comedies appeared),[12] but since then this neglect has been amended by the appearance of Rüdiger van den Boom's monograph, *Die Bedienten und das Herr-Diener Verhältnis in der deutschen Komödie der Aufklärung (1742–1767).*[13] This unfortunately came into my hands after my own manuscript was completed and under consideration by a granting agency and publisher, and thus its findings could not be taken into account in the body of my text. Van den Boom, keeping in mind the broad issues raised by Hegel's notion of "Herrschaft und Knecht-schaft," and proceeding thematically rather than chronologically, focus-ses on the interplay of inequality, superiority, and equality in the master-servant relationship itself, extending his discussion to a consideration of how far the stage relationship reflects that in real life.

The aim of this book is to present the servants in chronological per-spective as a contribution to the literary history of the period. In general terms, the changes in the conception of comedy, both at the beginning of the *Aufklärung* and during its course, are noted, but no systematic account either of *Aufklärung* comedy or of *Aufklärung* comic theory[14] is attempted. This is not a comprehensive survey of the servant figures on the German stage, for some texts were difficult to trace, and in any case, among the quite extraordinarily large number of plays performed at that time,[15] very many were translations or adaptations of foreign works. Discussion thus concentrates on the servants in the main original literary comedies of the period, and particularly on full-length plays, with men-tion of only a few of the many one-act comedies produced as *Vor-* or *Nachspiele*. The study traces the fortunes of valet and maid as dramatic figures, analysing their function within the plays and noting mutations in their characteristics, and commenting perforce on the relationship of master or mistress and servant.

A sociological approach is deliberately avoided, first as irrelevant to the overall purpose and second as dangerous ground when one is dealing with figures so firmly rooted in literary tradition. It is true that one has only to compare topics discussed in the moral weeklies and the popular moral philosophies with those treated by the comedists to conclude that the latter aimed to deal with real questions arising from the manners and morals of the age. But their means were often artificial situations and stereotype characters; realism in the modern sense was not part of their purpose. In fact, in the depiction of the servants there is a strong sense of *mundus inversus*. It would thus be as simplistic to interpret their often privileged status and influence in the stage household as more than a theatrical convention, as to assume that in those cases where they are exploited and abused (the seduction of Cathrine in Krüger's *Die Geist-lichen auf dem Lande,* for instance), the playwright is primarily using them for topical social comment.[16] The domestics belong to the lower class, but this is a minor consideration for the authors. Significantly, Gellert's *Das Loos in der Lotterie,* which brings in II, 6 a strong plea for better treatment of servants, introduces none as characters. To see a direct reflection of contemporary society in plays where servants *are* depicted is fraught with danger. No doubt servants in real life often did have their ears boxed by their masters, but if this happens, or is threatened, in the comedy, it is more the continuation of a tradition than a comment on social conditions, an element that the audience has come to expect rather than a deliberate imitation of life. (And unlike the real servant, the comic actor was paid extra for the blow!) In the nineteenth century, servants are still as much a part of middle-class households as in the eighteenth, but in the comedy they are in general reduced to insignificance. This might reflect the age's greater informality in family life, the more intimate relationship of parents and children, but the prime cause is more likely that a long literary tradition has played itself out.

A chronological study of the servants in *Aufklärung* comedy—indeed, of *Aufklärung* comedy itself—must end with both a bang and a whimper: a high point is reached with Lessing's *Minna von Barnhelm,* but at the same time one is uneasily aware that the comic spirit is fading. As Eckehard Catholy points out, we often tend to consider as great comedies those examples we view from the same perspective as "drama" or tragedy, whereas in its essentials comedy is not a closed form, but an open celebration of laughter for its own sake, actively involving the audience.[17] To discuss the *Aufklärung* valet and soubrette, descendants of the capering *lustige Personen* of the popular stage of many centuries, is ultimately to outline the beginning of the process whereby modern comedy acquired literary respectability at the expense of pure fun.

# ACKNOWLEDGEMENTS

I should like to express my appreciation to my friend and colleague Dr. E.J.H. Greene for his quiet encouragement of my work on this topic over some years and for the stimulus I have derived from his own research; my interest in the German comic servants coincides with some aspects of his much more broadly based study of European comedy. His book *Menander to Marivaux: The History of a Comic Structure,* which I was able to read in manuscript, provided many helpful insights. My thanks go to Dr. Eckehard Catholy for several useful suggestions, which I have incorporated into my text. Practical aid with such chores as blocking plays, bibliographical searches, and checking quotations was given over several academic sessions by a series of part-time graduate service assistants at the University of Alberta, and my thanks are due particularly to Miss Latha Tampi for her painstaking and intelligent help while the book was being cast in its final draft and amended, and to Mr. John Ellis for his meticulous aid when it was being prepared for the press. Dr. Hans Runte kindly verified a couple of points for me in the Bibliothèque Nationale in Paris. Finally, I am grateful to Mrs. Norma Gutteridge, Ms. Sylvia Vance, and Mrs. Katherine Koller Wensel of The University of Alberta Press for guidance on improving the manuscript and preparing it for publication.

Among several German librarians who patiently answered my inquiries about rare texts, I should like especially to thank Dr. J. Stoltzenburg, Library Director at the University of Konstanz, for helpful information. I am indebted to the Harvard University Library for photocopies of J.C. Krüger's works, to the British Library for microfilms of plays by G. Fuchs, C. Mylius, and C.F. Henrici, and to the Herzog August Bibliothek, Wolfenbüttel, for comedies by A.G. Uhlich and C.F. Weiße, also on microfilm.

My text includes, mainly in Chapters III, IV and V, parts of an article published in *Seminar*[1] and reprinted now with the permission of the editor, and uses in Chapters III and IV respectively parts of papers read to the Canadian Society for Eighteenth Century Studies, University of Laval, March 1975 ("The Servant in German Comedy between 1735 and 1748") and to the Lessing Society workshop held during the conference of the American Society for Eighteenth Century Studies, University of Victoria, May 1977 ("Lessing's Lisettes").

I should like to thank the Germanisches Nationalmuseum, Nürnberg, and Insel-Verlag, Leipzig, for kind permission to reproduce illustrations. I should also like to express my appreciation of the help of Mr. Dieter Fratzke and the Lessing museum, Kamenz, in tracing and obtaining material.

This book has been published with the help of a grant from the Canadian Federation for the Humanities, using funds provided by the Social Sciences and Humanities Research Council of Canada.

To my husband, Salvos, a citizen of the land where European comedy began, my thanks for his loving support.

Alison Scott-Prelorentzos

# NOTE ON TRANSLATIONS

My own translations for block quotations in German are given at the end of the book. Short German quotations within the text and those in the Notes are not translated.

Plays are cited according to act, scene, and page numbers (scene and page numbers only for one-act plays), except for Lessing's *Nathan der Weise*, where references for act, scene, and verse are given. Acts are in roman numerals, while scene and page numbers are arabic.

# I

## The Ancestors of Enlightenment Comedy

### Weise, Reuter, Henrici, and König

In the seventeenth century the *lustige Person* enjoys his heyday. He is the spirit of laughter, the embodiment of the comic for its own sake. His name and immediate ancestry vary: Harlequin of the *commedia dell'arte;* Pickelhering from the English theatre (Italian troupes had been touring Germany, particularly the south, since 1568, and the *Englische Comödianten* entered northern Germany in 1585);[1] Hans Wurst of Austrian extraction; and the clown types in the German tradition going back to Hans Sachs and beyond.[2] These are only some of the main lines of his pedigree. In fact, his origins are much older, for the comic peasant or servant is the most constant figure in the European theatre, and in a broad context we can view him in the seventeenth century as a descendant of the slaves of Greek and Roman comedy. His comic effects are but tenuously linked to plot;[3] his humour is coarse and physical; his main occupations are eating, drinking, and love-making; and his forte is extemporizing. He appears not only in farce or comedy, but also in the serious drama, the *Haupt- und Staatsaktionen.* He assumes various guises and fulfils many different functions in particular plays; Harlequin, especially, often serves a young master and helps thwart an old one,[4] and has a female counterpart in Colombina. But the *lustige Person* is a neutral, non-specific figure, for he is basically always the same, and his audience expects to recognize him immediately whatever his temporary role. Just as he stands for the spectator outside normal judgement on human behaviour, being characterized by what Hinck calls "moralische Indifferenz,"[5] he is separate from the rest of the cast, hovering on the edge or front of the stage, an intermediary between stage action and audience, "der Schauspieler schlechthin."[6]

Our study begins when there is an attempt to integrate this figure into the action in particular plays and make him a specific part of the constellation of characters. In this way, writers of comedy endeavoured to give a definite shape to their works, which even then may seem still quite loosely constructed to a taste bred on eighteenth- and nineteenth-century examples. Comedy was moving away from the formlessness and improvisation of the seventeenth century toward the literary comic genre proper.

Practically all commentators on Christian Weise (1642–1708) point to his attempts at integrating the traditional clown figure,[7] and place him at an interim stage between Baroque and Enlightenment, describing his plays as a mixture of the aims and characteristics of these two periods. Weise unites the influences both of the popular *Wanderbühnen* and the new literary theatre of, for instance, Molière.[8] In addition, Weise is a special case. As headmaster in Zittau, with its strong tradition of student dramatics, he was writing plays (some sixty in number) between 1679 and 1705 for the annual three-day, three-play festival. After a biblical drama and a historical play the last slot was usually filled by a freely invented comedy; this last contribution concerns us, and we must see these plays as conditioned by circumstance. They were broadly conceived and contained a great many characters, since parts had to be found for a large number of boys. Normally performed only once, they were rarely produced elsewhere in a normal theatrical setting, and hardly ever revived in later years, although one or two were still read in the early eighteenth century: *Bäuerischer Machiavellus,* 1679, for instance, had several reprintings up to 1725.

Nevertheless, Weise's work belongs to the development of literary comedy and is not simply part of the sub-genre of the *Schuldrama.* This is because, in the middle of his "galantes Zeitalter," as Lessing later put it,[9] Weise uses realistic prose, representing a refinement and purification of style in the midst of *Barockschwulst.* The lower bourgeoisie becomes the real centre of interest (for instance, the small-town politics of Querle-quitsch in *Bäuerischer Machiavellus*), though other social levels are represented. He introduces comic figures who, while exhibiting clear traits of Harlequin and Pickelhering, are integrated into the action, such as Mierten in *Ein wunderliches Schauspiel vom niederländischen Bauer,* 1685.[10] In *Bäuerischer Machiavellus,* the plot on the earthly, non-allegorical level revolves around filling the vacant post of Pickelhering and the petty in-trigues and manipulations that surround the three contenders for the job:[11] the *lustige Person* is thus presented clearly as a deliberately assumed role. In addition, partly perhaps because of the need to write a large number of parts, Weise distributes the comic function among several characters. In the *Schauspiel vom niederländischen Bauer,* these exist on three levels: the court servants, the village servants (Lars, the innkeeper's man, and Lauxson, servant to a brandy-distiller—both rough and rude), and those in the play-within-the-play, a *Singspiel.* In the latter, the func-tion of Fatuum, "ein lustiger Bedienter" (Latin *fatuus,* meaning stupid), is not only to poke fun at his near-namesake, the divine messenger Fatum (Latin *fatum,* meaning fate or prediction), but also to attempt to thwart Fatum's efforts on the gods' behalf to bring about the union of Amandus and Burgundia: here we have, atypically, a servant in opposi-tion to the young lovers. Of course, Fatuum fails miserably.

To some extent, however, Weise's converted clown figures repre-sent common sense, down-to-earth realism, and average opinion in a lower middle-class setting. In this sense—though we must not exagger-ate the similarity—they anticipate the servants of the Saxon comedy under Gottsched. Weise's realism in general has a basis of ambivalence. His moral is often founded on criticism of the peasants and small-town characters. He seems to be saying that, on an allegorical level, they repre-sent the peasant in all men and the lowest, roughest human characteristics (although it is possible to read some criticism of the aristocracy between the lines of the *Schauspiel vom niederländischen Bauer*).

Yet, his village scenes are his best, full of life, with crude but articulate characters, beside whom his stilted nobles and allegorical figures make a poor showing.

Certainly Weise thought of his plays as having a practical usefulness for both the young players and the audience, in teaching about the real "political" world beyond the theatre. This view also informed much of the theoretical writing on the comedy at the end of the seventeenth century and the beginning of the eighteenth, as Werner Rieck has shown.[12] Weise by no means leads his plays to a clear moral conclusion in the Gottschedian sense, for he often leaves us with the picture of a world where order and reason do not prevail. But at least a moralizing tendency is present, foreshadowing the later period.[13]

The plays of Christian Reuter (1665–ca. 1712) also present something of a special case, in that his major comedies (probably never actually performed) are satires derived very directly from personal experience. Satires on particular people and a particular place — Reuter's landlady and her family, and Leipzig — reflect the pretentiousness of the petty bourgeoisie and the tension between town and gown. Like Weise's comedies, these prose depictions of the bourgeois milieu are realistic, with perhaps a more skilful development of individual characters than Weise's, though the plots are rather weak. Harlequin in person, along with Lisette,[14] makes an appearance in the two brief sketches, *Des Harlequins Hochzeit-Schmauß* and *Des Harlequins Kindbetterin-Schmauß*, appended by Reuter to his first *Schlampampiade* (though he is not their author), and in the two longer original plays there are several servants. In *L'honnête femme oder die Ehrliche Frau zu Plissine*, 1695 (with its echoes of Molière's *Les Précieuses Ridicules* on a much cruder level?), we meet Laux, "ein lustiger Bothe aus Hamburg" (who nevertheless speaks Saxon dialect!);[15] Servillo, "ein Weinschenken-Junge"; and Ursille, a cook at the beck and call of Schlampampe, the "honest woman." Laux reveals his ancestry, the *lustige Person,* for his link with the main story-line is tenuous. He brings a message to the inn, but his main role consists of two solo scenes. In the first of these, I, 9, his comments on himself and his profession are intended for pure comic effect and only peripherally address the situation at hand:

... ja es gläubts wohl einen kein Mensche wie sauer es uns armen Bothen wird/und der Verdienst ist sehre sehre schlecht/ich bin nun in acht Tagen bald ein 50. Meilen gelauffen/daß ich Blasen an den Fußsohlen habe wie Hüner Eyer groß/und wenn ich ein klein bißgen starck zehre/so ist das Bothenlohn/was ich in acht Tagen verdiene/in einen Tage durch die Gurgel gejagt/ ja wenn die Kräffte nichts wegnehmen? was hilffts wir können nicht alle Edelleute seyn. (I, 9, 23)[16]

The main source of comedy in the first Schlampampe play is Schlampampe herself,[17] who has the major part; the three servants have quite small roles. But in the sequel, *La Maladie et la Mort de l'honnête femme, das ist: Der Ehrlichen Frau Schlampampe Krankheit und Tod,* 1696, the landlady is more talked about than giving tongue herself and the two servants have large parts. Lorentz, "Schlampampe lustiger Hausknecht," appears and speaks most frequently in the play, followed by Schnürtzgen, the maid (the gossip Camille appears as often as Schnürtzgen, but does not have as large a speaking part). Moreover, Lorentz is firmly integrated into the household, though he too shows his derivation from the stock figure. When he is sent to the doctor with a specimen of Schlampampe's urine, and drops the bottle and substitutes his own sample, the author exploits a motif connected with the clown from the *Fastnachtspiele* of the sixteenth century onward. Just as Weise's comic figures sometimes extemporize, so Reuter's occasionally speak directly to the audience. Nevertheless, Lorentz and Schnürtzgen are very much part of the plot, abreast of the latest happenings. Their scenes together are not only comic, but also provide commentaries on events and fill in details. Schnürtzgen's role is a more subordinate one—she carries messages and so on—but Lorentz has an important function in that he relates the latest excesses of Schlampampe's family to the "discreet" cousin Camille, thus ensuring that each detail will soon be the talk of the town. Schnürtzgen and Lorentz end the play in III, 21 with a brief dialogue after the other characters have exited. Lorentz speaks the closing words, slipping out of his specific role in what may strike us today as almost Brechtian fashion (though Reuter is in fact following a time-honoured tradition), to become the comic actor mediating between stage and audience:

Weil demnach sanffte ruht die ehrliche Schlampampe/
So geht ihr Leute nur fein wiederum zu Hauß/
Und wenn der Tod auslescht uns unsre Lebenslampe/
Hernach ists mit uns auch/wie dieses Schauspiel/aus.

(III, 21, 172)

At the same time as Weise and Reuter were writing, literary comedy was enjoying a golden age in France, largely owing to the works and influence of Molière:

Comedy had been developed more slowly than tragedy, but it had now reached a stage much in advance of the Latin plays, which had hitherto been almost the only classical examples available to dramatists who did not want to follow the medieval farces. Terence and Plautus had enjoyed an influence in Renaissance Europe far in advance of their true worth. But Molière had now shown how comedy could be at the same time dramatic and satirical, and how it could hold up twin mirrors, to character and to manners.[18]

Molière and his successors and the Parisian Italian theatre integrated the humble comic figure into cast and plot as personal servant, producing new stock figures of valet and soubrette. When, some decades later, in J.E. Schlegel's *Demokritus, ein Todtengespräch,* 1741, Regnard (1655–1709) is asked why in his play Demokritus takes his servant Strabo into exile with him, he replies,

... es [ist] nicht Gebrauch bey uns..., einen Herren aufzuführen, der keinen Diener hätte; weil uns allzuviel Gelegenheit aus den Händen gienge, lustige Dinge zu sagen.[19]

The servants became a firm part of the household and the family, acquiring gaiety and wit and developing a lighter touch and, while they clearly belonged to the lower social orders, they showed a bourgeois tinge. By the turn of the century in France, a conventional role for comic servants had been established, representing a fusion of French and Italian elements. This influenced the new beginnings of comedy in Germany:

> ... die entscheidenden Konsequenzen jener Überlieferung der Commedia dell'arte werden auch für das deutsche Lustspiel wirksam: die Durchsetzung des reinen Intrigen-, Überraschungs – und Verwechslungsspiels mit satirischen Elementen, mit den Intentionen einer Stände und Sitten-, Mode (Frauen)- und Aktualitätssatire.[20]

Published collections of the plays performed by the *Wanderbühnen* in Germany up to 1670 contained only English or Dutch pieces, but the *Schaubühne Englischer und Französischer Comödianten*, 1670, printed some Molière comedies, and there were several translations of many of his plays into German between 1694 and 1721.[21] The plays of the Italian theatre in Paris became known in Germany as elsewhere through Gherardi's *Théâtre Italien*, 1700, used by troupes and quite widely read (as was later the *Théâtre de la Foire ou l'Opéra Comique*, 1721-37).

The Saxon comedy proper did not begin until the 1730s, after Gottsched's heavy theoretical spadework in the *Critische Dichtkunst*, 1730, but discussion on how to revitalize and purify German literature was evident in the moral weeklies of the 1720s, which were already looking at literature from the point of view of its social role and moral effect. In this decade there were two comedy writers of interest, C.F. Henrici, whose pseudonym was Picander, and J.U. König, both writing in Saxony and both acquainted with Molière and the *Théâtre Italien*. Like Weise and Reuter a generation earlier, they represented a mixture of the old and the new.[22] Both were clearly aware of the need for reform. At the same time, both were influenced on the literary level by the French, or French-Italian comedy to the west, and on a practical level from the south by the many Italian troupes touring Germany. At the beginning of the century Dresden and Leipzig had been centres for the Italian theatre.[23] In very general terms, the aims of König and Picander were new, but their means largely old, rooted in the traditional improvised comedy, the realm of Harlequin and Pickelhering.

Picander (1700–1764), himself an interesting mixture, being both the author of texts for J.S. Bach (the *Matthäuspassion,* for instance) and the creator of extremely vulgar and crude comedies, seems at times to approach later Gottschedian principles. In his prefaces, he clearly aims at some sort of reform of the genre, but believes that this reform should be carried out on a farcical level.[24] His plays borrow directly from Gherardi, and the characteristics of the *Stegreifkomödie* are evident: beatings, night scenes, mistaken identity, and so on.[25] The farcical element emerges from his copious stage directions; as Brüggemann shows, Picander leaves "einen ziemlich großen sprachfreien Spielraum" for the *lazzi* of Harlekin and Peter in *Der akademische Schlendrian* in particular.[26] Comedy here does not derive from character. The *Vorbericht an den Leser* of the 1726 edition of his plays explains that Picander wants to concentrate on criticizing human foibles in a lively way, and like Reuter, he singles out Leipzig society, with much personally observed detail:

> Eine Comödie und ein Stachel-Gedichte sind Kinder einerley Mütter. Wen beyde die Laster in einer lebhafften Farbe und heßlichen Kleidung nicht vorstellen, so sind sie von ebenso kahlen Geschmack, wie ungelsalzene Heringe. (2ᵛ) [27]

But it is equally manifest that his purpose is not a strictly moralizing one in the way in which Gottsched will understand the matter:

> ... also muß auch ein Moraliste..., seine beißenden Pillen mit lachendem Munde vorhalten, und mit angenehmen Scherze einreden. Dahero ist die lustige Person in einer Comödie unentbehrlich, weil die satyrischen Wahrheiten dadurch nicht so trocken, auch nicht zu empfindlich werden. (3–3ᵛ)

The consequences for the servant figure are obvious. In *Der akademische Schlendrian,* 1725, Harlequin, Ließgen, and Peter are amoral types, and Harlequin, "der Diener," has still much of the clown in his make-up:[28] he is both superior and inferior, indispensable to his master, Galanthomme, to whom he speaks as an equal, yet blamed immediately when things go wrong, and in the end, always a loser. In the first scene he delivers himself of a severe commentary on Galanthomme's character and their precarious situation (I, 1, 2), but almost at once is ready to support his profligate employer in a new dubious enterprise, the courtship of Frau Vielgeldtin. Galanthomme has the idea; Harlequin fills in the practical details. Preoccupied with his physical well-being, he is full of tricks, as in this night-scene:

LIEßGEN: Bst! Mr. Donat, seyn Sie es?
HARL.: Ich heiße zwar nicht Mr. Donat, wo es aber was zu Fressen giebt, da heiße ich alles. (IV, 2, 78)

He is involved in plenty of physical action and many farcical situations. In III, 4, he cheats the farmer and almost literally leads him by the nose. In V, 4, he rushes on stage, falls down, and breaks a bottle—such precipitous entrances were typical of the traditional *lustige Person*. In I, 5, largely behind the backs of their masters, he and Ließgen indulge in comic by-play, as in this excerpt:

*(Nach diesen Reden, nimmt Harlequin von dem Bey-Tisch eine Pfeiffe, und zopfft Ließgen heimlich mit einem Papier in der Hand, ihm solches anzuzünden, diese versagt es mit einer sauern Mine; Endlich nimmt Harlequin sein Feuer-Zeug mit Schwamm aus den Schubsack, und schläget selbst Feuer an, gehet bey seite und dampffet wie ein Lands-Knecht:)* (I, 5, 13–14)

As to the size of his role, Harlequin shares the honour of first place in number of appearances with Lisette and Frau Vielgeldtin, but has the most to say. His relationship with Ließgen is a mixture of co-operation and tension. She aids him in his schemes for her own reasons, but recoils from his courtship of her and flirts with others. Anything but respectable herself, Ließgen nevertheless anticipates the maids of the Saxon comedy in her often moralizing comments on the way of the world and the ways of her mistress. The language of Harlequin, Ließgen, and Peter is vividly colloquial.[29] Ließgen is intended to reflect quite realistically the speech characteristics of her *métier* in Leipzig, as Harlequin's long list of her "Leib- und Sprichwörter" shows (I, 7). The servants are extremely outspoken, while being themselves the target of considerable verbal abuse: Vielgeldtin's reference to her maid as "die garstige Trolle" (I, 4, 10) is typical. Peter, who has a much smaller role than the other two, is also a trickster, who in a trice can turn into a moralist. He dislikes and despises his master, Capriol, yet helps him in questionable affairs. In IV, 4, after a conversation in which he constantly makes fun of his snobbish and affected employer, he proffers this lofty advice:

> Wenn ich aber an eurer Stelle wäre, so machte ich mir daraus gar keine Schande, sondern vielmehr eine Ehre, von Geburth zwar niedrig, an Tugend und Eigenschaften aber vornehm zu seyn. (IV, 4, 75).

Harlequin is given the last word of the play. Over the letter explaining Galanthomme's abandonment of Vielgeldtin, Stockblind, and Vielgeld,

> (... *krazen sich im Kopffe, und gehen mit langsamen Schritten ab. Wenn sie fort, schleichet Harlequin nach, und krazet sich auch im Kopffe und saget:*)
> > Ja! ja! Wie wir es treiben, so gehts.
> > Es ist so der gemeine
> > Schlendrian. (V, 13, 110–11)

His comment is not hypocritical. Picander wants his spectators to shake their heads at the vices of his bourgeois characters, but to do it while laughing at his servants — both pranksters and preachers — who are at the same time outside moral judgement. The Saxon comedy will generally make the servants subscribe to the same moral code as their masters. In Picander, particularly this play, most of the bourgeois figures are unprepossessing and vicious rather than simply foolish. Their language is just as vulgar as that of their servants, who are not merely comic, but almost refreshing in their candid amorality.

Die Weiber-Probe, 1725, includes only an unimportant part for a French merchant's servant, but in Der Säuffer of the same year, there are, in addition to a similar insignificant figure, three servants with substantial roles: Ließgen, maid to Antonine; and two thinly-veiled Harlequin-types, Mischmasch, "Lustiger Diener des Polyzythus," and Hocuspocus, "Lustiger Diener der Dorinden." Mischmasch has by far the biggest part in the play, appearing in twenty-eight of the thirty-six scenes and having one and a half times as many speeches as the next most important character, his master Polyzythus. Mischmasch is completely unscrupulous. Dissatisfied with his life as servant to a drunkard, to whom he has lent money and for whom he has gone to the pawnbroker's to trade clothes to buy wine and beer, he makes it clear that he sees through Polyzythus in a long monologue at the beginning of the play. This type of one-man exposition was traditional in the popular extemporized comedy, but later in the eighteenth century, exposition was generally handled through dialogue in the first scene, often a conversation between one of the bourgeois characters and a servant in which the problematic situation is more gradually delineated. Mischmasch does not want to reform Polyzythus. Rather, he threatens to leave if Polyzythus renounces alcohol, tempts him into drinking again, and tricks him into breaking his word to Antonine. He tells hypocritical lies to Valentin, Polyzythus's father, and manipulates the world around him constantly. He generates much farcical action, including the traditional episode of the urine bottle and a comic scene with the doctor (III, 1 and 2). At the end of act III, he temporarily gets his come-uppance when all the other characters on the stage turn on him and rob him as a punishment for his lies, but he bounces back unabashed in act IV, where the servants' capers are particularly marked when the rest of the characters become melodramatically tragic.

Hocuspocus and Ließgen have moderately sized roles, the former mainly as a go-between for Dorinde and Polyzythus. He and Mischmasch play a scene, I, 6, in which their gallant phrases to each other are presumably a parody, in the tradition of the *commedia dell'arte*, of the over-refined manners of the gentry.[30] Much is made of their rivalry over Ließgen. In *Der akademische Schlendrian* the servants abet adulterous relationships, but here they more traditionally support the courtship of single young people. Ließgen's plan for her mistress to marry Orontes rather than Polyzythus runs counter to Mischmasch's schemes, and he has a poor opinion of her motives and her whole profession:

MISCHMASCH:   Regula: Wer einem Cammer-Käzgen die Hände
versilbert, erlangt alle guten Tugenden. (I, 2, 8)

It is hinted that Ließgen is no better than can be expected, having had a
child by the tutor. Indeed, she does strive to rise higher in society and
pretends to speak French, but when Mischmasch uses coarse language
and tries to strike her, she descends to his and her own true level and
*"prügelt ihn zum Theatro hinaus"* (II, 7, 36). Ultimately she prevails. At
the end of the play, Mischmasch and Hocuspocus literally pull her to and
fro between them, and when the masters and mistresses have paired off
and left the stage, they fight over her. But meanwhile, she departs, and
they are left alone.

Johann Ulrich König (1688–1744), court jester in Dresden before
becoming court poet there in 1729, also used traditional elements in his
servant figures, and introduced Harlekin and Scaramuz in one play. Like
that of Reuter and Picander, König's satire is local and strictly topical,
yet shares the new trend to realism. His plots are more tightly constructed (a close comparison is not possible, because we would be
measuring his one-act plays against their longer works), and he conveys
a clearer message of restraint and common sense. Picander's language
was the sort that Gottsched wanted to refine, but König's was more
moderate in tone and fairly natural. He was concerned with standards of
taste and decency, as is apparent in *Untersuchung von dem guten Geschmack
in der Dicht- und Redekunst*, 1727. Gottsched, who had nothing but contempt for Picander, praised König extravagently at first and dubbed him
a "German Molière," though by the time of the Bodmer-Breitinger controversy there was a complete break between them. König was entirely
out of sympathy with Gottsched's strictures on opera.[31]

An interesting servant figure appears in König's early *Singspiel, Die
Österreichische Großmuth oder: Carolus V,* 1712. The elderly, crude, man-
crazy Sybille, servant to the delicate Clarise, tries to make love to the
page Alisto, who only spurns her with insults.[32] The one-act *Die
Verkehrte Welt,* 1725, which remained in the repertoire of German
troupes until the 1760s, is based on a French *Singspiel* from the *Théâtre de*

*la Foire: Le Monde Renversé.* Harlekin and Scaramuz,[33] the main figures, are presented not as "real" characters, but as theatrical stock figures or "masks" very familiar to König's Dresden audience. They appear as two Dresden actors who journey forth to discover the topsy-turvy world. Although König enlivens his piece by showing Utopia's ridiculous side, he is faithful to the theatrical tradition of this oft-used theme. The topsy-turvy world is as rational and virtuous as the real world is corrupt. Husbands are always faithful, wives always loving—and the theatre is held in high esteem!

> Alle ihre Stücke sind voller Neuigkeit, Veränderung, scharfsinnigen Ausdrücken, feinen Satyren, und immer abwechselnden versteckten Sitten-Lehren, jeder Auftritt ist mit den andern durch einen geschickten Zusammenhang der Umstände und Verwirrungen künstlich verknüpft. In ihren Zweydeutigkeiten steckt nichts unhöfliches, man hört keinen ungesalzenen oder zur Unzeit angebrachten Schertz.[34]

This *Wunschbild* reflects König's concern with form, and also his avoidance of obvious moralizing and his desire to present lively action; his *Der Dreßdner Frauen Schlendrian*, 1725, fulfils this intention. A one-act play conceived as a *Nachspiel*, it is also based on a foreign model, this time a piece from the *Nouveau Théâtre Italien*. Valentin, the servant, has one of the largest parts and, like Picander's Mischmasch and Harlekin, furnishes the exposition by opening the play with a two-page monologue on the idiosyncracies and idiocy of fashionable women, and on the difficulties of his life. Indeed, he is roughly treated by his "elegant" mistress, Frau Rechts und Links. "Fauler Esel!" "Rind-Vieh!" and "Einfältiger Schöps!" are among the designations that come flying his way in scene 3. But very efficiently, he brings out her own foolishness. In scene 8 during a long dialogue, Valentin tries again and again to find out why Frau Rechts und Links considers herself mortally insulted by Bedachtsam, and finally discovers that the offender had once asked her in company how old she was. Valentin also plays a practical role. Unable to read or write, he has inventiveness and native wit, and undertakes to help Ohnesorge court Jungfer Sittsam, which involves a parallel plan to marry off Frau

Rechts und Links to Sittsam's guardian, the tactless Bedachtsam: "verlasset euch auf mich," he declares to the young man, "Solte mir dieser Anschlag mißlingen, so habe ich schon einen andern im Kopfe" (4, 10).[35] His first scheme goes awry when Bedachtsam discovers him, in the disguise of a woman selling cosmetics, passing a love-letter to Sittsam. But Valentin tries again and in the end the desired result is achieved.

He is often crude. Ohnesorge, slow to see the point of one of Valentin's strategies, is told, "Herr, ihr seyd ein dummer Teufel!" (8, 23). To Sittsam, who lives up to her name by wishing to dismiss the maid who let Ohnesorge into the house in Bedachtsam's absence, he exclaims:

> Ey Jungfer, das ist nicht herkommens; andere Jungfern behalten ihre junge Mägde eben deswegen, warum ihr die eure wegjagen wollt. Seyd doch nicht so seltsam. (12, 30)

Then he turns her intention to his own advantage by begging that the double marriage be a triple one and the maid "dismissed into his bed." The play ends with Valentin adding his own candid twist to the conventional expressions of joy:

> OHNESORGE: O! unvermuthetes Glück!
> SITTSAM: O! unerwarteter Ausgang!
> VALENTIN: O! Nagelneue Braut! . . .
> BEDACHTSAM: Auf! Zur Trauung!
> OHNESORGE: Auf! Zur Hochzeit!
> VALENTIN: Auf! zu Bette! (12, 31)

Within a decade, Caroline Neuber, in her *Deutsches Vorspiel*, 1734, will inveigh against the fantastic and crudely comic elements, both present in König, and will work under Gottsched's aegis for a refined and more realistic comedy. Elements of the farcical Harlequinade, theoretically, will be utterly rejected. Yet paradoxically, the comic figures of Weise, Reuter, Picander, and König, especially the servants of the latter two, all of them indebted to the popular theatre of improvisation, pave the way for the new realism, for they are employed to point out the vices and foibles of a clearly defined lower middle class. The purpose of Gott-schedian comedy will be unashamedly moral and its means satiric, and precisely here do we have the link, certainly not acknowledged and probably not perceived by Gottsched. The comic writers—and the theo-rists, too—of the sixty years before the *Critische Dichtkunst* understood comedy primarily as satire. This helped to define the scope and the limits of the genre as practised in the early *Aufklärung*.[36] Gottsched may be seen as the culmination of a trend, the point where the gradually merging lines of theory and practice meet. The servants from Weise to König are the children of the comic masks and have risen in the world. Among the farcical or (in König) fantastic elements, much realistic observation of ordinary life emerges. But while they are largely integrated into the action of the plays, they are themselves not yet fully part of that milieu, though this is less apparent with female servants. They are still *lustige Personen* capering on the edge of society, commenting on morals, but free of morality's demands. In the Gottschedian Saxon comedy, where the society portrayed is in general much more staid and virtuous, the servants acquire a new respectability. Two generations separate them from the popular clowns and buffoons of the seventeenth century, and new genteel blood has come into the family. But valet and soubrette, as we shall see, still owe something to their livelier forebears.

# II

## The Saxon
## Satiric Comedy

### Theory and Practice

Apart from some general remarks about language and the social status of characters, Opitz had said very little about comedy in his *Buch von der deutschen Poeterey,* 1624, and later theorists in the seventeenth century tended also to comment more fully on other poetic forms, reflecting perhaps the paucity of observation on the genre in the extant works of Aristotle.[1] Gottsched's *Versuch einer Critischen Dichtkunst vor die Deutschen,* 1730, which replaced Opitz's book as the definitive German work on poetics, devoted much more space to comedy. In the broad scope of eighteenth-century theatre, comic forms predominated. On the literary level, Gottsched subscribed to the dictum that tragedy is the highest form of poetry, but in practice, comedy eventually proved a more suitable and potentially effective vehicle for his didactic purposes (*CD,* 354).[2] The so-called Saxon satiric comedy written under his aegis represented, for all its shortcomings, a greater achievement than the tragedy of this first generation of the Enlightenment. If Horace Walpole was right when he said that "this world is a comedy to those that think, a tragedy to those that feel,"[3] then to the early *Aufklärer* with their view of the world as a rational structure and life as inherently amenable to order, comedy must have been the more congenial of the two genres.[4]

Terence, Gottsched's favourite comic poet, was a dramatist who significantly made no concession to popular taste in his drawing-room comedies. Gottsched followed in the tradition of the Protestant school comedy, for which Luther had advocated Terence as model, and which was still important in the eighteenth century for the performance of comedy. Gottsched's views on the genre were linked to his practical efforts, undertaken at first with Frau Neuber and her troupe and later with J.F. Schönemann, to raise the literary and artistic level of stage productions, to bring literature and the living theatre closer together, and to make the stage respondent to and worthy of a growing class of cultivated bourgeois. Ironically, the children of the latter, Lessing among them, condemned Gottsched outright, raising the cry of "Theater für das Volk" and misjudging his aims because they seized on his limited artistic talent.[5] We must remember that when he began his reforms, there was no sophisticated, knowledgeable theatre-going public and no well-established dramatic repertoire. Thirty years later, while condemning Gottsched's methods, Lessing conceded that he had faced a difficult situation:

Man kannte keine Regeln; man bekümmerte sich um keine Muster. Unsere *Staats-und Helden-Aktionen* waren voller Unsinn, Bombast, Schmutz und Pöbelwitz. Unsere *Lustspiele* bestanden in Verkleidungen und Zaubereien; und Prügel waren die witzigsten Einfälle derselben.[6]

Gottsched, then, could not base his theories on a German comic repertoire from which he might choose what to discard and what to preserve. Such a store of older original plays, which remained part of the living theatre at least up to the end of the century, existed in France and England before 1730,[7] but not in Germany, where there were simply isolated examples — Gryphius, Reuter, Henrici — none of them completely to Gottsched's taste. While he had hopes for the future, for the present he had to base his programme on what he considered the best of European comedy, particularly the French, and to advocate its performance in the German theatre as an interim measure, (*CD*, 359–60).[8] His

*Deutsche Schaubühne,* 1741–45, a sort of contemporary repertoire of the "reformed" stage, contains in its first three volumes translations of foreign comedies dating from 1666 to 1736 and in its last, three examples of the Saxon comedy composed with his blessing, but no German comedy written before his reforms.

In addition, Gottsched had to contend with fairly widespread disapproval of the stage. Lessing's parents' dismay at the news that their son attended performances of comedy was typical of many Germans who considered the theatres to be "Temples of Satan" (a phrase from the rhetoric of the full-blown controversy on the subject in the first decades of the century in England), just as in France in Molière's time and for a century afterwards one school of thought held comedy to be the great corruptor.[9] Gottsched's insistence on overtly didactic drama must be seen in this context.

Since he wished to forge a literary comedy to replace the popular pieces with their "leeren Possen,"[10] his discussion of the genre in the *Critische Dichtkunst* leads clearly to the conclusion that the servant figure must be affected. In a comedy that aims at verisimilitude, a *lustige Person* who turns up in all manner of plays, in various guises but basically, and to Gottsched monotonously, ever the same, who provokes laughter simply by tumbling onto the stage, who undermines the unity of the action by being "nur mit einem Bein in der Handlung,"[11] is inconceivable. Thus, Hans Wurst and the traditional Harlequin are rejected, though in the *Critische Beyträge,* 1734–35, Gottsched does praise examples of the new refined Harlequin by De Lisle (*Arlequin Sauvage,* 1721, and *Timon le Misanthrope,* 1722) and Marivaux (*Ile des Esclaves,* 1725) in plays written for Luigi Riccoboni's *Nouveau Théâtre Italien* in France, which had advanced far beyond its popular origins. The latter, however, still strongly influenced not only the repertoire but also the acting style of German troupes, and so in the end Gottsched could not advocate even the reformed Harlequin for the new German comedy. Radical surgery was necessary, though the Neubers, not Gottsched, were responsible for the oft-mentioned "banishment ceremony" of 1737.[12] Morhof, Schottelius, and Leibniz had spoken against the farce, but Gottsched was the first to do so with vehemence. Thus we find him condemning the practice of ad-libbing, rooted in the Italian comic tradition and imitated in

Germany, as responsible for the decline of the comedy (*DS* II : 13).[13] Disguise is sharply criticized. In short, the comic for its own sake, the visually comic, comedy of gesture and physical movement, all are repudiated.[14] Since these elements had been particularly pronounced in the servants, it follows that the latter were now to become respectable characters, restricted to being vehicles for satiric comment or common-sense advice and, theoretically, forbidden the element of pure fun.

The Prologuist of Fielding's *The Modern Husband*, 1731, might have been echoing Gottsched when he declared,

> Though no loud laugh applaud the serious page,
> Restore the sinking honour of the stage,
> The stage, which was not for low farce designed,
> But to divert, instruct and mend mankind.[15]

Similarly, Caroline Neuber, in her appeal to the Saxon court on 21 April 1734, stressed improvement rather than laughter as the aim of comedy.[16] Thus comedy as Gottsched conceived it, and as many of his followers practised it, tends to seem like dramatization of social maxims as found in the then popular works of the *Weltweisheit* type, his own and others'.[17] *Prodesse et delectare* is its motto:

> Die Komödie ist nichts anders, als eine Nachahmung einer lasterhaften Handlung, die durch ihr lächerliches Wesen den Zuschauer belustigen, aber zugleich erbauen kann. (*CD*, 348)

For, as he remarks in *Die vernünftigen Tadlerinnen:*

> Komödien sind oft bessere Beweggründe, vom Bösen abzustehen als die besten Vernunftschlüsse der Sittenlehre. Freilich müssen die Stücke danach beschaffen sein. Die Tugend muß stets als belohnt, das Laster als bestraft vorgestellt werden.[18]

He demands regular structure and adherence to probability, just as for tragedy, but the form should be prose (or at least "prosaic") and the milieu bourgeois—aristocratic figures could be permitted on occasion, but never princes or great heroes (*CD*, 355–56, 217). These last requirements derived from a comic tradition reaching in part back to Aristotle's time and strengthened by the practice of the sixteenth and seventeenth centuries, but Gottsched believed that they could be proven as necessary in the nature of the genre (though in his comments on A.D. Richter's "Regeln und Anmerkungen der lustigen Schaubühne" he raises some questions concerning strict social classification).[19] Characters should be "general," as should the follies portrayed (*CD*, 354), which are asocial, rather than amoral, strictly speaking. This meant that comedy-writers were to portray types, concentrating on one major characteristic only, rather than whole characters. It was a retrograde step, as Hinck points out, since over fifty years before Molière had created fully rounded figures.[20] The audience's reaction is to be, in Mary Beare's phrase, "ein verstandesmäßiges Verlachen,"[21] that is to say, reason recognizes that the actions and attitude of a character are absurd. Betsy Aikin-Sneath calls the resulting laughter "the verdict of the group mind,"[22] for the norm by which folly is judged is the structure of accepted modes of thought and behaviour of the society of the time, and the outcome must be to conserve society in its *status quo,* hence Gottsched's conviction of the valuable function of comedy in schools (*DS* IV : 20). This view of Gottsched's provokes a basic question: is the ridiculous in his sense in fact laughable? Do we really laugh at such social absurdities, or is our reaction more often a sneer? In any case, as Steinmetz has suggested, the effect is to produce something very much akin to "Schadenfreude,"[23] an idea not limited to Gottsched and his circle, but rooted to some extent in the current rationalist philosophical conception of the comic.[24] The audience's reason is intended, in Gottsched's view of the comedy, to provoke laughter at the deviation from the norm. At the same time a tremendous demand is made of the rational faculty, namely that it accept a miracle cure at the end of the play! A ridiculous character has only to recognize his folly to effect a complete and permanent reform. As Gottsched explains in his *Weltweisheit,* the foolish man is at odds with both society and his own inherent nature; in the end he finds himself again, and an educative process has taken place.[25]

Since "das Lasterhafte" in comedy is "das Unvernünftige," and in general all characters except the bearer of the foolish trait represent "das

Vernünftige," the servants' role is from the outset circumscribed, since any comic function they have must perforce be entirely in the service of reason. They may not be the exponents of pure comedy. Nevertheless it may be argued that the Saxon comedy-writers unconsciously preserved remnants of buffoon elements traditionally connected with the servants, simply because the strength of tradition in both the writing and acting of comedy had made such elements inherent. The answer is that theory and practice are two different things, and that when they merged in Germany, the comedy, while strongly influenced by Gottschedian precepts, was also heir to a tradition that included, for instance, the whole of Molière as a compendium of characters, themes, and motifs, Gherardi's *Théâtre Italien*, and Holberg, who had been influenced both by the more "refined" French comedy and by the more robust Italian tradition. Gottsched had criticized Gherardi heartily, inveighing against the Italian theatre—"Romanstreiche, Betrügereyen der Diener, und unendlich viel abgeschmackte Narrenpossen" (*CD*, 342)—and considered much of Destouches superior to a good part of Molière. (He was in distinguished company, since Boileau, Bossuet, and Fontenelle had balked at those of Molière's plays that contained farcical elements.) As for Holberg, in that he specifically commissioned Detharding to translate three of his comedies for the *Deutsche Schaubühne*, Gottsched himself showed that defining a genre is one thing and illustrating it another, while his warm advocacy of Destouches brought a comedy before the German public that was beginning to move away from the strictly satiric genre, whether Gottsched himself was aware of this or not.[26]

Modern critics writing on *Aufklärung* comedy have been able to show again and again that consciously or unconsciously its authors retained characteristics of the *Stegreifspiel;* Hinck goes so far as to speak of an "Umfunktionierung" of *commedia dell'arte* types.[27] Most agree in seeing the clearest traces of the older popular comedy in the servant figures, for instance, in the fact that many plays are not tightly constructed and the servants are involved in scenes where comic effect, despite Gottsched's strictures, is made for its own sake.[28] Strangely enough, Gottsched's own sketch for a comedy in the *Critische Dichtkunst* reads more like a scenario from improvised comedy than a draft for a staid satiric play, with its night setting, assaults, and beatings, except that it does not sound very funny.[29] The Saxon comedy, except on rare occasions, lacks the spontaneity and exuberance of the *Stegreifspiel*. It is much more sober and much more sophisticated. The humour, even in the more risqué writers such as Krüger, is toned down, and is manifested, as Aikin-Sneath comments, "in innuendo and in indecency of situation, but not of expression," while the sexual element is "not primitive and spontaneous, but . . . rationalized."[30] Language is sometimes more refined than in the pre-Gottschedian era but, more important, it is "realistic" in exploiting colloquial expression and metaphor, particularly in the speech of the servants, and fulfils Gottsched's didactic aims rather than his specifically linguistic ones.[31] In fact, some *Aufklärung* comedies, including those of Frau Gottsched, are surprisingly vulgar in expression, perhaps because a "respectable" colloquial language for the literary. depiction of the everyday scene was slow in developing. All in all, the comedy writers were often unwittingly subject to a tradition stronger than their conscious and somewhat circumscribed goals. As A.W. Schlegel declared over half a century later:

> Hanswurst, als allegorische Person, ist unsterblich, und wenn man ihn noch so sicher begraben zu haben glaubt; so kommt er unversehens in irgendeiner gravitätischen Amtskleidung wieder zum Vorschein.[32]

In fact, just as the German stage was being pressed into the service of literature and enjoined to reject improvisation, the "literary *commedia dell'arte*" of Carlo Goldoni (1707–93), which revitalized the servant figure, was beginning to be known.

One important distinction must not be forgotten between the new German literary comedy (and the theatres it influenced in particular seasons) and the larger sphere of the German stage in general. Hinck quotes Schmid's *Chronologie des deutschen Theaters,* 1775, to show how strong the popular influence of the Italian comedy was, not only in the days of Gottsched's reforms, but well into the 1760s.[33] Extemporizing was a firm tradition, in which even Caroline Neuber indulged, according to Schmid. Moreover, in Germany as in England, the eighteenth century was the heyday of the Harlequinade. Gottsched's invective against Hans

Wurst and the Neubers' ceremonial banishment of that figure in 1737 did not mean that he or his more sophisticated relative Harlequin disappeared from the theatre.[34] Later productions by the Neubers included a clownlike character called Hännsgen, and performances of Lessing's *Miß Sara Sampson* in Vienna in 1760 and 1763 replaced the valet Norton with Hans Wurst, while in Hamburg in 1741, Schönemann, fresh from a Leipzig season highly praised by Gottsched, put on Harlequinades and even *Staatsaktionen*, along with Holberg, Molière, and Borkenstein's *Bookesbeutel*. The critic Friedrich Schulz reported that Döbbelin complained that when he went to Berlin in 1766, he found "nur Hanswurst und wieder Hanswurst und alle Tage Hanswurst; aber wie erstaunte ich, als ich auch Nicolai, Ramler, Mendelssohn, *Lessing* unter den Zuschauern fand."[35] The Harlequin actor was not only highly regarded, but got extra pay for what he "suffered" in the physical by-play: so much for a box on the ears, so much for getting his face blackened, and so on.[36] A factor when Caroline Neuber took up the cudgels against farce was her rivalry with the Harlequin actor, Müller. Nevertheless, as Steinmetz points out, the crude clown disdained by Gottsched was the same in name only as the Harlequin mourned by Lessing in the 17th *Literaturbrief*.[37] Neither was he perhaps the same figure H.P. Sturz had in mind in 1767 when, bemoaning the dearth of truly German manners in the German comedy, he remarked: "Wir haben eine Originallaune, die als Karikatur betrachtet nicht ohne glückliche Züge ist, ich meine die Possen des Hanswurst."[38] And Lessing, rather in the manner of his attitude to Shakespeare's disregard for the unities, defended Harlequin theoretically, but did not adopt him as such in his own plays, not even, as Hinck notes, in his fragmentary adaptation of Goldoni's *L'Erede Fortunata (Die Klausel im Testament/Die glückliche Erbin)*.[39]

The production of original German comedies in the *Aufklärung* did not begin until the 1740s, when a generation of writers born mostly between 1710 and 1725 turned out in the space of a few years the corpus of works known as the Saxon comedy. Since Gottsched had proposed the presentation of translated foreign models as a temporary solution, let us first look at the selection of these he printed in the first three volumes of the *Deutsche Schaubühne*, presumably as representative of the best available — presumably, because the prefaces to the individual volumes contain no programmatic statements, simply superficial comments on individual plays. Fénélon's "Gedanken von den Lustspielen," printed in volume I, like the companion piece on tragedy, as an introduction to the genre, provides as preface to a comparison of Terence and Molière only generalizations that must have seemed platitudinous even in the early eighteenth century. For example, "Die Comödie stellt die Sitten solcher Leute vor, die im Mittelstande leben: also muß sie in einer nicht so hohen Schreibart abgefaßet seyn, als das Trauerspiel" (DS I: 34). It is thus impossible to deduce what guided Gottsched in his choice of these plays: two comedies by Dufresny, two by Destouches, one by Molière, one by Saint-Evremond, three by Holberg, and a translation of a French version by Destouches of a play by Addison. Clearly, Gottsched's role in the *Schaubühne* as a whole was more than editorial, since some contributions were directly commissioned by him and others submitted tentatively for his evaluation and amendation or revised extensively at his suggestion.

These works are more significant than a set of translations might be in another context, because for a while they were representative of comedy on the reformed Gottschedian stage for the previous decade and established certain traditions on which the German playwrights then built. The first pertinent question for the present study is, then: were there any changes made by the translators that suggest a different view of the servants? Hardly, for apart from unimportant structural alterations (three-act plays were reorganized into five acts, and acts were divided more systematically into scenes, so that each new entrance made a new scene), the main change was the "Germanization" of personal names, particularly in the French plays, and sometimes of placenames or geographical references. In his prefaces Gottsched singled out this practice for comment more than once and felt that it gave "ein deutsches und einheimsches Ansehen" (DS I: 12) to make Lisette in Dufresny's *La Joueuse* into Josephe in *Die Spielerinn*, Perrette in Saint-Evremond's *Les Opéra* into Cathrinchen in *Die Opern*, or Pasquin in Destouches's *Le Dissipateur* into Christian in *Der Verschwender*. Holberg, for instance, attracted Gottsched because he had fashioned something unmistakably Danish out of conventional comic themes and characters. Gottsched did not grasp that it was a question of more than a simple change of locale, and his own changes touch only the surface. He was, however, deeply serious about creating something "German." Later in the century he was unjustly branded for having forced French taste onto German literature, for he was by no means enamoured of all things French, finding German thought philosophically sounder and German morals better. A propos of his wife's *Die Hausfranzösinn*, he castigates German families who insist on importing French tutors to educate their children to admire French culture and despise their own (*DS* V: 12). But a characteristically and self-consciously German middle-class milieu on which to focus was not to hand, and thus, to quote Holl, "er wollte ein nationales Lustpiel schaffen und blieb am Internationalen haften."[40] That is, he was caught in a web of international stereotypes, except possibly where the servants are concerned, if we extend Lappert's conclusion about Lessing's early plays to the Saxon comedy in general:

> In den Dienerszenen gewinnt sogar, wenn auch in engen Grenzen, *heimisches Kolorit* Gestalt. Zuzeiten sprechen die Diener wirklich "deutsch" und handeln so, wie sich, nach den Vorstellungen der Zeit, ein ungebildeter Deutscher verhält. Die Hauptpersonen bleiben ... "international."[41]

The foreign plays in the *Schaubühne* are not exact translations, but that is due more to a lack of skill on the translators' part than to any systematic effort to produce "original" works. Thus the renderings are remarkably faithful,[42] and in the three volumes there are only two minor additions affecting the servants; these are nevertheless odd enough to warrant special mention. In IV, 4 of Molière's *Le Misanthrope*, Alceste's servant Dubois searches in his pockets for a letter, and *"après avoir long-tems cherché le billet,"* [43] concludes that he has left the letter at home. In her translation, Frau Gottsched expands the search of Dubois's counterpart Johann to produce a greater comical effect:

> (*Er suchet ihn lange, und da er ihn nicht finden kann: so packet er seinen Ranzen aus, worinn er allerley alte Lumpen hat, und schmeißt sie über das ganze Theater. ...* )

In addition, whereas Molière does not indicate how Dubois is dressed,

Frau Gottsched clothes Johann somewhat à la Hans Wurst:

*Johann mit Stiefeln und einer Capuse, und einem großen Ranzen auf dem Rücken, in dem über dem Rocke geschnallten Degengehenke hat er einen großen Zettel stecken. . . .* (DS I: 312)

There is no basis in any Molière edition of the period for such additions. Richel speculates that Frau Gottsched may have been "attempting to relieve the tension of the foregoing confrontation" in thus turning the valet into the "rejected clown." [44] In the first scene of Dufresny's *Die Widersprecherinn*, the same translator adds extra words to one of Herr von Gutleben's speeches to the effect that Michel, his gardener, was his servant when he was at university (an interesting touch, since Greene remarks of the original that Lucas "performs the dramatic function of valet and soubrette"),[45] and that Michel's mother was formerly his nurse (*DS* I: 498). These small interpolations are intriguing, for the one gives rise to visual comedy and the other adds a human element to the master-servant relationship: neither is characteristic of the Gottschedian comedy in theory or practice, though the former in particular does occur in works by certain authors.

Since changes from originals to translations are negligible, the next question is: what is the character and function of the servants in these faithful renderings that presently formed the starting point for writing original German comedies? In the Molière play, a rather special case, the servants are insignificant, being largely bearers of messages. The Destouches-Addison comedy is unusual in a different way, with subordinate roles for *sommelier*, coachman, and gardener and substantial ones for the housekeeper and steward, but no specific parts for valet, soubrette, or house-servant in the usual sense. The three plays of Holberg contain a great many servants (in *Bramarbas*, for instance, there are five named ones) who not only have considerable roles as confidants and/or intriguers, but also indulge in some visual comedy and much verbal comedy (a speech of one and a half pages is not unusual).[46] In general there is a folksiness about Holberg's servant figures, which attests to his fusion of the sophisticated comedy of manners with an older comic tradition, and provides an example of how, unconsciously, the reformed stage inherited some slapstick elements. The plays of Dufresny, Destouches, and Saint-Evremond present the stereotyped sophisticated valet and soubrette, who are then taken over by the Saxon comedy. Supporters of their masters' causes, frequently looked to for advice, though often motivated by personal gain, they play prominent roles: Josephe in *Die Spielerinn* by Dufresny appears as often as the title figure and has the third-largest speaking part among the ten characters; in Destouches's *Der Verschwender* only the title figure appears more often than Cathrine, who also has the second-largest speaking part, leading the rest of the cast by a wide margin. The servants are regarded as enormously influential, for example, Cathrinchen in Saint- Evremond's *Die Opern*, IV, 3, "die das ganze Haus fast regieret" (*DS* II: 142).[47] They are pragmatic, worldly wise, and sometimes a little hard — with one notable exception — the servant Christian in Destouches's *Der Verschwender*, who, echoing exactly his original, Pasquin, proves in a moving scene that he is the only person to feel genuine compassion for his bankrupt master. Christian exemplifies how Destouches began to modify the purely satiric comedy with sentimental and morally edifying elements.

On the whole, the translated comedies in the *Schaubühne* attest to the French-Italian or, even more broadly, the western European convention of the servants to which German comic playwrights fell heir. The general outline follows. The servants are prime movers in the plot to further the young lovers' cause, being more quick-witted than the parents or guardians and more practical and less scrupulous than the young people, who, particularly the female, cannot envisage open defiance of their elders and comport themselves like the historian Gibbon in a similar situation: "I sighed as a lover, I obeyed as a son." [48] Originally rooted in the often crude characters of the improvised comedy, the servants, particularly the female servant, bow to the demands of the late seventeenth and early eighteenth century and become more refined in speech and deportment. But they largely retain their "moralische Indifferenz," belonging to neither vice nor virtue.[49] Often they have their own sub-plot, a courtship between valet and maid, in which the practical and sometimes sensual contrasts with the purely spiritual attraction that binds the bourgeois lovers, but there is rarely a rival in love for the maid, as there often was in the popular comedy. The main plot is usually a peg on which to hang the comedy's purpose, satire on some social foible in one of the characters (more often than not in one of the older characters), and here the servants' comic role, their gift for ridicule or simply for comic remark, comes into play. Thus the servants, ever present in the *commedia dell'arte*, the purpose of which was not satiric, are still crucial in comedy where satire is the order of the day. The reason lies in the fact that in both they stand apart from the world to which the other characters belong, though, paradoxically, in the comedy of manners isolation goes together with amalgamation:

> Diese *Distanzierung* erlaubt es ihnen, satirische Attacken zu reiten, ihre gleichzeitige *Integrierung* ist die Ursache dafür, daß sie das mit den Mitteln tun, die das neue bürgerliche System zugleich tragen und verteidigen: mit denen der tugendorientierten Vernunft.[50]

This is the new tradition, the set of conventions surrounding the servants. How does German Enlightenment comedy, after all largely derivative, use it? Occasionally it reproduces almost a text-book example, and on the whole it adopts many of the servants' character traits, those of the soubrette particularly, while the male servant is often somewhat rough-hewn in comparison with the French valet. The general formula still applies. The servants—whether they are personally attractive or not as characters—align themselves on the side of the young people, occasionally altruistically, but generally regarding the presents and tips they will receive if young love triumphs as their just due.[51] The maid's advice is especially valued. Usually at least a year or two older than her mistress and always more knowledgeable about the world, she is held to be "in Ehstandssachen besser beschlagen" [52] than anyone else in the household. While the young lady speaks of her own loved one, the maid speaks of romance and sweethearts in general. At the same time there is considerable variation amongst the Saxon comedy writers where the role given the servants in the action is concerned. S.E. Schreiber claims that the Gottschedian pattern calls for the servants to be "duped and outwitted" by their masters,[53] but this is hardly borne out by the plays themselves, where these figures are often insulted—in a few cases, perhaps, badly treated—but not in the end outwitted. Rather, the

French-Italian pattern of the servant outwitting his elderly master generally holds true in those cases where the servants have a part in the action; but in some plays their role is sharply reduced and in one or two they are peripheral figures. Such variations are above all significant in the comedies of Frau Gottsched, which retain certain traditional characteristics (the female servant is, for instance, pert and self-assured), but in which the servants have a lesser role in the plot.

The biggest part for a servant in Frau Gottsched's comedies is that of Cathrine in *Die Pietisterey im Fischbein-Rocke*, 1737, a satire on religious mania that pre-dates the Saxon comedy proper, being largely a translation of Bougeant's *La Femme Docteur*, 1730.[54] There is no valet in this play (an unnamed "Diener" appears in one scene), but the role of Cathrine (in the original, Finette) is fairly substantial: she is present in fifteen out of forty scenes, and shares with her young mistress and the latter's sensible uncle third place in the ranking of speaking parts, after the dupe Frau Glaubeleichtin and the hypocrite Scheinfromm. Level-headed and quick-witted, Cathrine raises laughs in scenes where her function is to bring out the foolishness or the dishonesty of others, for instance, in her encounter with Scheinfromm in II, 2. But she is not the chief source of comedy, for the satirized figures unwittingly provoke the loudest laughter against themselves. Perhaps the funniest scenes in the play are the first two in act IV, where the three female fanatics try to outdo each other in describing their inward self-examination in flowery Pietistic jargon. And though important as a go-between for her mistress and others, Cathrine is not the author of the dénouement. *Die Pietistery*, like most of Frau Gottsched's plays, is what Horst Steinmetz calls a "binomische Komödie,"[55] a type popular in the early *Aufklärung*, in that it presents not individual foibles, but a contemporary social malaise and two types of "foolish" character: the villain, here not only a hypocrite, but a criminal swindler who is routed at the end, and the dupe, who is nevertheless no hypocrite and who is not exposed but rather led back to social virtue and good sense. The religious mania that has threatened to destroy the happiness of Frau Glaubeleichtin's household during her husband's absence is temporary. Frau Glaubeleichtin was sensible once and is so again in the last scenes of the play; this reform is brought about, not by the intrigue of servants, but more appropriately by the guidance of her brother-in-law, Herr Wackermann, a figure of equal social status. The dénouement in V, 7 involves even some initiative on the part of the "cured" Glaubeleichtin herself.

In *Die ungleiche Heirath*, 1743, Hanne and Jacob break with tradition in that they are brother and sister; but they are not very important in the action (nominally they are helping von Zierfeld to intrigue against Wilibald), appearing only in five and six scenes respectively of the play's total forty-one, although when on stage, they have a good deal to say, Hanne in particular. In their one scene together, III, 9, the comic effect of her lecture to her slower-witted sibling on the niceties of the ranks of aristocratic servants is subordinate to its relevance for the satire on the pretentiousness and emptiness of the upper class, a main theme of this comedy.[56] Fundamentally these two are decent people, with a certain good sense and enough wit to poke fun at exaggerated snobbishness.

*Die Hausfranzösinn*, 1744, is a satire on another kind of snobbishness, the practice of some middle-class Germans of hiring French employees, and so the three examples of the latter—Mad[ame] la Fleche, de Sotenville, and the valet La Fleur—have a particular function.[57] They kidnap their patron's daughter and thus provoke him into realizing the error of his ways, a lesson reinforced by the views of his sensible half-brother, Herr Wahrmund. Of the three, the governess and the old French officer have the major parts, while the valet appears only twice and in one scene says nothing. The function of the German Erhard, an elderly family servant rather than a young valet, is one of contrast: he is loyal, and he contributes to the discomfiture of the French characters by playing a trick on them.[58] But again, this is a limited role, for he appears in but nine of the play's forty-seven scenes and speaks relatively little (twenty-four speeches).

In the one-act *Der Witzling*, 1745, Paul's role is negligible (he appears for part of two scenes and speaks once), and Heinrich's in *Das Testament* of the same year, Frau Gottsched's only completely original comedy, is not much greater: he is on stage in three scenes and speaks four times. There are no female servants at all in these last two plays.

The role of the servants in Frau Gottsched's plays thus diminishes as time goes on, or rather, the servant figures are really dispensable for her. Of the two plays in which they have fair-sized parts, one, *Die Hausfran-*

*zösinn,* is a special case, and in the other, *Pietisterey,* a translation-cum-adaptation rather than an original play, the author inherited the character along with the rest, and significantly this is the only comedy of hers in which the servant's role is at all comparable to that in the French comedies. Moreover, Frau Gottsched never uses the servants' courtship motif, so these figures have no subsidiary action of their own. Characteristic of her comedies is the increasing tendency for the conflict to be played out among characters of equal social status, but representing differing views of life. Caroline in *Das Testament* is the culmination of this development; she is the most individualized of all Gottschedin's figures, a rather serious young woman of principle who does not fit into the *ingénue* convention, and this play in general may show something of the development toward "serious" comedy visible in Destouches. Thus, in the works of Frau Gottsched, directly influenced by her husband's theories, the significance of the servants decreases in inverse proportion to the importance attached to the reform or re-education, rather than the mere discomfiture, of the character who bears the social foible.[59] Frau von Tiefenborn in *Das Testament* is not reasonable, but she is not the butt of ridicule, and in this play the servant's role dwindles to a nominal one. The characters in Frau Gottsched's plays who function as commentators are largely of the same age and social rank as the satirized figure, and witty mockery is not their prime concern. Perhaps one may see a connection here with Gottsched's view of the nature of the comic: in the *Critische Dichtkunst* he declares, "das Lächerliche der Komödie muß mehr aus den Sachen, als Worten entstehen"(*CD*, 356), thus downgrading one of the traditional characteristics of the servants, namely their ready wit. But the chief reason for this modification of the servant tradition may lie in the overriding concern to educate the audience and to convey a moral precept, in comic clothing certainly, but also in a morally irreproachable way (this despite the frequent vulgarity of Frau Gottsched's language, her well-developed "Schimpfwortvokabular").[60] If the satirized character came to his senses as a result of an intrigue fostered by a servant, who would thus have to be allowed to practise deceit successfully and even to be praised for it, then a high moral tone would be hard to sustain. Traditionally in the comedy, questionable means served a moral rational end, but for Frau Gottsched both means and end must be good.

*Das Testament* is sometimes regarded as marking the transition to senti-mental comedy, but in fact what we have here is a variation on satiric comedy, rather than something new. The early *Aufklärung* sought to entertain and to instruct. It is hardly surprising that the latter gained the edge over the former in the comedies discussed so far, written by the chief literary disciple of the man who, in his discussion of tragedy in the *Critische Dichtkunst,* more than once enjoined: First choose a moral!

However, other Saxon comedy writers did use servant intrigue, though in the case of the one who stressed most openly and emphatically the moral aim of comedy, we find a similar dearth of servants. Hinrich Borkenstein (1705–77), in the foreword to *Der Bookesbeutel,* 1742, bemoans the fact

> daß noch an den mehresten Oertern unsers Vaterlandes, die Zotten und Unflätereyen des Harlekin, die Betriegereyen und Ränke Scapins, statt der Wahrheit, wo nicht ganz und gar, doch zum Theil die Oberhand behalten.[61]

Since his own play, he claims, performed by the Schönemann troupe in Hamburg, had been applauded by all those who favour reason and good taste, he hopes that more such works might be produced to convince the public that "die gesunde Vernunft und der gute Geschmack"[62] should replace vulgar farces. (Borkenstein presumably knew that Schönemann also put on Harlequinades with great success in the same season.) There are no servants with individual roles in *Der Bookesbeutel*: the "zwo Mägde" listed at the end of the *dramatis personae* sit spinning in the first scene, singing together with the mistress Agneta and her daughter Susanna, and leave, never to return, at the end of the second scene. The conflict of the comedy is played out between the three satirized charac-ters (Grobian, Agneta, and Susanna) and the five sensible ones (Sitten-reich, Charlotte, Carolina, Ehrenwehrt, and Gutherz), all middle-class figures. A speech by Susanna in I, 7 suggests that this ill-conducted household includes corrupt servants — the cook, coachman, and nurse — who indulge, for instance, in *Hahnrey-Spiel.*[63]

All of Frau Gottsched's servants have German names, but Christlob Mylius (1722–54) borrows his for *Die Schäferinsel,* 1749, from the French comic repertoire, though his Lisette and Valentin, because of their master's retreat into a pastoral life, have from the beginning of the play been forcibly re-christened Chloe and Mops. Under a superficial rustic veneer, however, they retain their traditional character and role, to the eventual undoing of their master's plan to withdraw from the world forever, and bring the young lovers together. Mops is direct and a bit simple. Chloe out-talks and outwits him, and even beats him in one scene. No longer "Magd," but "Schäferinn und treue Freundinn" of Doris, Chloe's origins show through: at first she cannot grasp her outlandish new name—is it "Kohle," or maybe "Lohe"?[64] She expresses herself rather vulgarly at times, gives worldly advice to her young mistress, and resolves the play's conflict by a trick.

This play is in verse and in three acts, and in another play, *Der Unerträgliche*, Mylius uses disguise for comic effect: all of these elements had been questioned by Gottsched. Mylius had begun as Gottsched's faithful disciple, for which he was posthumously ciriticized by his cousin, G.E. Lessing: "sein Geist war in Gottscheds Schule zu mechanisch geworden." [65] Mylius's two early prose comedies are indeed uninspired pieces, particularly *Der Unerträgliche*, 1747, which has a lightweight plot ridiculing an over-friendly bore. Jule, the maid, does not appear in the first two acts, and altogether speaks much less than the other five characters. There is little coherence in her role. In her first scene she is an assenting chorus to Leonore's raptures on her sweetheart (one can, of course, interpret her exaggerated agreement as a parody of those raptures).[66] Then she is suddenly active and articulate, repelling the unwelcome suitor Unhold in III, 2 and berating him in terms that Leonore herself naturally cannot use ("Knasterbart, Schweinigel, Mäuseschießer, Schubsack").[67] After this she relapses into passivity, allows herself to be dressed up as a lady and used to make fun of Unhold for the diversion of the two pairs of young lovers, thereby exposing herself also to ridicule. There is no male servant in the play. However, Unhold, on the surface a variation of Theophrastus's Tiresome Man (who is potentially much funnier), has been interpreted by some commentators as a made-over *commedia dell'arte* figure because of his disguises as pedant and braggart soldier and his forced marriage to the maid at the end.[68]

*Die Ärtzte*, 1749, a highly exaggerated satire on medical practitioners inspired by Krüger's *Die Geistlichen auf dem Lande*, begins with a comic scene between the two contrasting male servants, the "dummer Pinsel" Matthes and the sophisticated Fridrich, which provides the exposition and reminds us of the Italian comedy.[69] However, Mylius does not exploit the character contrast further, for Matthes, who appears only in the first half of the play, has but a minor role. The cook Dorchen comes on stage in one scene only, though her pregnancy and the delivery of her baby are important to the plot. Fridrich has a substantial part, is completely devoted to the true interests of his masters and indignant at the hypocrisy of the doctors Pillifex and Rezept, whose exposure he helps to bring about. But this does not mean that he represents a new type of "human" servant, for he is a somewhat unconvincing paragon, drily witty and articulate to the point of speaking exactly like the "vornehme Personen" in long sentences and formal phrases. His importance ends with the exposure of the charlatans in act IV and he retreats to the background while, in the last act, the young lovers resolve their personal differences themselves.

"Die treuherzige und gute Rosel"[70] in *Die Klägliche,* 1747, by Gottlieb Fuchs (1720–99), is a much more sympathetic figure, really devoted to Charlotte: "Der redliche Mensch [Rosel] will durchaus nicht von der Charlotte lassen, so gut meynt sie es," declares Charlotte's suitor, Leander (V, 1, 86). Yet she is still a worldy-wise and unsentimental character. Her complaints to Charlotte in the first scene about the latter's mother, Frau Dittrichin, "die Klägliche" of the title, furnish the exposition of the play's problem; this account of abuse is a remnant of the popular comedy and found relatively rarely in the Saxon comedy. Rosel's intention to give notice provokes a protest from Charlotte, which attests to her maid's importance:

> Besinne dich doch nur, wie vertraut Leander und ich mit dir gelebt haben. Bist du nicht stets recht unser geheimder Rathgewesen?
> (I,1, 7)

Rosel's role is in fact greater in the first half of the play, when she takes the place of the absent Leander as Charlotte's protector and applies defence tactics. In act IV Leander returns and proceeds to the offensive.

Nevertheless, Rosel has the largest part: she is on stage in just over half of the scenes and her appearances are distributed evenly over the whole of the play. She has by far the largest speaking part (one hundred and twenty-three speeches compared to her mistress's forty-nine, for instance), though some of the pedant Holzwurm's speeches, in keeping with his character, are much longer than hers.

Rosel has rough common sense and a tongue to match; she can hold her own with any of the other characters, even the learned Magister Holzwurm, whom she makes look ridiculous. She is rude to Frau Dittrichin and impatient with the spoiled Fritzgen—her advice is, send the boy to school to be licked into shape. She tries to argue the old miser Geldlieb out of his plan to force marriage on Charlotte by painting a vivid and unappetizing picture of such a *mésalliance* between youth and age.[71] In V, 3, however, the author seems to have this usually ironic commentator become suddenly naïve when, learning that the sweethearts and their servants are to flee to India, she objects that she cannot swim! The explanation lies in a general characteristic of the servants in the satiric comedy: they are wise and far-seeing about their immediate concerns, love-affairs, family relationships, and the daily life of the household, but their horizon does not extend beyond, and in other matters they are often semi-literate.[72]

Heinrich, "Bedienter der Frau Dittrichin" according to the *dramatis personae*, is in fact servant to Charlotte's suitor Leander, and thus not present until the fourth act brings his master's sudden return from abroad. He appears for the first time in IV, 4, but then is present in two-thirds of the remaining scenes of the play, with a speaking part equal to that of Charlotte or her unwanted suitor Geldlieb distributed over the whole play. He is outspoken and witty: his master, he says to Rosel, "will aus Desperation in alle Welt hinausgehen, und ich als ein treuer Diener bin auch mit desperat" (IV, 5, 77). He, too, is seriously devoted to the young people's cause. Atypically, not he, but Johann, who has no part in the play, is Rosel's sweetheart. Friederici, who praises Fuchs's lower-class characters fulsomely, sees unspecified traces of Hans Wurst in Heinrich, while others, such as Brüggemann, find in Kühnwitz (not a servant but a young pupil of Magister Holzwurm) characteristics of the uncommitted *Spaßmacher*.[73]

"Die Welt liebt den Betrug, drum muß man sie betrügen": this exit line of Sophie, "das Mädchen im Hause," in III, 9 (*DS* VI: 454) of *Der Unempfindliche*, 1745, by Adam Gottfried Uhlich (1720–56), expresses the practical philosophy of the majority of the servants in the Saxon comedy, but those in this play carry it further than most. Uhlich's comedy gains its effects from deceit, intrigue, a false letter, and false news. Sophie has only the fourth-largest part in a cast of eleven (after the henpecked husband of the title, his wife, and Morgenschein, their candidate for their daughter's hand), though her role is more substantial than that of her young mistress. Ernst, the valet, has a modest part but is kept busy behind the scenes and has, as Friederici has shown, a significant function in the last scene, where his final deceitful trick, meant to be helpful, almost destroys the happy ending.[74] A rather crude figure, he is openly disrespectful to his master, and drunk on occasion. From the beginning Sophie is the mouthpiece for the "verdict of the group mind," whether she is commenting satirically on fashion and foreign modes or on her master's weakness:

Wer sich gutwillig läßt die Frau Befehle geben,
Und stets thut was sie will, der ist nicht wehrt zu leben. (I, 1, 401)

(A poor look-out for Ernst, since he is completely under *her* thumb!) Her remarks on events frequently have the flavour of "I told you so." Compared to the sentimental heroine, she is utterly down-to-earth:

Ich schlag auf einmal los; ich seh, ich red, ich liebe.
Die Zögerung macht nur allmählich kalte Triebe. (I, 1, 403)

The servants are critical of the parents and ready to help the young sweethearts, but when in I, 2 Ernst arrives with news that Lottchen has been promised to Morgenschein, they urge her to agree: he is old and will die soon, and then her beloved von Schimmerreich will get not only her, but Morgenschein's money as well. Lottchen indignantly repudiates this advice, but Sophie nevertheless uses the notion later in an effort to turn Morgenschein against the arranged match (II, 8, 437 f.). Sophie is rather hypocritical, for elsewhere she bemoans the passing of the good old days when moral precepts meant something. As the above remarks may suggest, Uhlich's play, though regular in structure and superficially fulfilling Gottsched's requirements (the verse is certainly "prosaic"!), reveals its debt to the popular theatre, particularly in the pronounced amorality of the servants and the thoroughness of their intrigues.

*Der Unempfindliche*, since it was included by Gottsched in his *Deutsche Schaubühne*, has become for literary historians the best known of Uhlich's comedies. He also wrote many adaptations of foreign works, which need not concern us here, and one more or less original play, which again reveals elements of farce, the one-act *Der Schlendrian oder des berühmten Bookesbeutels Tod und Testament*, 1746. Like the longer play it presents stereotype characters drawn with rather heavy-handed exaggeration and, in the case of the servants Anne and Ernst, the same unattractive deviousness. Bookesbeutel and his wife have the largest parts, there is one very minor role, and the other five characters, including the servants, have medium roles, just over half as substantial as the principals'. Anne abets Frau Alrune in her deception of Bookesbeutel, but plays a double game, while Ernst, who has a certain simple common sense, pretends to be a superstitious fool like his master. Their main scene is a somewhat improbable encounter between Anne and the pedantic Magister Boockesbeutelius, whose courtship she encourages in order to get funds to set up house with Ernst. Ernst eavesdrops, jumps out of hiding at the crucial point to dart between the pair, receives the kiss the Magister intends for the maid (a clear borrowing from farce), and then proceeds to blackmail him![75]

Theodor Johann Quistorp (1722–?), whose full-length comedies follow a well-established European tradition in satirizing the medical and legal professions, offers a plethora of servant figures, but relegates the female to a subordinate role. Lehnchen in *Die Austern* appears in one scene only and Cathrine in *Der Hypochondrist* has one of the smaller parts in the play. The male servants, more prominent, though they are not the authors of the dénouement, are constantly coming and going, carrying messages, making reports, and some have strong farcical characteristics. They are outspoken and often garrulous, for instance, Johann, the long-winded barman in *Die Austern*, 1743. The other servant in this *Nachspiel*, Peter, appears only in seven scenes out of twenty-seven, but has the second-largest speaking part because of a long third scene with Liebegern, which aims at comic effect from the tension between the impatient and irritated master and his good-tempered but bungling servant (with more than a bit of Hans Wurst in his make-up).[76] Willing to do his best, Peter always keeps one eye on his financial advantage. He has a part in the main action in that, by failing to deliver a message, he unwittingly contributes to the frustration of Liebegern's plans for a pleasant evening with two young ladies. *Die Austern* is not at all a satiric-moralizing play — the plot is slight, no real vice is involved, and the aim is apparently un-Gottschedian laughter for its own sake. It and Quistorp's longer plays contain more stage directions than is usual in the Saxon comedy, an indication of a desire for pure comic effect; more often than not, these directions involve the servants.

Dietrich, valet of the young suitor Zierlich in *Der Bock im Prozesse*, 1744, is dubbed by Hinck a *servo furbastro*:[77] "so wüßte ich keinen verschlagenern Kopf . . . als ihn," says his master in V, 1, "er hat mehr Streiche in seinem Kopfe, als mancher achzigjähriger Advocat in seinem Mantel" (*DS* V: 357). However, he gets little chance to use his talents, for he appears but briefly in two scenes. As for the other servants, "unser Haus ist unten und oben davon ganz voll," declares young Zankman (I, 1; *DS* V: 253), citing this as a result of the legal mania which has taken hold of his father under Scheinklug's influence. Of these "sechs Tagediebe," to quote Zankmann's sister Suschen (I, 7; *DS* V: 263), four make actual appearances in the play. One, the Gerichtsdiener Claus, has a negligible role, but his colleague Martin, while not appearing in the first act, is present in well over half of the scenes in the rest of the play. His function is that of foil: a simple but sensible fellow, forced to act as domestic court usher and process server by his foolish master, he plays along without any notion of the meaning of the Latin phrases and legal jargon he is required to parrot, and his very naïvety points up the pretentiousness of it all. Heinrich and Johann make few appearances and speeches, but these are concentrated at particular points in the action, and so their functions are important. The parlous state of the household is exemplified through "den gottlosen Hausbothen" Heinrich (I, 7; *DS* V: 263). Having orders to treat prospective clients brusquely, he manhandles Frau von Eigensinn in act I and thereby provides Zierlich and young Zankmann with the pretext for having the trouble-maker Schein-klug arrested at the end of the play. Johann's role is partly expository, as he pokes fun at the elder Zankmann by telling in I, 9 of the "cases" the latter has made out of trivial events involving the household's domestic animals, at the same time shrugging his shoulders at such idiocies:

Ja, nun, wo sollten wir arme Leute bleiben? wenn es unter den Reichen nicht Thoren gäbe, die unser mehr in Brod nähmen, als sie gebrauchten? ... so lebt doch mancher davon; und ich selbst auch. (*DS* V: 269–70)

Like Heinrich and Johann, the maid Lieschen appears in a few early scenes and then not again until the latter part of the play. She is the sympathetic confidante of her young mistress in act I, but her assistance there is limited to boosting Suschen's courage and persuading her that to defy her father and refuse to marry the elderly Scheinklug is no sin, but simply good sense. In act V she is of more practical help when she manages to free herself after old Zankmann has locked her up with Suschen, explains the situation to the two young gentlemen, and abets them in their trick on Scheinklug.

So far Quistorp's male servants have tended to be somewhat self-serving, but Heinrich, valet of the title figure of *Der Hypochondrist*, 1745, has, under a rough exterior, a genuine concern for his foolish master. Appearing in just over half the scenes of the play, with the third most substantial speaking part, he is an outspoken character, lively, something of a wag, and at the same time a representative of common sense, for he sees through the two quacks who vie for permission to treat his employ-er's melancholy. Though put in his place by the hypochondriac's father, Herr Gotthard, when he offers his sensible views on the reasons for the son's state of mind, he good-naturedly agrees to support Herr Gotthard's plan to cure Ernst by providing him with a bride of a pronouncedly merry disposition. Driven to irritation by Ernst's irrational anxieties and repeated declarations that he will kill himself, he responds to his "so muß ich mich gar erhenken" at the end of V, 2 with the callous retort: "Ey Possen! thun Sies, wo Sie das Herz haben!" (*DS* VI : 384), but is concerned enough to remain behind the scene and rush in to save the young man when he actually carries out his threat, thus naturally also turning the suicide attempt into a comic, even farcical episode. Earlier, Heinrich had read out a "prescription" for marriage as a sure cure for hypochondria, but that Ernst eventually follows this advice is brought about by Jungfer Fröhlichinn herself, who effects his cure miraculously in a few speeches by the light of pure reason! "Ihre vernünftigen Vorstellungen curiren mich viel besser, als alle Brunnen und Recepte," Ernst declares (V, 5; DS VI : 393), though Heinrich is still needed to prod his timid master to give tongue to his proposal of marriage. The valet has the last words of the play, as he literally pushes Ernst off to bring the good news to his own father and the father of his bride:

> Gehen Sie! gehen Sie! Ich bitte Sie um des Himmels willen. Werden Sie nicht wieder wunderlich . . . nun Ihnen die Jungfer eine halbe Unze Witz in den Kopf praktisiert hat. (DS VI : 396)

Johann Elias Schlegel (1718–49) joined Gottsched in criticizing the Italian comedy of intrigue, but his literary horizons were broader than those of the Leipzig circle. In his *Gedanken zur Aufnahme des dänischen Theaters* (written in 1747, though not published until 1764), he makes the following comparison:

> Der Franzos belustiget sich an dem Geschwätze eines Kammermägdchens und eines Lackeyen, welche in manchen seiner Stücke die klügsten Personen sind. Der Engländer läßt sich nur selten zu diesen Kleinigkeiten herunter, und er sieht die Thorheiten der vorgestellen Personen ein, ohne daß er die Glossen der Bedienten darzu nöthig hat.[78]

Commenting on the monotonous repetition of the same characters in traditional satiric comedy, he regrets that its chief attraction usually lies in the intricacies of the plot, which, moreover, follow "auf die List einiger Bedienten . . . und nicht auf die Folgen von den Charakteren der Personen."[79] The discussion of the genre in the *Gedanken* shows that Schlegel was moving towards a new comedy, one that would speak to the heart as well as to the intellect. This development has not yet taken place in his earliest comedy, *Der geschäfftige Müßiggänger,* 1741, which commentators from Moses Mendelssohn onwards[80] have frequently regarded as the first truly original German comedy, but which was written under Gottsched's aegis and printed in the fourth volume of the *Deutsche Schaubühne* in 1743.[81] A strictly limited role for the servants seems to have been Schlegel's intent at this early stage.

Apart from four servantlike figures (Goldschmidsjunge, Tabletkrämer, Lakay, and Materialistenjunge), who appear in one scene each only and have one or two brief speeches, *Der geschäfftige Müßiggänger* has two servants in the household itself, the maid Cathrine and Friedrich, the valet of the idler Fortunat. In IV, 4, Cathrine makes the traditional declaration to her mistress, Frau Sylvesterinn, that she rules the house (*DS* IV : 346), but though she is always pert and critical, this claim collapses when we look at her part in the play, for the conflict and its resolution arise indeed directly from the character of Fortunat. Friedrich's and Cathrine's roles are among the smallest. The valet appears in eight scenes only of the forty-four, and apart from the occasional pointed comment, his main function is to carry messages; Cathrine comes on stage only six times, though she has more and longer speeches than Friedrich. A certain comic effect is achieved in act II when the pair disagree over whose job it is to tidy up a room, and in three scenes, II, 13, IV, 4, and V, 1, Cathrine makes much of the fact that she fills two positions in the household, maid and cook. All this has perhaps some bearing in a contrastive way on the purposelessness and formlessness of Fortunat's existence, but if so, Schlegel's aim seems to be to satirize yet another type of foolish behaviour as well (just as he pokes fun at the arid orderliness of Frau Richardinn and Lieschen), for the servants appear ridiculous in their quibbling. There is hardly a "sensible" character in the play, and the servants have a small part in the presentation of an absurd society.

"Bediente! Mägdchen! He!" cries Jacob at the beginning of *Die stumme Schönheit* and Cathrine retorts offstage: "Nun! nun! wer ist denn da? Geduld! wir trinken Thee."[82] Thus even the servants are involved in the innovative use of rhyme, which, in opposition to the main school of thought against comedy in verse, marks this play of 1747.[83] In Leonore the work also reveals, however sketchily in a one-act play, something of Schlegel's "new" woman, with qualities of heart as well as good sense, but nevertheless its overall effect is satirical, and as far as the servants are concerned, it belongs in the present discussion. If, as Staiger says,[84] the real theme of this comedy is the art of conversation, then Jacob and Cathrine are merely peripheral figures, their "conversation" largely functional. Jacob appears in four scenes only (of twenty-five) and has the second-smallest speaking part; Cathrine is on stage more often, seven times, and has a slightly larger role, and toward the end of the play she hides Laconius in a closet. But in the thematic structure, the series of contrasting pairs of characters and contrasting pairs of principles or qualities, the servants have their function. In the opening scene, for instance, the country bumpkin Jacob knocks to beg admittance of the city-bred, sophisticated Cathrine, and later, in scene six, in front of a silent Charlotte, they play their most substantial scene, with the disdainful soubrette rejecting the advances of the "dummer Teufel."[85]

The unfinished comedy of 1724, *Die Pracht zu Landheim,* was intended as a satire with the "Deutsch-Franzose" theme, snobbish pretentions based on an exaggerated veneration for French culture, with miserliness as a subsidiary trait in Frau von Landheim, but—unusual at that time—no love-plot.[86] Since the pretentiousness involves a desire to keep several smart servants and the miserliness dictates doing so without spending extra money, the village tailor, cobbler, and hosier who are pressed into unwilling service without pay as hunter, footman, and postillion have a special comic role, particularly Hans the tailor, a naïve wag whose quips underline his mistress's folly. The largest part (appearances in two-thirds of the extant scenes) falls to the share of Lisette, called in II, 4 variously "Madmösell Geheimderäthinn" and "die gottlose Französinn." [87] Occasionally witty, always unscrupulous, she exploits her masters' idiosyncracies for her own advantage. Though she has assumed the role of the fashionable French maid, she was christened plain Liese, and knows but a few French words and phrases, one of which, "Coquin," she suggests as the new name for the valet Christian—appropriately enough, for he is a rascal who eventually makes off with a large quantity of household goods. A minor character as the play stands in its fragmentary form (had it been completed, he would probably have appeared in more scenes), Christian is nevertheless a source of comedy because of the complicated jargon to which, as a former lawyer's clerk, he is addicted.

In the one-act *Der gute Rath,* 1745, which has a Danish setting, the maid Pernille is used for satiric effect to underline the inconsistency in the attitude of the central figure, Raadfast. Other short plays and fragments offer no servant parts of any importance, and *Der Geheimnisvolle* and *Der Triumph der guten Frauen,* which are not in the purely satiric mode, will be dealt with in the next chapter.

Schlegel sets out in the plays discussed so far to limit the role of the servants, except in the case of *Die Pracht zu Landheim,* the theme of which necessarily involves them heavily, but that is not his only change, for he has altered his attitude towards them also. No longer are they clearly identified with reason and good sense, perhaps because Schlegel is not concerned to teach in an extremely obvious way, but to produce something entertaining from which the moral will emerge.[88] Except possibly for Pernille and the country characters in *Die Pracht zu Landheim,* the servants are not likeable, and most of them are objects of criticism and some degree of ridicule. The female servant predominates, and in general Schlegel has adapted the servant figures to the particular needs of individual plays.

While Johann Christian Krüger's dates (1722–50) put him squarely into the period under discussion in this chapter and his frequently satiric purpose makes his inclusion logical, he nevertheless stands apart from the Gottschedian school of comedy. The social foibles portrayed by the latter are generally rather slight and, despite the attempt to localize, might be observed in any society; even Quistorp's treatment of doctors and lawyers is rooted in a time-honoured comedy tradition and contains few directly topical details. But Krüger's satires on clergymen and aristocrats are to some extent exposures of contemporary abuses: *Die Geistlichen auf dem Lande* was banned and gave rise to considerable controversy. And in these plays there is no sense at the end that the world has been restored to order, for behind the foolishness or criminality of the figures in the foreground opens a vista of more general corruption.

Moreover, Krüger's practical contact with the stage as a member of Schönemann's troupe made him open to a greater robustness of expression, a livelier dramatic presentation (including the use of surprise and disguise, for instance), and a larger variety of types of plays than existed in the canon of the Saxon literary comedy. Ingredients found in varying measure in his works are the *commedia dell'arte,* the French-Italian comedy, the satiric comedy, the "Rührstück," the fairy-play, and Marivaux (twelve of whose plays he published in German translation in 1747–49).[89] In his servant figures, therefore, there are old and new elements and sufficient diversity that it is impossible to bring them under one rubric.

While the servants in the plays discussed so far in this chapter clearly belong to the lower classes, their specific social status has not been specially emphasized. In Krüger's three-act *Die Geistlichen auf dem Lande,* 1743, it is vitally relevant that Peter and Cathrine are common folk, for the religious hypocrisy and corruption portrayed in this play are seen on two levels: in the clergymen's unwelcome wooing of the aristocratic Wilhelmine (that is, on the customary level), and in the misfortune they and their calling cause in the state in general, repaying with ill-usage the respect that the peasants accord them. This is the difference between *Die Geistlichen auf dem Lande* and *Die Pietisterey,* despite certain obvious parallels. In Frau Gottsched's comedy only a small sect has temporarily managed to pervert the thinking of a few silly middle-class women and there is no attack on the pastoral profession in general; in Krüger's, although the two hypocrites do not succeed and Frau Birkenhayn's eyes are opened at last to their iniquity, their exposure does not bring a radical cure for what has been portrayed as a general malaise, and Muffel, in fact, is somewhat ironically *not* deprived of his living at the end. Meanwhile, Peter and Cathrine have been depicted as victims of corruption on this second level: Cathrine, the housekeeper, is pregnant by her employer Muffel, who then tries to bribe his servant Peter into marrying her through the promise of a dowry. In the action of the play, these facts are used later as a means of shocking Frau von Birkenhayn into realizing the true character of her protégés and ending her insistence on marriage between Muffel and her daughter Wilhelmine. Krüger certainly does not dwell on the subject of corruption as a main theme, yet from time to time general social criticism surfaces. In Cathrine's serious indictment of the clergy in her last speech in the first scene of the play, she complains that "wir arme Leute" are forced to put trust in ignorant deceivers (I, 1, 9).[90] That the poor, and hence the servants, are held to be of no account is periodically suggested, and later in the play there is a revealing moment when, after the disguised Peter has thrown off his mask, Frau von Birkenhayn declares: "Ey, das ist ihr Peter? ich habe ihn niemals so genau angesehen, sonst hätt ich ihn wohl kennen müssen" (III, 12, 133).

Analysis of the comedy's structure reveals a peculiarity in Cathrine's role. She dominates act I, where she appears in seven consecutive scenes of the eight and has the largest speaking part; after this she disappears to come back briefly in the second-last scene of the play. She is not involved at all in the problem of Frau von Birkenhayn's determination to have a clergyman as her son-in-law, the basis of acts II and III. Thus, lacking the function of confidante, and concerned only with her own situation, she is atypical of the servant.[91] Peter, while appearing in only nine scenes of the play's total of thirty-one (and not at all in act II), has the second-largest number of speeches, and it is he who undertakes, with the backing of the sensible Herr von Roseneck, to "cure" Frau von Birkenhayn by revealing Muffel's and Tempelstolz's escapades in highly dramatic fashion.

The play is an odd mixture of comic effect and serious comment. It opens with a conventional comic scene of tension between male and female servant; Cathrine calls Peter "ein Tagedieb" and accuses him of drinking. But in the next scene the serious dimension manifests itself in the revelation of the betrayal of Cathrine by Muffel. Here, however, the comic and the serious are constantly interrupting each other. Cathrine's attempts in I, 3 to recall to Muffel the circumstances of the seduction are made funny rather than pathetic by his repeated interpolation of pious words. For a while she seems desperate, but at the end of the scene she is in tone the typical soubrette when she agrees to the suggestion that she marry someone else, the dowry to be supplied by her seducer:

O ja, das ist mir zehnmal lieber, als Sie, und ihr geistlicher Stand. Denn haben sie mir erst den Korb gegeben, so geb ich ihn Ihnen hiermit wieder. Wenn Sie aber jemanden das Glück gönnen wollen, so muß es Peter seyn. (I, 3, 16)

In I, 5 her reluctance to reveal her secret to Peter is exploited comically in dialogue, particularly in the use of the analogy of the large and small "Butterkuchen." But here too there are flashes of seriousness, as when she admits: "Hier wurd ich endlich mehr von meiner Schwäche, als von der Stärke seiner falschen Beredsamkeit, überwunden. . . ." (I, 5, 28).

As for Peter, his immediate reaction to the story is to ask what kind of a figure Muffel cut during his wooing (I, 5, 23), and this is followed by the odd effect of Cathrine's speech at the end of her recital, when she explains that Muffel, who had come to her room ostensibly to pray with her, departed immediately after the seduction without finishing the prayers: "Ich selbst hätte die übrige Zeit lieber mit dir, Petergen, zu-bringen wollen" (I, 5, 28). In short, Cathrine is a woman in a desperate sit-uation, but furnished most of the time with the character and dialogue of the traditional comic maid with nothing else on her mind but getting her young mistress happily married and pocketing a few good tips along the way. But in this play it is Peter, not she, who is instrumental in furthering Wilhelmine's and Wahrmund's cause. After I, 7 we do not see Cathrine again until the second-last scene of the comedy, where she is a mixture of sensuality (harping on the masculine physical charms of the unknown theology student) and shamefacedness (she throws her apron over her head and runs offstage when the assembled company is told that Muffel seduced her). The end of the play brings no apparent solution to Catherine's predicament, unless we are to assume that Muffel will be forced to make an honest woman of her.[92] This reinforces the impression that Krüger by no means intends to portray Cathrine's situation in its full seriousness; rather, it is subordinate to the action involving Wilhelmine. On the other hand one need not completely write off the wider social implications.[93]

Peter, who declares of himself, "Ob ich gleich dumm aussehe, so habe ich doch einen polirten Kopf" (III, 2, 95), is also a mixture,[94] and this is shown particularly with reference to Cathrine's difficulty. In III, 1, when Frau Brigitte arrives and inquires about the household, Peter uses it for comic effect:

BRIGITTE: Also bestehet seine ganze Haushaltung nur aus drey Personen?

PETER: Nein, aus vieren. Ich bin eine Person, mein Herr ist auch eine, aber Cathrinen muß ich gewisser Ursachen wegen für zwey Personen rechnen. (III, 1, 83)

Yet, in act I, with quite genuine indignation, he has refused to be part of Muffel's cowardly plan to solve the problem of Cathrine's pregnancy. In the second scene of the third act, he declares,

> ... aber ich bin mehr ehrgeitzig, als geldgeitzig, ich verlange sie nicht, ob ich gleich nur ein armer Baurenknecht bin, (III, 2, 93)

to which Brigitte remarks that the clergyman Tempelstolz would not have had such scruples. Peter's language is vivid, his wit is crude, and at times he appears somewhat naïve (in his comments on hell in the first scene of the play, for instance), yet many of his apparently artless comments are potentially satirical, as when he explains why he believes clergymen have secrets:

> ... und ich glaube es denn, weil unter zehn Worten, die unser Herr sagt, sehr oft neune sind, aus welchen kein Mensch klug werden kann. (I, 1, 9)

Both servants parody the language of their masters, and Peter sometimes provides straightforward commentary, for instance, when he describes the constant quarrelling that goes on in Muffel's house:

> Ich habe mein Lebestage bey Bauern und Krügern genug gedient, aber so viel hab ich in keinem Hause zanken gehört als hier. Ja bey dem Cartenspiele unsrer betrunkenen Knechte geht es viel friedlicher zu, als wenn ihrer zwey oder drey Geistliche bey meinem Herrn zusammenkommen. Man sollte schwören, sie wären dazu ins Amt gesetzt, daß sie sich in ihrem Leben brav herumzanken sollten. So viel Geistliche in unserm Hause sind, so viel Ketzer sind auch allemal drein, denn einer macht den andern dazu. (III, 2, 86)

In *Die Candidaten,* 1748, Krüger builds a complicated structure, uses a plethora of motifs, has a constant eye to theatrical liveliness, and again, by means of comic technique, treats a serious state of affairs. Corruption is rife both among the aristocracy and the bourgeoisie, and individual advancement depends on the whims of the great and the willingness of the middle class to flatter and kowtow. When the Count declares:

"nichts ist an einem Bedienten löblicher, als ein gefälliges Gemüth" (III, 8, 67), he is actually referring to his children's tutor, Arnold. Reflecting conditions of employment in the eighteenth century, both Arnold and Hermann, the secretary, are treated no better than servants, but they do not fit into a strict definition of the term. Caroline, the Countess's maid, presents another problem, for she is in reality a noblewoman who has gone into service due to her family's misfortune, and though the revelation of her true identity is not made until the end of the play, the reader or spectator realizes very early that she is not what she seems. She does exhibit some slight traditional traits of the soubrette, such as a certain practicality, as when in I, 1 she defends her flattery of the Countess against Hermann's criticism. But there can hardly be any doubt that she is a lady—the tone and style of her language bear witness to this, as do her lofty sentiments. What genuine maidservant would give tongue to such thoughts as "Die Hochachtung bleibt doch allemal das festeste Band zwischen zweyen Seelen" (I, 2, 11)? When she has to have recourse to intrigue, it is for her "eine gewisse Art eine Erniedrigung" (II, 5, 51). Like her suitor Hermann, she is a sentimental and sensitive figure, and despite her temporary lowly status as maid and her real rank as Fräulein von Wirbelbach, she is a true example of the best of bourgeois values. When she repulses the Count's advances, he describes her as "zu widerspenstig, zu bürgerlich, zu gewissenhaft" (III, 3, 60). Because she values above all the last two qualities, in the end she renounces the advantages of her family's reinstatement to marry the bourgeois Hermann, whose heart is "mehr als Adel und Reichthum" (V, 8, 120). The motif of the older character lusting after the maid used by Krüger here and in *Die Geistlichen* is frequently found in the *commedia dell'arte,* but rarely appears in the Saxon comedy.

Johann and Valentin are a contrasting pair of genuine servants. Valentin has a slight part, and reveals in I, 7 the Count's ill-treatment of his lackey, but also, in the scene with Johann, IV, 1, the lackey's snobbish contempt of his less sophisticated confrère (who nevertheless gets the better of him). Johann's is a substantial part and includes some elements of the Harlequinade; although he does not come on stage until act III, he has overall the second-highest number of appearances and speeches. He is sent on a spying mission by his master Valer, eavesdrops on several scenes, is the source of a good deal of comic play, and acts in general as a rather naïve commentator on events, constantly shaking his head in wonder at the intricacies of the action, suggesting the country bumpkin come to town and amazed by the busyness of life there. He is not treated well by his aristocratic master, for whom, it seems, he formerly procured women. In III, 1, for instance, the abuse and threats of violence come thick and fast: "Verdammter Hund! . . . Bestie! . . . du Canaille! . . . Hund! . . . Narr!" (III, 1, 52–54). In fact, Johann is far from being a fool, and even in this scene, though he weeps over his plight, in a comic way he manages to defend himself. He is no village simpleton, no mere buffoon, but possesses a sincere naïvety, a good heart, and a gift for sharp observation. In IV, 2, he tries to make plain to the slow-witted Chrysander that the Count is only willing to give him the vacant post because of his hopes for a liaison with Chrysander's compliant fiancée. Johann has the closing speech of the play, in which he comically expresses his astonishment at the complicated situations of which he has just been a part, but his last words—"Ihr Herren Candidaten, befleißiget euch auf gute Canäle" (V, 8, 120)—point also to something more serious. While the corrupt characters have been held up to increasing ridicule, and by lucky chance the worthy candidate, Hermann, has in this case succeeded, power is still on the whole in the wrong hands, and advancement is achieved by shady means.

In Cathrine of *Die Geistlichen* the confidante function is entirely lacking and in Caroline's one lengthy tête-à-tête with her mistress, II, 1, her ironic contempt for the Countess is abundantly clear to the reader or spectator. Appropriately, Krüger's one Lisette fills this gap. She appears in another work of his with a firm satiric intent, the unfinished *Der glückliche Banquerotirer,* of which only act I and the first scene of act II were completed. "Ha! ha! ha! Da haben wir noch eine Nachkomödie nach der Maskerade," she cries (I, 4, 478)[95] when she and Frau Pandolph, returning masked from a ball they have attended in secret, are taken for ghosts by the terrified Pandolph and his servant Peter. Her words reflect the tone of this play, in which farce predominates. Lisette's very name and her character underline this, for she belongs to the ancient guild of self-assured and unscrupulous maidservants, she aids and abets her mistress in the deception of her master, and she completely confuses Peter.

Crispin, the valet of Frau Pandolph's admirer, appears in the list of characters, but not in the existing scenes; he was meant perhaps to form with Peter a contrast pair of clever/stupid male servants. Pandolph is gullible and timorous and Peter, with his slow wits and literal mind, provides a constant comic reinforcement, with some traits of Hans Wurst. For instance, he takes the lay-figure Frau Pandolph has left in her bed to be the lady herself, suggests that they may be able to bring her to life again by shaking her to start the blood circulating, and, once persuaded that it is just a doll, is nevertheless frightened out of his wits at being left alone with it (I, 7, 483).[96]

Unless Krüger meant her to undergo a change of heart later in the play, Frau Pandolph may be labelled a frivolous, hypocritical creature. But it is characteristic of the "good" figures in the two plays discussed previously that they are not only rational, but also sensitive and high-minded, and the young women in particular, like those of Schlegel's later plays, are, in contrast to the general run of *ingénue* in the Gott-schedian comedy, serious, articulate, and full of fine feeling.[97] In the fairy-play *Der blinde Ehemann,* 1747, and in the two plays with a village setting, *Der Teufel ein Bärenhäuter,* 1748, and *Herzog Michel,* 1748, the same sentimental element is manifest.

Marottin in *Der blinde Ehemann* shows Krüger's conception of the new refined Harlequin figure, under Marivaux's influence, making, in Hinck's words, "einen natürlichen, verspielten, nahezu ländlichen Har-lekin."[98] Temporarily valet to the Prince, for whom he seems to be a kind of court fool, he is really in the service of the fairy Oglyvia, who treats him fairly cavalierly, striking him dumb for a while and casually turning him into a tree in one scene when she does not want him to hear her conversation with another character. Since Marottin has to play several scenes in dumb show, he does not have one of the largest speaking parts, but he appears more frequently than any other character, and has the practical task of bringing about the situation Oglyvia desires. In the play's mixture of sentimental and farcical elements, Marottin is largely the source of the latter, but it is delicate farce. For instance, in I, 8 Marottin and Florine flirt together literally behind the back of Florine's husband Crispin, with Marottin, unable to speak, miming his admiration for Florine and dodging nimbly out of sight whenever Crispin turns in their direction. In the following scene, II, 1, the stage directions indicate how Marottin re-enacts events:

> *Marottin bezeiget indessen durch allerhand gaukelnde Gebährden seine Freude über die Begebenheit mit Florinen.... Marottin fährt fort, Gebährden zu machen, als wollte er dem Prinzen seine Begebenheiten erzählen.* (II, 1, 244)

He is involved in similar capers in II, 7, although his speech is now restored, when with Florine as partner he mimes for Crispin the supposed courtship of the Prince and Laura, while at the same time he further indulges his fancy for Florine.

Marottin is thus the source of visual comic play and intrigue. But while he is amoral and sensuous, in comparison to the high-minded Laura, Astrobal, and the Prince, he speaks — once Oglyvia has given him back his tongue — the same language and on the same level as they do. This is reflected in his discussion with the Prince in II, 1, on the conflict between love and virtue. Marottin is meant, of course, like Harlequin, to be outside normal moral judgement, and so at the end of the play, while Florine is "condemned" to feel ashamed of their dalliance, there is no punishment for him.[99]

Marottin is the only servant, properly speaking, but Crispin, brother-in-law to the title figure and equerry to the Prince, shows traces of traditional servant characteristics: his name, his naïvety, and in particular his actions in the first scene where, pretending to share a bottle of wine with his host, the blind Astrobal, he constantly refills his own glass only.[100]

In *Der Teufel ein Bärenhäuter,* there is only one servant, Peter, although Jacob, now a prosperous tenant farmer, relates in the first scene how he built his nest-egg from his time as servant to the local landowner during the latter's university studies, when he turned all his master's escapades to his own profit. Peter, servant to the lascivious and hypocritical sexton Ruthe, appears only in three scenes and the concluding "divertissement" and is the least important character; his main function is purely farcical. Ruthe has been beaten and tied up, and in their rendezvous in scene II, Peter and his lady-love, Ruthe's wife Anna, thinking he is a log, sit down on him.

"Vom Herzog Michel . . . ," writes Lessing in *Hamburgische Dramaturgie*, no. 83, "brauche ich wohl nichts zu sagen. Auf welchem Theater wird er nicht gespielt, und wer hat ihn nicht gesehen oder gelesen?" [101] This playlet with three characters is a dramatization of the short story by J.A. Schlegel and has much in common with Marivaux's *L'Héritier du Village*. The servant Michel and Hannchen, his employer's daughter, owe something perhaps to the Harlequin-Columbine tradition. [102] Michel has caught a nightingale, and like the milkmaid of the fable, spins in his fantasy a vision of increasing fortune and social status, whereby his betrothed Hannchen will become his "Mattrasse." He is foolish and naïve, but yet tender and sentimental.

With Krüger's servants, the key is liveliness. Occasionally they may have a part in the plot; yet their role is not primarily to be comic advocates of good sense, but to add verbal and visual comedy to the proceedings. Since comic business was traditionally the province of male servants, they are more prominent than the maids in Krüger's plays. His comedies point up elements that are missing from those composed more strictly according to Gottschedian precepts, especially since Gottsched chose to banish, rather than to refine, Harlequin and his kin. In Krüger's plays we find both coarseness and delicacy, but the former is much more characteristic of the bourgeois or aristocratic figures than of the servants; in some of the humble figures there prevails a delicate innocence and charming naïvety.

The variety found in Krüger's comedies is not typical of the Saxon comedy, which assigns to the servants a fairly circumscribed role (though their importance varies from play to play) and modifies their purely comic element. Though some of them show flashes of sheer merriment, on the whole they are integrated into the sober purpose of their setting: the realm of wit merges into the realm of instruction. In some measure these remarks might apply to the servants in the French comedy of manners, too, as valet and soubrette settle into stock figures, and their counterparts in the German plays partly inherit their tone. But characteristically German in the Saxon comedy is the small-town atmosphere, a prevailing provincial spirit, and a pervading domestic cosiness. Transported northward from the great metropolis of Paris, most often to that "Klein-Paris," Leipzig, the servants lose not only their big-city gloss, but their air of being somehow timeless, supra-national figures. Less sophisticated than their French cousins, perhaps, they are at the same time often more truly bourgeois.

The plays considered so far are plainly satiric in intent. But in the mid-1740s variations of the genre already appear in which this element is modified or disappears, and, as we shall see in the next chapter, the servants' role alters accordingly.

# The Comedy of Feeling

## Schlegel, Gellert, and Cronegk

Johann Elias Schlegel, "der . . . dem deutschen Theater die meiste Ehre gemacht hat,"[1] is a transitional figure. Nurtured in the Gottschedian school, with which he never openly broke, he showed in his early critical writings and particularly after he finished his studies in Leipzig in 1742 and moved to Denmark a year later, that his views differed from those of Gottsched on the subject of rules, imitation, the importance of the impact of drama on the audience, and the quality of the "irregular" English theatre. Schlegel was a friend of Holberg, translator of Destouches, and admirer of Marivaux. From his "Schreiben über die Komödie in Versen," among other essays, emerges clearly the notion that comedy is no less noble a genre than tragedy. *Gedanken zur Aufnahme des dänischen Theaters* outlines several possible variations of the comic genre, rather than simply the one form, purely satiric comedy. Schlegel speaks of the "higher" comedy, which can involve "die edeln Empfindungen des Herzens," where "die Fehler der Hauptperson so beschaffen sind, daß sie die Hochachtung des Zuschauers nicht ausschließen."[2] Above all, comedy is to be for the heart as well as the head.

In *Der Geheimnißvolle*, 1747, and even more so in *Der Triumph der guten Frauen,* 1748, this leads to a deepening and softening in the main female figures, who become representatives of true feeling. It follows that they will hardly resort to servants' intrigues to solve their problems—and yet in these two plays, despite Schlegel's strictures on comic servants in the *Gedanken* and elsewhere, the role of the maid in particular has expanded. With Schlegel here, as later with Lessing in *Minna von Barnhelm,* the servants' importance increases as direct moral teaching recedes, but laughter is still the aim. Schlegel's soubrette has changed, for she shares something of what is new in the portrayal of her mistress: tender feeling and an independence of character, which is more subtle than superficial cocksureness. While retaining some of her time-honoured traits, she is affected by the new humanizing trend and reveals a flash of the "edeln Empfindungen."[3]

When Cathrine in *Der Geheimnißvolle* calls herself "eine rechte Grundsäule des ganzen Hauses" (I, 6, 209),[4] with a finger in all affairs, we believe her at once, for she appears more often than any other character (in twenty-six of the play's thirty-nine scenes) and has the second-highest number of speeches, almost as many as the title figure Abgrund. *Der Geheimnißvolle* treats a character trait which, like Tellheim's conception of honour, is foolish in its exaggeration, but not necessarily contemptible in itself and indeed, given the circumstances, comprehensible.[5] Abgrund has lost faith in his fellow man, and while the constant frustration of his attempts to keep himself to himself is comic, his good qualities are stressed from the beginning. At the end, though his father's forgiveness leads to the happy resolution of the action, he is not miraculously cured; secretiveness and distrust are tendencies that will remain in him, but for which his bride Amalia, like Minna for Tellheim's seriousness, will provide a constant antidote. Abgrund is thus a new type of character, and so, too, is Amalia, with her sensitive concern and deep sincerity. These qualities are brought out in her scenes with Cathrine (six in all), for Cathrine, completely in sympathy with her mistress's feelings, nevertheless provides a contrast and acts as foil. In V, 1 she asks what guarantee Amalia has that von Abgrund is no deceiver:

AMALIA: Mein Herz.
CATHRINE: Ach das arme Herz! Sagen Sie ihm nur daß ich keinen

gutherzigern, aber auch keinen schwächern Bürgen kenne, als das ist, und daß es bey der Bürgschaft sehr zu kurz kommen dürfte.

AMALIA: Mein Herz kann sich in tausend andern Dingen irren; aber darinnen nicht.

CATHRINE: Allemal in denjenigen Dingen am ersten, wovon es am gewissesten zu seyn glaubet. (V, 1, 297–98)[6]

Though in such scenes Cathrine is completely unsentimental, she is nevertheless part of the new presentation of the love-interest in that she is prepared to analyse the workings of the heart at all.[7]

In many ways, however, she is the traditional *Zofe*. She likes to worm out secrets and is convinced of her ability to get to the heart of any mystery: "alles, was geheim heißen soll, ist eine Sache, die mich angeht" (I, 1, 191), she assures Amalia, and later stands guarantor to von Schlangendorf for Johann's innocent ignorance:

SCHLANGENDORF: Aber wie kannst du behaupten, Cathrine, daß er nichts weis?

CATHRINE: Weil er mir nichts gesagt hat, und ich glaube, die Wahrheit auszupressen. . . . (V, 6, 316–17)

She is astonished at Amalia's lack of curiosity; she answers for Amalia in one scene with her father; and in her relationship with her sweetheart Johann she is dominant, indulging in sharply witty word-play, while he expresses a rather naïve wisdom. This courtship provides the urgency of the situation: Cathrine makes clear from the beginning that she wants to marry as soon as possible, but von Schlangendorf needs her help first in getting his daughter betrothed.

A born schemer, Cathrine spies—and tries to use Johann as a spy, too, declaring, "Denn das ist dein Beruf" (II, 1, 192)—but she does it on behalf of both her elderly master and young mistress. In the beginning she is supposed to be talking Amalia out of loving Abgrund, but eventually father's and daughter's aims turn out to be the same, and so Cathrine is in effect working for the good of her "victim" Abgrund, to see him happily united with Amalia. Here the servant is no buffer between parent and child, for the father is not a ridiculous figure and there is no generation conflict between Amalia and von Schlangendorf. In the end, the problem is simply how to get the enamoured yet reluctant Abgrund to declare his love, and it is the unwanted suitor Glocke who does the intriguing. In V, 3 Schlegel shows the meeting of the old and the new in Cathrine, for she is sentimental enough to shed some genuine tears with and for Amalia, and for a few moments loses her aplomb (though we should note the contrast between the qualities mistress and maid respectively praise in Abgrund!):

> AMALIA: ... Er war bescheiden, er war ehrerbiethig; und man mag sagen, was man will! Er war gewiß vernünftig und gesetzt.
>
> CATHRINE: Er hatte Augen, so feurig also sechs Paar andere; ganz allerliebste breite Schultern, und kleine Hände, man hätte sie küssen mögen.
>
> AMALIA: Ich war versichert, daß er mich aufrichtig liebte.
>
> CATHRINE: Und ich wollte meine Ehre zum Pfande setzen, daß Sie seine erste Liebe gewesen wären. ...

But her weakness lasts for a few moments only, then she stops crying and declares:

> ... Aber sind wir nicht wunderlich, daß wir weinen, und uns mit seinem Andenken plagen, da wir ihn vielleicht niemals wieder zu sehen bekommen werden? ... (V, 3, 305)

And a few scenes later, V, 7, she is back in her usual role, provoking Abgrund so that he makes open avowal of his love for Amalia. She speaks the last lines of the comedy, which are, characteristically, a dig at the unsuccessful suitor Glocke.

In the Preface to his *Theatralische Werke*, 1747, Schlegel confesses his difficulty with the male servant in this play; because of Abgrund's secretiveness it would be illogical to provide him with a confidant.[8] The solution he found was to make the relationship of Abgrund and Johann one of constant tension. Johann's role is not insubstantial, for he appears in eleven scenes and has the third-largest speaking part (after Abgrund and Cathrine). Moreover, much of the visual comedy focusses on him (there are, for instance, no fewer than six disguise episodes in this play). Abgrund and Johann exchange clothes as part of the former's attempt to avoid recognition, but Johann is an unwilling partner in his master's strategies and their encounters border on the hostile, with Abgrund suspicious that Johann will give him away and Johann speaking boldly, even cheekily, to his master.[9] Largely comic, he too has his moment of humanity when, goaded by Abgrund's behaviour, he would like to leave him, but, "ein guter Narr," decides to stick by him (IV, 7, 295).

In contrast, Heinrich, the valet in Der Triumph der guten Frauen,[10] a superficial creature, is impertinent towards both the maid Cathrine and his master Nikander. He has only one moralizing moment when he points out to the latter that the money he is about to splurge on an evening with a "kleinen artigen Mägdchen" (III, 3, 384–85) might more sensibly be used to pay off debts. An unsympathetic character, he is a bit of a dandy in his speech, as when in II, 5 he tries to imitate his master's lady-killing technique. Heinrich's is a minor role, but Cathrine appears more often than any other character (in twenty-eight of the forty-eight scenes) and though her speaking part is by no means the largest, she does have the first and the last words of the play, with her closing remarks a gloss on the title:

> . . . Ihr Herren Ehemänner, ihr möget so wild oder so ausschweif-
> end seyn, als ihr wollt. Eine gute Frau findet schon Mittel, euch
> wieder zurechte zu bringen. (V, 10, 448)[11]

She is central to the action: particularly important as confidante to Juliane since the latter's unreasonable husband Agenor has cut her off from other society, she is also trusted by Philinte and is the only character who knows that "he" is really Hilaria in disguise; Agenor and Nikander claim her aid; and Heinrich makes her the object of impertinent gallantries. Her prominence is interesting since at the same time this play provides a good example of how the mistreated character, here Hilaria/Philinte, takes over the critical function both of the earlier servants and of the disinterested commentator figures (such as Wackerman in Die Pietisterey).[12]

However, in the discussions of love and human feeling, which are equally as important as outward action in this comedy, Cathrine has some part, too. When fighting for a good cause, she is not averse to a little harmless deception: "weil denn die Wahrheit nichts nütze ist, so helfe die Lügen!" (II, 4, 362). Otherwise she is the soul of honour, repulsing Agenor's advances, completely devoted to Juliane and Hilaria, and, what is new in the stage-tradition of her character, not in the least mercenary. Rational and sharp, she has a strong sense of justice, revealed in II, 2 in her pointed remarks to Agenor about his treatment of his wife. In Cathrine, the traditional wordly-wise soubrette has become in fact the voice of conscience. Nikander calls her "Du kleiner Prediger" (II, 7, 366). But, while valuing the ideal qualities of the heart, she retains some scepticism about human beings in reality: in the last scene she acts as a nice counterbalance to the general mood of reconciliation and sweetness by hinting doubts of the permanence of the sudden miraculous improvement in Agenor and Nikander.[13]

Paradoxically, in these two plays, the servants are by no means less funny for being more serious-minded. The plays themselves are lively, using such devices as disguise, and the new sensitivity does not mean solemnity.[14] We have moved away from the purely satiric comedy, but there are laughs aplenty. It is a different matter when we come to Gellert.

With Schlegel tears are but brief interruptions to a cheerful outlook on life: with Gellert they are an integral part of such an outlook. In *Die zärtlichen Schwestern* a character speaks of virtue, which "uns durch Liebe und Freundschaft das Leben zur Lust macht" (III, 11, 72): this "Lust" is often enjoyed by the figures in Gellert's comedies through a mist of tears.[15] The audience, too, is to be moved, for Gellert declares in the Preface to the *Lustspiele* of 1747:

> Sollten einige an der "Betschwester," dem "Loose in der Lotterie" und den "Zärtlichen Schwestern" überhaupt tadeln, daß sie eher mitleidige Thränen, als freudige Gelächter erregten: so danke ich ihnen zum voraus für einen so schönen Vorwurf.[16]

In his inaugural lecture in Latin as Professor of Poesie, Eloquenz und

Moral at the University of Leipzig in 1751, Gellert chose to speak "Pro comoedia commovente," to put the case for the new genre, comédie larmoyante, which had caused such violent arguments in France (and itself become the subject of comedy, for instance in Destouches's L'Envieux), while its relative, the English sentimental comedy, was dominating the London theatre.[17] Three years after Gellert's lecture, Lessing published a German translation of it in the Theatralische Bibliotheck, matching it with one of Abbé Chassiron's Réflexions sur le Comique-larmoyant and adding some comments of his own. Without doubt this was a question of topical interest to German readers, but hardly a very controversial one, for from the beginning Gottsched had admired Destouches, had not objected in 1737 when Koch, while still a member of the Neuber troupe, translated Voltaire's "serious" comedy, L'Enfant Prodigue, 1736, and had voiced no overall opposition to the new form, except to say in the 1751 edition of the Critische Dichtkunst that such plays should not be considered a branch of comedy proper, but rather a separate genre with the designation of bourgeois tragedies or tragicomedies.[18] The Critische Dichtkunst did in general reject the ideas of Dubos, whose Réflexions Critiques sur la Poésie et la Peinture, 1719, had stressed the power of poetry to move. More specifically, Gottsched disapproved of love as a theme for comedy, but even so, in the German examples of the sentimental play, there is basically nothing inconsistent with his major tenets on the comic genre. Despite all analysis of feeling and stress on heart, sentimental comedy is still "the Musick of the Mind," not emotion run riot, and Gellert hears the human heart speaking a "doch stets verständliche Sprache."[19] Gellert did not think of himself as a reformer (for he did not reject satiric comedy), nor as a great innovator, but simply wished to explore a potential area of the non-tragic drama.

The comédie larmoyante thus made a relatively peaceful and smooth entrance onto the German literary scene in the late 1740s, with translations of Destouches and Nivelle de la Chaussée and the comedies of Gellert. Though the latter stood alone in Germany in the mid-eighteenth century as an exponent of the purely sentimental form, most comedy from his time onwards was influenced and modified in a general but positive way by the new trend. We find from now on a mixture of the comic and the sentimental tone, a humanizing of the satiric element, a development toward greater sensitivity and refinement in the female figure, and a stress on the heart as moral arbiter. Some of all this is in Schlegel's last plays, as we have seen, and is accompanied by an increase in the importance of the servants. In Gellert's case they all but disappear, for while his plays—"wahre Familiengemälde," as Lessing called them[20]—stress particularly everyday household affairs and the trivia of family life, he is at pains to present this life as positive and dignified.[21] The only type of servant character who would fit in is the aged family retainer or the devoted nurse, but Gellert's plots do not need them.[22]

The contrast in the satiric comedy between the sensible and the ridiculous becomes with Gellert one between the genuine and the false, between tender feeling and materialistic concerns. But even in his earliest plays, *Die Betschwester,* 1745, and *Das Loos in der Lotterie,* 1746, there are no servants (though comments on the master-servant relationship occur in the latter play), nor are any to be found in the *Singspiel, Das Orakel,* 1745, or the two pastoral plays, *Sylvia,* 1745, and *Das Band,* 1747. In *Die zärtlichen Schwestern,* 1747, a servant appears in III, 6, hands over a letter, and speaks two short sentences, but he is not listed among the *dramatis personae,* nor is the nameless servant in the one-act play *Die kranke Frau* of the same year, who comes in with Herr Richard in scene 20 and is sent off on an errand without having opened his mouth.[23]

Gellert's sentimental hero and heroine, passive in their calm acceptance of circumstances and in their unselfishness, are active in another sense, for they determine the outcome, if only by a quiet adherence to an attitude. They strive to behave as conscience dictates, and do not need, indeed would disdain, intrigue, for they are fully prepared to renounce personal desire in the name of high principle. And there is another practical reason for the virtual disappearance of the servants. The soubrette in particular has been made superfluous by Gellert's frequent depiction of two young middle-class females: for instance, Christianchen and Lorchen, friends in *Die Betschwester;* or Lottchen and Julchen, sisters in *Die zärtlichen Schwestern.* When the satiric comedy portrays a pair of sisters, it usually contrasts them as a nice/nasty pair and makes one deeply jealous of the other (Luischen and Dorchen in *Die Pietisterey,* for instance), but Gellert's young women are mutually sympathetic, and being each other's confidante, need no maid to lend a willing ear to their troubles. Gellert also uses monologue more frequently than other comedy writers of his time.[24] In *Die zärtlichen Schwestern,* indeed, a general spirit of trust and affection prevails between all characters, with the exception in the second half of the play of the hapless deceiver Siegmund.

But Gellert is an extreme example, and the purely sentimental comedy does not develop further as such, whereas the sentimental *element* in satiric comedy becomes ever more important. An example from the 1750s is J.F. von Cronegk's *Der Mißtrauische* (published posthumously in 1760, but written between 1750 and 1754 in Leipzig), and a modification of the servants' role is evident here too, though at first glance they may seem to be merely late examples of Saxon stereotypes.[25] The valet Philipp speaks of himself in the first scene as a former country bumpkin who has settled in town and become more sophisticated;[26] he has wit and common sense enough to act as foil to the chronically suspicious Timant, his master: "Ich habe nicht so viel Verstand, als mein Herr, aber mehr gesunde Vernunft" (II, 4, 47). Lisette, in Philipp's words "ein schlaues, listiges Ding" (I, 1, 12), is quick-witted, equipped with a sound knowledge of human nature, and very sure of herself: " . . . ich irre mich selten" (II, 1, 27). In keeping with tradition, she and Philipp are themselves carrying on a courtship and stand in the conventional relation to one another: while he is clearer-sighted than his master, he is slower-witted than Lisette. She is devious where he is open, as when he speaks frankly of Timant's irrational behaviour, and she replies:

> Pfui, schäme dich, von deinem Herrn so übel zu reden! Mein gnädiges Fräulein ist auch manchmal wunderlich genug! Nun ist sie in den Damon sterblich verliebt; das habe ich ausgeforscht: und doch will sie ihrem närrischen Vater gehorchen, und deinen närrischen Herrn nehmen. Sie muß den Verstand eben verloren haben: aber siehst du, ich bin verschwiegen; ich rede meinem Fräulein nichts Böses nach. (III, 4, 47)

The servants are responsible for much of the comic effect, especially in the first half of the play. Lisette has the makings of an intriguer, being adept at plumbing hidden emotions in others. She remarks to Philipp of Damon and Climene: "Ich weiß schon, wie ich es anfangen will, daß ich allen beyden ihre Geheimnisse herauslocke" (I, 3, 15). And she makes good this claim. Not to Climene first of all, but to the maid Lisette, does Damon admit that he loves Climene (II, 1), and at the end of the following scene, Lisette, having also wormed Climene's secret out of her and satisfied herself that the pair are in love as she conjectured, remarks complacently: "Es gehört Kunst dazu, einem solchen Paare die Geheimnisse seines Herzens abzulocken" (II, 2, 31).

The stage should now be set for Lisette, abetted by Philipp, to further the lovers' cause, fully justified since the "official" claimant to Climene's hand, Timant, is clearly more obsessed with his suspicions and his rights than truly in love with her. However, not only do we find Philipp, a few scenes later (II, 5), trying to undo the effect on Orgon of Timant's procrastination about his marriage:

PHILIPP *läuft ihm nach, und saget ihm:* Er liebet sie auf mein Wort. Handeln Sie, als wenn er alles gestanden hätte [,] (II, 5, 37)

but also, apart from delivering messages, neither servant has any role to play in the resolution of the action, which is brought about by Damon's noble self-sacrifice, Orgon's recognition of it, and finally Timant's relinquishing of Climene in the face of the proof of his friend's loyalty to him. Lisette and Philipp are still much in evidence, since one or both is on stage in all but five of the thirty-five scenes of the play. Philipp appears more often than any other character and has the second-largest speaking part; Lisette is the third most frequently appearing character, though her speaking part is only moderate. They are vocal as commentators on the action. For instance, Philipp, left on stage alone at the end of V, 4, declares,

Nun, das heißt durch Thorheiten sein Glück gemacht. Mein Herr bekömmt Climenen! Die närrischen Leute sind doch allemal die glücklichsten. (V, 4, 84)

But manipulation of events is no part of their role. If, with Gellert, when the world of practicality gives way to the world of sentimentality, servants all but disappear, here, with Cronegk, they adapt themselves to the world of principle and feeling and identify themselves with it. Increasingly, as *Der Mißtrauische* progresses, there is evidence of the servants' real fidelity, quite different from the attitude of most of their counterparts in the satiric comedy of the 1740s, where identification with the young masters' or mistress' cause does not spring from emotional attachment to them, but from the practical motive that the masters' affairs are the outlet for the servants' energies, their legitimate sphere of action. Moreover, Philipp in Cronegk's play has every justification for feeling irritated and disrespectful:

> Was da nicht für Geduld dazu gehöret, mit einem solchen Herrn umzugehen! Ich bin zu ehrlich für ihn; er ist eines so guten Bedienten nicht werth. Wer zu mistrauisch ist, verdienet, betrogen zu werden. (II, 6, 38)

Timant may deserve to be deceived, but it never happens. Philipp sticks by him to the point of declaring, torn between loyalty and a desire to quit his service:

> Ich thäte es gern: aber fast habe ich das Herz nicht. Wenn Sie mir versprechen, anders mit mir umzugehen: so will ich Ihnen überall folgen, und sollte es auch in den Krieg seyn! Ich habe Sie lieb, ob ich schon manchmal ein loses Maul habe. Ich will ein Gefährte Ihres Glückes seyn. (IV, 6, 72)

"Ich thäte es gern: aber fast habe ich das Herz nicht": the heart is involved, and not only the head (or the pocket), as with so many of her stage predecessors, is also shown by Lisette, who weeps as Damon speaks of giving Climene up despite his love (IV, 1), tries to comfort him and strengthen him in his virtuous resolve, and weeps again at the sight of Climene's distress in the scene of parting (V, 5). A Lisette in tears? This in itself is a small revolution in eighteenth-century comedy.

The general similarity of *Der Mißtrauische* to his brother's *Der Geheimnisvolle* was noted already by J.H. Schlegel,[27] and Lessing also comments on it in the *Hamburgische Dramaturgie,* no. 52, remarking incidentally that both plays would arouse pity or revulsion rather than laughter, because the type of character portrayed reveals a petty nature.[28] Specific parallels involving the servants include Johann's expression of fidelity to an unappreciative master and Cathrine's joining in her mistress's tears. But Philipp's loyalty is given much fuller play by Cronegk and Lisette's tears do not turn to comic comment within moments, but are evidence of her continuing state of mind.

In terms of effective presentation, Cronegk's play reveals many weaknesses, for his characters are largely stereotypes, rather than fully fleshed-out people. Not only does Damon's renunciation verge on the unconvincing, for he seems more concerned with his own image as a noble friend than with his beloved's happiness, and Climene's passive obedience to the insensitive Geronte provoke impatience, but also the two aspects of the servant characters, the traditional and the new, have not been successfully fused. It is almost as if they played different roles in the two halves of the comedy, but without any psychological basis for the change. Their very language seems to alter midway, particularly that of Lisette, whose initial pertness gives way to a sentimental tone; in effect, she begins to speak exactly as Damon and Climene do. From a literary-historical point of view, nevertheless, the portrayal of the servants in this work makes it a half-way house between the earlier Enlightenment comedy and Lessing's *Minna von Barnhelm*.

# IV

# Lessing's
# Early Comedies

Although Cronegk's *Der Mißtrauische* can be called a half-way house between the Saxon satiric comedy and *Minna von Barnhelm,* and in a sense
also stands midway between the early Lessing and *Minna,* Lessing's
youthful comedies are sufficiently varied that the development cannot be
reduced entirely to such simple terms. In some ways the plays discussed
in the last chapter represent an advance over those Lessing wrote between 1747 and 1750, and in other respects his plays already reach beyond them.

The comedy was Lessing's first love. The interest he had felt at
school already flowered into enthusiasm when he arrived in Leipzig in
1746 and came into contact with the live stage. "Meine Lust zum
Theater war damals so groß," he was to say in 1754, "daß sich alles, was
mir in den Kopf kam, in eine Komödie verwandelte,"[1] and writing to
his father in April 1749, protesting against the contention that a comedy
writer could not be a good Christian, he admitted being tempted by the
ambition of becoming a German Molière.[2] A letter to his mother three
months earlier, an *apologia* for his way of life in the previous two years,
reveals that the comedy had been of even greater importance, for before

the Leipzig theatre inspired him to try his own hand at writing plays, it had first taught him about life:

> Die Comoedien kamen mir zur erst in die Hand. Es mag unglaublich vorkommen, wem es will, mir haben sie sehr große Dienste gethan. Ich lernte daraus eine artige und gezwungne, eine grobe und natürliche Aufführung unterscheiden. Ich lernte wahre und falsche Tugenden daraus kennen, und die Laster ebensosehr wegen ihres lächerlichen als wegen ihrer Schändlichkeit fliehen. Habe ich aber alles dieses nur in eine schwache Ausübung gebracht, so hat es gewiß mehr an andern Umständen als an meinen Willen gefehlt. Doch bald hätte ich den vornehmsten Nutzen, den die Lustspiele bey mir gehabt haben, vergessen. Ich lernte mich selbst kennen, und seit der Zeit habe ich gewiß über niemanden mehr gelacht und gespottet als über mich selbst.[3]

Lessing at twenty years old was already widely read in the European literary comedy from the Greeks to his own day and was to broaden this knowledge continually in the next decades. But just as important in his life (and in his writing in a less obvious way) was his abiding love of the comic stage itself, extending with enthusiasm to its most popular aspects. Lessing had a lifelong appreciation of a good belly-laugh! It was reported of his Breslau period that he rarely missed a performance of a clever burlesque and declared more than once, "daß er viel lieber eine gesunde rasche Posse, als ein lahmes oder krankes Lust- oder Trauerspiel sehen wolle!"[4]

Lessing's first major piece of literary criticism focusses on comedy: in the *Beiträge zur Historie und Aufnahme des Theaters,* 1749–50, edited by himself and Mylius, the greater part of his contribution has to do with Plautus. The account of the life and works, the fairly strict translation of *Captivi,* the critique purporting to be by a Gottschedian, and Lessing's reply to it form together a considerable tribute to his favourite comic writer. There is no open break with Gottsched, nor any repudiation of the "regular" drama, but Lessing's defence of Plautus shows that he is tending towards a modification, through serious elements, of the purely satiric comedy:

Was ist aber die Absicht des Lustspiels? Die Sitten der Zuschauer zu bilden und zu bessern. Die Mittel die sie dazu anwendet, sind, daß sie das Laster verhaßt, und die Tugend liebenswürdig vorstellet. Weil aber viele allzuverderbt sind, als daß dieses Mittel bei ihnen anschlagen sollte, so hat sie noch ein kräftigers, wenn sie nämlich das Laster allezeit unglücklich und die Tugend am Ende glücklich sein läßt: . . . Wahr ist es, die meisten komischen Dichter haben gemeiniglich nur das erste Mittel angewendet; allein daher kömmt es auch, daß ihre Stücke mehr ergötzen als fruchten. Plautus sah es ein, er bestrebte sich also in den Gefangenen ein Stück zu liefern, ubi boni meliores fiant, da er seine übrigen Spiele den Zuschauern nur durch ein ridicula res est anpreisen konnte.[5]

When we turn to Lessing's practice in these early days, we find that his comedies have something for every taste: sentiment in *Damon oder die wahre Freundschaft*, 1747, satire in *Der junge Gelehrte*, 1747–48, and *Die alte Jungfer*, 1748, laughter of a gentler sort in *Der Misogyn*, 1748, and serious themes grafted onto a traditional comic structure in *Die Juden*, 1749, and *Der Freigeist*, 1749.[6] Sometimes he reaches back to earlier traditions, naming the female servant Lisette, making her the one stock figure in his early plays,[7] and restoring to her something of her pre-Gottschedian French-Italian sparkle and not a little of her old crudity at times; he adopts current fashion in the shape of the Saxon satiric comedy, while at the same time revealing an interest in the new sentimentality; and he points to the future.[8]

Let us look first at the three short plays, the two one-acters *Damon* and *Die Juden*, and *Die alte Jungfer*, which is in three acts but is not much longer than the other two. It shows the clearest traces of the *commedia dell'arte* with its delight in comic situations without regard to moral considerations. There is no male servant as such, though Peter, "der Gebackensherumträger," plays a role that is rather similar: he is persuaded, for instance, by Lisette to disguise himself as Jungfer Ohldin's suitor in order to further the maid's intrigue. Though he appears only once in act I and then six times in act III, Peter has almost as large a speaking part as Lisette herself. In the really rather unprepossessing cast of characters, he is the only attractive figure, a naïve but colourful character, attesting to the continued survival, under another guise, of the Harlequin tradition.[9] His expression is lively without being coarse and he provides visual comedy, for instance in I, 5, where he tries to prevent Lisette from stealing cakes out of his basket. Lisette is present in sixteen of the twenty-three scenes, as often as the title character, though her speaking part is not quite as large. In this play the maid is not backing a pair of hapless lovers, and neither side in the conflict can lay claim to virtue. Lisette's intrigue with Lelio, the spinster's mercenary cousin, to prevent the marriage fails, but right by no means prevails, for Captain von Schlag's marriage proposal itself is motivated purely by an urgent need for money, and in either case the bride is victim. Moreover, the end of the play implies that Lisette, whose promiscuity has already been hinted at in II, 4, will reconcile herself to her failure by having an affair with the bridegroom.[10] Shrewdness and pertness in this Lisette border on the crude and cruel, and her language is not so much witty as coarse and suggestive. There is scarcely any differentiation between the various characters' speech, however (whereas in other early comedies Lessing exploits contrasting linguistic levels). Here all express themselves in similar colloquial fashion and Jungfer Ohldin addresses Lisette as crudely as the maid does her.[11]

The Lisette of *Damon* (in which there is no male servant) speaks more gently; her chief characteristic is not unscrupulousness, but practicality or a complete lack of sentimentality. In this she is a true foil for her mistress and for Damon, especially since her second speech in scene 2 suggests that she, unlike them, sees through Leander from the start.[12] She opens the play by bemoaning the dullness of the household: "Gesellschaft ist das halbe Leben!" (1, 707).[13] She is lively, and her language contrasts sharply with her mistress's sentimental tone, for it is brisk, peppered with generalities on human nature and verging sometimes on the platitudinous, though vivid enough in its simple proverbial force:

> Liebe bleibt Liebe. Eine Königin liebt nicht edler, als eine Bettlerin, und eine Philosophin nicht edler, als eine dumme Bauersfrau. Es ist Maus, wie Mutter. (2, 712)

When she talks of "heart" (as in scene 1), we can read "common sense," and she constantly counters others' expression of feeling with her worldly-wise attitude. To Damon, who thinks that the widow's inclination will eventually lead her to choose one or other of her suitors, she retorts: "... Neigung? Als wenn ein Frauenzimmer nicht für alle wohlgemachte Mannespersonen einerlei Neigung hätte" (2, 712); and echoing Leander's flowery phrase, she comments, "Den Gegenstand Ihrer so zärtlichen Liebe—Sie meinen doch meine Frau—nicht?" (4, 716).

She is the second most frequently appearing character (in six out of ten scenes) and has the second-largest speaking part,[14] but her role in the play overall is rather lopsided. Her chief function is to set the plot in motion with her proposal to test the suitors' feelings by announcing that the more financially successful of the two will win the widow's hand, a plan only half-heartedly assented to by her mistress.[15] Even this limited commission Lisette oversteps in scene 4 with her advice to Leander, but this is necessary to bring out the ignoble side of his character. This done, her role is virtually over, for although she reappears later in the short ninth scene to confirm to Damon Leander's treachery, she says not a word in the tenth and final scene, where all the characters are present. The problem of the play is resolved in that scene on a completely different plane, when the widow ignores all mercenary considerations and bestows her hand on the unselfish and noble-hearted Damon.

In *Die Juden* there is a different type of "servant" in the persons of Krumm and Stich, not valets, but nevertheless employees of the Baron, "rare examples of rural figures to appear on the German comic stage at this time," as Metzger points out.[16] Stich appears in one scene only, but the bailiff's role is more substantial, revealing the mixture of serious and comic characteristic of this play. Not a rogue, but an out-and-out villain who would not hesitate to do murder, his is the loudest voice raised in condemnation of the Jews (scene 2), but at the same time his attitude is exploited for comic effect, as he mimes the pickpocketing he claims is typical of the Jews while simultaneously relieving the Traveller of his snuffbox. Comic patter characterizes both the miscreants' opening scene together and Krumm's speeches in scene 2.[17] In this scene there is a recurring word-play around the concept of servant and service, producing comic irony since the "servant," Krumm, is merely hypocritically obsequious, while the "master," the Traveller, shows true consideration for and service of others.

Although she appears in less than half of the play's twenty-three scenes, Lisette has the second-largest speaking part. More than a third of the comedy is over before she comes on stage, but from her first word: "Nu?" (9, 392), she is completely in character — quick-witted, brusque, her role a traditional one for the soubrette, to spy out the land and discover who the stranger is (though in actual fact she achieves little in this way). Her relationship to her mistress is an odd one, however, for "Das Fräulein" is no decorous young lady, leaning on her maid for advice about the ways of the world, but half tomboy, half disingenuous child, ignorant of social conventions, and she teases Lisette rather than being led by her.[18] Unlike most maids in the Enlightenment comedy, Lisette has two suitors for her favours (an echo of the Columbina tradition, perhaps). The one, Krumm, she treats haughtily in scene 11, until she notices "his" fine snuffbox, and then has the (for a Lisette of Lessing's) unusual experience of hearing her own disdainful words given back to her. However, by means of pretended tears, she comes into possession of the stolen box, and her presenting it to Christoph in the course of their suggestive flirtation leads to the dénouement. Her complete self-possession is illustrated by her answer to the Baron when he chides her for accepting gifts from a villain: "Ich habe geglaubt, von wem Sie Dienste annehmen können, von dem könne ich auch Geschenke annehmen" (21, 411).

Christoph, the Traveller's valet, has a part almost as large as hers.[19] In the second-last scene of the play he shows some decent feeling when he acknowledges his master's generosity, but otherwise he is crude, discourteous (speaking in one or two places as if *he* were the master),[20] mercenary, and none too honest, expressing his prejudice against Jews in a particularly heartless manner. He lacks any real interest in his master. They travel comfortably; "Um was brauch ich mich mehr zu bekümmern?" (14, 400). This unconcern precipitates the dénouement (whereas a similar trait in the unnamed lackey in *Minna von Barnhelm* serves to prolong suspense). His tale that the Traveller is a duellist fleeing from justice, invented to satisfy Lisette's questioning and thus acquire the snuffbox, helps to force his master's revelation of his identity.

Christoph and Lisette are stock characters, in a stock relationship to one another, but involved in anything but a stock comedy situation. In this play Lessing tries to portray a theme of serious social consequence, with tragic undertones, by means of traditional comic technique.[21] The two servants represent the latter. On their plane the action is resolved — the identity of the robbers who had attacked the Baron before the play begins is established and the theft of the snuffbox is cleared up. But all this simply represents the mechanics of the piece, the tenuous connection between the three groups of characters; plot and the play's major theme have not been fused, as they will be in *Nathan der Weise,* "die Handlung," as Hinck says, "[erhebt] sich nicht zur Höhe des Problems."[22] Lisette and Christoph have the last word, a brief flirtatious exchange, a comic echo of the serious theme, to end it all on a light, even suggestive note:

> LISETTE: Und wanns dazu kömmt, ist Er wohl gar auch ein Jude, so sehr Er sich verstellt?
> CHRISTOPH: Das ist zu neugierig für eine Jungfer gefragt! Komm Sie nur! (23, 414)

Perhaps this is a deliberate contrast to the impossibility of a "happy ending" in the main plot, which could only close with the Baron and the Traveller exchanging, at the end of scene 22, polite, but ultimately somewhat meaningless phrases?[23]

In each of the plays discussed so far, only one character appears and speaks more often than Lisette. In the three-act version of *Der Misogyn* Lisette, the only servant (Wumshäter calls in vain in the first scene for "den Schurken" Johann, who has gone off on some errand and stays away),[24] is present in twelve out of twenty-three scenes, but despite this her part is not large. After rare appearances in the first two acts, she is on stage for almost all of act III, but often silent.[25] As far as number of speeches goes, only one other character has a lesser role than she. But she is presented as a force to be reckoned with behind the scenes. The master of the house, Wumshäter, complains:

Meine Leute sagen mir auch gar nichts. Aber woher kömmts? Da hat mich der Himmel mit lauter weiblicher Aufwartung bestraft, und wenn ich ja einmal einen guten Menschen zur Aufwartung habe, so vergeht kein Monat, daß ihn nicht das verdammte Mädel, die Lisette, in ihren Stricken hat. (II, 3, 447–48)

And when she does speak, she makes a considerable impression. She alone speaks out boldly to Wumshäter. The play begins with a tense scene in which she provokes his first mysogynistic outbursts, and throws his words back in his teeth. She gets the better of him in every encounter; only she is astute enough to realize that Lelio and Hilaria are one and the same person; with her common sense she is a foil to Laura; it is she who announces triumphantly to Wumshäter in the last scene— "Sie waren gefangen" (III, 9, 470).

But though she has the last word of the play, there is earlier an unusual moment when Laura says to her: "Aber wie stehst du denn da, Lisette? Bist du versteinert? Rede doch!" (III, 6, 466). The traditional injunction to the soubrette is that she should talk less![26] Lisette has hatched no intrigue to thwart Wumshäter. The plot aims, not at making him seem ridiculous, but at overcoming his scruples and getting his blessing on the two marriages, and this the enterprising Leander and Hilaria accomplish themselves.[27]

In *Der Freigeist* there are two male servants, Johann and Martin, "Spitzbube" and "Dummkopf," according to Lisette (II, 4, 499),[28] so that we have three contrast pairs: masters, mistresses, and valets. Martin appears only in II, 5, a highly comic scene in which the two valets, having half-digested the views of their respective masters, carry on a "theological" dispute:

MARTIN: Du mußt mich für sehr dumm ansehen. Dein Herr ein Atheist? . . . Er sieht ja aus, wie ich und du. . . . und soll ein Atheist sein?

JOHANN: Nun? sind denn die Atheisten keine Menschen?

MARTIN: Menschen? Ha! ha! ha! Nun höre ich, daß du selber nicht weißt, was ein Atheist ist. . . . Ein Atheist ist — eine Brut der Hölle

... ein listiger Fuchs ... ein Esel ... ein Seelenkannibal. ...

JOHANN: Findest du etwas Erschreckliches, etwas Abscheuliches
an mir? Bin ich nicht ein Mensch, wie du? Hast du jemals
gesehen, daß ich ein Fuchs, ein Esel oder ein Kannibal gewesen
wäre?

MARTIN: ... warum fragst du das?

JOHANN: Weil ich selbst ein Atheist bin; das ist, ein starker Geist,
wie es jetzt jeder ehrlicher Kerl nach der Mode sein muß. (II, 5,
499–500)[29]

Johann appears in five scenes. He is instrumental in producing comic
dramatic tension in I, 4, when he tries to announce privately to his
master Adrast the arrival of the creditor Araspe. He is contemptuous of
Martin, and rude to his master, whose moral sensibility he despises,
declaring that he himself would deny his debts even if he had the means
to pay them (I, 5, 488). Thus he helps to underline the free-thinking
Adrast's moral worth.

The Lisette in this play is a shrewd observer of human nature, who
guesses at feelings either kept secret or not consciously realized and is the
means of making these feelings clear to the audience. She is always
briskly articulate. Her wit emerges in II, 3, where she interlards her
common-sense remarks with phrases copied from lofty religious arguments, and she contributes pure comedy in II, 5, when she jumps out
from hiding to put the fear of God (or the Devil) into the boastful
would-be free-thinker Johann.[30] Like Martin and Johann, Lisette provides comic relief from the seriousness of the central theme, but her role,
like theirs, remains decorative, and is not fused into the play to make a
whole.[31] Her appearances are sparse, for she is on stage in only eleven of
the thirty-five scenes and has in fact less to say than Johann (five characters have larger speaking parts than she). While she does have the last
line of the play, the words she speaks then underline the limitations of
her role. The conflict has been resolved with an exchange of bride and
bridegroom to form two contented, well-assorted couples—"Wie übel
ist unser eines dran, das nichts zu tauschen hat!" declares Lisette as the
curtain falls (V, 8, 555). But however limited her part is, surely she is
not, as far as the reader or spectator is concerned, the "superfluous

laugher" that Rentschler dubs her, for in this play, as in *Die Juden,* the servants' scenes provide almost the only comic moments.[32]

The plays discussed so far establish a rule that the maids have a much more significant role than the valets in Lessing's early plays; *Der Schatz* and *Der junge Gelehrte* provide important exceptions. In the case of the first, a re-working of Plautus's *Trinummus,* of course, Lessing inherited from the original a cast that contained no female characters at all. Minor parts are played by two porters, who appear in one scene each, and by Raps, whose social status is unclear, but who plays the type of part often assigned to a servant (his counterpart in Plautus is the title figure). He comes on stage only once, but it is the longest scene of the play. Philto and Staleno, who wish to practise deception in a good cause, hire him to disguise himself as a friend of Anselmo, a merchant nine years absent from home. Raps enters in bizarre costume and encounters Anselmo himself, unexpectedly returned — a perfect comic set-up. Moreover, he is the only figure characterized by a distinctive way of speaking through the use of puns, whereas Maskarill, valet to the young spendthrift Lelio, and a true Harlequin figure in character,[33] speaks exactly like his master. This valet has overall the largest part in the play, for while Staleno has a slightly bigger speaking part, Maskarill appears more often than he does, in nine of the eighteen scenes (whereas in Plautus's play the slave Stasimus has only the third-largest role). To his master and his master's guardian Philto, he is outspoken to the point of cheekiness. Utterly without conscience, he regards people and circumstances as material for his manipulative genius: "Man hat nie etwas Unrechtes begangen, so lange man noch selbst das Herz hat, es zu rechtfertigen" (5, 579). Philto calls him Lelio's "Anführer in allen Schelmstücken" (3, 572), and although Lelio's conscience has begun to prick him, Maskarill not only tries to steal from him, but responds to his self-recriminations and desire to provide his sister with a dowry by making fun of him, promising to help by "lending" him for ten years at no interest the seven years' wages Lelio owes him. But Maskarill is a non-realistic character, a rogue who is meant to be neither good nor bad, a figure from farce outside such concerns, for whom everything is a game. This is clear from scene 7, where his attempt to persuade Staleno that Lelio's farmstead, his last possession and intended as Kamilla's dowry, is tainted with a curse is made in such exaggerated fashion that he can hardly expect to be believed. His function is pure comedy of the moment. By similar comic exaggeration and use of false climax as in scene 5, he saves Lelio at the end by preparing the way for a reconciliation with Anselmo:

MASKARILL: Als ich Lelio Ihre glückliche Ankunft zu melden kam, fand ich ihn, mit untergestütztem Arme, im Lehnstuhle--

ANSELMO: Und in den letzten Zügen vielleicht?--

MASKARILL: Ja, in den letzten Zügen, die er aus einer ungerschen Bouteille tun wollte. . . . Er sprang auf, lief zu dem Fenster, das auf den Kanal geht, riß es auf--

ANSELMO: Und stürzte sich herab?

MASKARILL: Und sahe, was für Wetter wäre. . . . Er nahm [den Degen], und--

ANSELMO: Und tat sich ein Leides?

MASKARILL: Und--

ANSELMO: Ach! ich unglücklicher Vater!

### Achtzehnter Auftritt

MASKARILL: Und steckte ihn an. . . . Er stürzte die Treppe herab, . . . und warf sich nicht weit von hier (*indem Maskarill dieses sagt, und Anselmo gegen ihn gekehrt ist, fällt ihm Lelio auf der anderen Seite zu Füßen*)--zu den Füßen seines Vaters. (17, 601-18, 602)

Anselmo rewards him, however, by urging his son to send the good-for-nothing to the devil, and Maskarill's retort, which closes the play, indicates his picaresque and irrepressible nature:

Das ist unbillig!--Doch jagen Sie mich, oder behalten Sie mich, es soll mir gleichviel sein: nur zahlen Sie mir vorher die Summe aus, die ich Ihnen schon sieben Jahre geliehen habe, und aus Großmut noch zehn Jahr leihen wollte. (18, 603)

At first glance, Anton and Lisette in *Der junge Gelehrte* seem to be text-book examples of the servant-pair in the European comedy of manners.[34] From them stems a large part of the comic element, particularly from Anton, who is essential as foil to Damis to bring out the latter's ridiculous pedantry. The unsophisticated Anton must suffer his master's abuse, but scenes like II, 4 or III, 15 show that his common sense is capable of turning the tables on Damis's self-centred pretensions:

> DAMIS: Ich rede von der Republik der Gelehrten. Was geht uns Gelehrten, Sachsen, was Deutschland, was Europa an? Ein Gelehrter, wie ich bin, ist für die ganze Welt: er ist ein Kosmopolit: er ist eine Sonne, die den ganzen Erdball erleuchten muß —
>
> ANTON: Aber sie muß doch wo liegen, die Republik der Gelehrten?
>
> DAMIS: Wo liegen? dummer Teufel! die gelehrte Republik ist überall.
>
> ANTON: Überall? und also ist sie mit der Republik der Narren an einem Orte? Die, hat man mir gesagt, ist auch überall. (II, 4, 318)

Even the hint that Anton was the offspring of adultery (I, 6, 299), though serving in its context for comic effect, shows that he is part of real life, as opposed to the paper world of Damis's study; his language reinforces this impression.[35] On the other hand, Anton and Chrysander understand and even reluctantly respect one another, though Anton's attitude in their long scene, I, 6, may be interpreted as ironic, representing only surface agreement with Chrysander. Chrysander, too, is a figure of ridicule and mercenary into the bargain, but he is part of the real world and manages to get along quite well in it. He says to Anton: "Du bist zwar ein Gauner, aber ich weiß auch, man kömmt jetzt mit Betriegern weiter, als mit ehrlichen Leuten" (I, 6, 302), but Anton, despite his readiness to intrigue (motivated mainly by hopes of a handsome present enabling him to set up house with Lisette), does not strike one as a particularly unscrupulous character. Damis, with his lofty contempt for the simple man, deserves every trick Anton can play (such as his delay in handing over the letters in III, 14), and it is no surprise that at the end, unlike Timant's Philipp or Abgrund's Johann, Anton has had enough and bids his master adieu with the comment: "Je nun! wem nicht zu raten steht, dem steht auch nicht zu helfen" (III, 19, 374). Anton is the fall guy who manages to get a bit of his own back.[36]

With Lisette it is a different story. Anton wears "masks," adapting his role to his dialogue-partner of the moment, overplaying, for instance, his naïvety when speaking with Damis, but adopting a different tone with Chrysander. Lisette is always outspokenly Lisette. She is every bit as rude to Anton as to Damis, and for every "Idiote" or simiar insult he has to swallow from his master, he hears a "Narre" or "Dummkopf" from his lady-love, though he is her "goldner Anton" when she needs his help (III, 1, 337). In one scene Damis rudely orders him: "Halt dein Maul! . . . Schweig!" and when Anton then becomes aware of Lisette creeping along behind Damis and mimicking him, she repeats the injunctions in the same terms (III, 14, 359–60).[37] Lisette is quicker-witted, at least in their scenes together, more unscrupulous, and a match for both master and servant; Anton, at first an auxiliary to Chrysander's intrigue, soon joins forces with Lisette in hers, although she mistreats him to the end. Anton and Lisette are the source of much of the action, particularly Lisette (although Anton has a slightly larger part), and she might be speaking for all the soubrettes of European comedy when she airily puts the rhetorical question: "Kömmt denn wohl ohn unser einer irgend in einem Hause eine Heirat zu Stande?" (II, 10, 327). Almost everyone tries to enlist Lisette's valuable talent for intrigue at some point in the play— Chrysander, Damis, Valer, even Juliane in a limited way— and she chooses to aid the one who will promise her greatest advantage.

Lisette with her unsentimental practicality can break the bubble of lofty thoughts and feelings and provide comic relief:

> VALER: [referring to Damis] Seinetwegen würde ich dieses Haus fliehen, ärger als ein Tollhaus, wenn nicht ein angenehmerer Gegenstand—
> LISETTE: So gehen Sie doch, und lassen Sie den angenehmern Gegenstand nicht länger auf sich warten. (II, 2, 311)[38]

More than that, her practicality is placed over against noble feelings which are fine in principle, but out of place in the struggles of daily living. "Eine wunderbare Moral!" is Lisette's retort in II, 1 to Juliane's declaration that in order to show herself worthy of Valer, she must give him up in obedience to her uncle's wishes (II, 1, 306). For Lisette every person has his price, money is what makes the world go round (II, 2), and those, like Valer, who are transparently honest and think all others equally scrupulous, are simply naïve. Lisette's ends are "good" — clearly it is right that Valer and Juliane should marry, rather than that Juliane should be sacrificed to Damis — but this is just happy chance. And in her own mind, Lisette's aims fully justify unscrupulous means. It is simply good practical sense. "Ei, was Betrug?" she asks when her scheme is challenged, "Wenn der Betrug nützlich ist, so ist er auch erlaubt" (II, 15, 336).

Lisette has a minor set-back in I, 4, when her intriguing fails because of Damis's foolishness, but it is in the gentle Juliane of all people that she meets her match. In *Damon*, as we have seen, it was the "sentimental" characters, the widow and Damon, who directed events in the end by their very adherence to "unpractical" values. And in *Der junge Gelehrte* the outcome is even more striking: Lisette's intrigue with the false letter (dishonest means) promises to bring about Juliane's marriage to Valer (worthy end), but Lisette's very conviction of her own leading role leads to its failure. For when she openly boasts of the deception (III, 10, 355), Juliane learns of the plan and refuses to be a party to a trick practised on Chrysander. The tradition of the active, manipulative servant, reaching back through the *commedia dell'arte* to antiquity, collides with something new, the element of virtuous sentimentality. Intrigue versus uprightness, pragmatism versus feeling — and feeling wins. The dénouement of the Valer-Juliane situation is brought about by Juliane's gesture of gratitude to Chrysander, incidentally a thoroughly undeserving object of it, so that the reader must sympathize a little with Lisette! Juliane and Valer renounce money that is rightfully hers, a most untypical gesture in the rationalist age where a canny financial sense was regarded as a virtue. It is true, of course, that whereas in the conventional comedy situation of the time, blocking the lovers' marriage by their elders often also involved withholding money needed to make the marriage possible, this is not so here, for Valer can afford to take Juliane without a dowry.

Even more uncharacteristic for Enlightenment comedy is the fact that while Damis's pretensions are exploded, Chrysander's acquisitiveness is left uncorrected. Indeed, materialism, his basic motivation, seems sanctioned by events, that is, the ending is in part non-moralistic, not in keeping with the fate of the elderly schemers in the French comedy of manners or the German Enlightenment comedy.[39] The point is that, though mercenary and rather ridiculous, he is socially integrated and no outsider like his son. Twenty years later, Lessing remarked in the 99th number of the *Hamburgische Dramaturgie* (apropos K.F. Romanus's *Brüder*):

> Ich weiß überhaupt nicht, woher so viele komische Dichter die Regel genommen haben, daß der Böse notwendig am Ende des Stückes entweder bestraft werden, oder sich bessern müsse. In der Tragödie möchte diese Regel noch eher gelten; sie kann uns da mit dem Schicksal versöhnen, und Murren in Mitleid kehren. Aber in der Komödie, denke ich, hilft sie nicht allein nichts, sondern sie verdirbt vielmehr vieles. Wenigstens macht sie immer den Ausgang schielend, und kalt, und einförmig.[40]

*Der junge Gelehrte* proves that already in 1747 Lessing was more concerned with reality than with moral teaching in comedy. And reality seems to mean also that even clever intrigue has its limits, for the answer to Lisette's rhetorical boast quoted above, "Kömmt denn wohl ohn unser einer irgend in einem Hause eine Heirat zu Stande?" must be: "In diesem Falle — doch!"

However, theatre-goers seeing *Der junge Gelehrte* for the first time might well, a week later, retain vivid memories of the sprightly Lisette and the clever Anton and have to force themselves to call Juliane to mind from her appearance in only six scenes out of the forty-two.[41] Her last appearance is half-way through the final act, so that her generous gesture is not made in person, but by Valer. On the other hand, there are only six scenes where neither Lisette nor Anton is on stage (and in one of these Lisette is eavesdropping in a closet). Lisette, with the third-largest speaking part, is present in twenty-two scenes and hidden in four more, while Anton appears in twenty-four scenes. Damis, on stage in twenty-eight scenes, appears more frequently than either of them individually, but Anton actually has a greater number of speeches. Anton and Lisette, in fact, represent Damis's world—Damis is far more frequently seen with them than with the other bourgeois figures: with Anton because he is his valet, and with Lisette because she insists on constantly butting in, although forbidden to enter his study. Thus, despite the twist to the ending just described, one is left with the impression that the servants are prime movers. Then, too, the love of Valer and Juliane is secondary to the main emphasis on Damis. In the overall effect, Damis's exaggerated pedantry, Chrysander's pomposity, and the caperings of the two servants all but hide the fact that, in Juliane's refusal to deceive and Valer's backing of her, Lessing has modified the satiric comedy by introducing an aspect of the sentimental drama. Curiously enough, however, Lisette does not appear in the last five scenes of the play, exiting in triumph with an "Adjeu" at the end of III, 14, having goaded Damis to the utmost. It is left to Anton to seek confirmation that Valer does indeed intend to give Lisette a dowry (III, 18, 374). Damis and Anton played the first scene, and now they have the last, but Anton has only the *second*-last word, for Damis, disillusioned and angry, stands alone on the stage at the end, a slightly tragic as well as a comic figure.

After he finished *Der Freigeist* in 1750, Lessing did not complete another comedy until *Minna von Barnhelm*, 1767, though he worked on ideas for a dozen or so. In general in Germany there was a gap in the production of original comedies in the 1750s (apart from Cronegk's *Der Mißtrauische*, there are two by C.F. Weiße), though the number of comic plays *performed* steadily increased, translations and adaptations still forming the bulk of the repertoire. With the exception of *Die Matrone von Ephesus*, which will be discussed in the next chapter, those of Lessing's comedy fragments dating from the late 1740s to the mid-1760s containing servants belong to the satiric mode, and these figures provide further evidence of points already noted in the finished comedies.[42] In seven fragments the maid is Lisette: *Der Leichtgläubige*, 1748?, *Tarantula* and *Weiber sind Weiber*, 1749, *Der gute Mann*, 1753, *Der Vater ein Affe*, 1753?, *Die Klausel im Testament/Die glückliche Erbin*, 1755, and *Der Witzling*, 1763. In *Der Schlaftrunk*, 1756, she is Finette. A Toinon is listed in *Palaion*, 1750, and a Hedwig in *Vor Diesen*, 1756, but neither appears, and though it is dangerous to make firm conclusions on the basis of fragmentary pieces, it may be significant that in these two plays the heroine herself is pert and quick in repartee. One play alone lists no maid: *Justin*, 1750, an adaptation of Plautus's *Pseudolus*, where the title figure is a servant and two other male servants are included. Overall, however, the female servants are far more important than the male, for in some plays there is no valet and only in three has he any significance: in *Der Leicht- gläubige*, where Johann makes common cause with Lisette; in *Der Schlaf- trunk*, where Anton displays a naïve wit; and in *Die Klausel im Testament- /Die glückliche Erbin*, where Pasquin is more than a match for Lisette and is particularly articulate, skilfully imitating Lelio (I, 7). The Lisettes of the fragments are active figures. For instance, the maid dominates the four extant scenes of *Der Vater ein Affe*. In *Der Leichtgläubige*, *Tarantula*, and *Weiber sind Weiber* they are brisk, practical, and materialistic com- pared to their gentle mistresses, and very sure of themselves. In *Taran- tula*, Lisette declares:

> Es liegt Lisettes Ehre dran
> Daß sie es halten kann
> Was sie verspricht. (scene 3)[43]

They are mercenary: in *Weiber sind Weiber* Segarin wishes to entrust his suit to Lisette, convinced she can bring off his marriage before nightfall, but she refuses when it becomes clear that her only reward will be his eternal gratitude. Significantly, in *Der gute Mann* Lisette takes a hand in the situation against the wishes of her young mistress and therefore fails as an intriguer.

An important aspect of Lessing's use of servants, and one which he exploited more fully than his predecessors, even Schlegel, is their liveli- ness. What strikes one on comparing his early comedies with almost any example of the Saxon comedy between 1735 and 1748 is how much more truly dramatic Lessing's plays are, with their quicker tempo and brisker dialogue.[44] A comparison of *Trinummus* with *Der Schatz* brings this out clearly. Plautus's play moves slowly, and speeches and soliloquies, which are frequently extensive direct comments on manners and morals, are quite long.[45] Lessing's characters express themselves more succinctly and never let up on comic effect or snapping repartee. There is a tremendous quick-moving liveliness to his play,[46] and the language is varied and vivid. The Porter in scene 12, for instance, peppers his remarks with proverbial sayings, while Raps in his scene with Anselmo makes constant comic play with words. The following is a much sharpened version of the original speech in Plautus:

> Sein Sie wer Sie wollen, wenn Sie nur nicht der sind, der ich nicht will, daß Sie sein sollen. Warum waren Sie dann nicht gleich Anfangs der, der Sie sind? Und warum wollen Sie denn nun der sein, der Sie nicht waren? (II, 595)[47]

There is altogether great fun with words in this play: the tension in scenes 1 and 5, for example, is purely verbal, and Maskarill's last trick, his narration of Lelio's "suicide" in scenes 17 and 18, quoted above, is a matter of the effect of the words.

Compared with this, how flat seems the dialogue in a comedy by Frau Gottsched, for instance. Let us look at contrasting examples. Act II, scene 2 of *Die Pietisterey im Fischbein-Rocke* consists of a long dialogue between the villainous hypocrite Scheinfromm and the maid Cathrine, in which Cathrine's function is to find out his plans and make him look ridiculous at the same time. Her method is first to make a series of rather heavy-handedly ironic rejoinders, in which she apparently expresses her agreement with his views, while indicating her contempt to the audience by her tone:

HERR SCHEINFROMM: So seyd ihr also meiner Meinung?

CATHRINE: O freylich!

HERR SCHEINFROMM: Nun, so will ich euch was offenbahren: Ich habe selbst die Frau Glaubeleichtin bisher abgehalten, ihre Tochter zu verheyrathen.

CATHRINE: Ey! Ey! wer hätte das dencken sollen? . . .

HERR SCHEINFROMM: Aus Eigennutz thue ich das alles nicht; von diesem Laster bin ich durch die Gnade Gottes schon lange Zeit befreyet. Nein, ich thue es aus bloßem Eyfer vor Jungfer Luischens Seeligkeit.

CATHRINE: O! das sieht man wohl. (II, 2, 44–45)[48]

Then, towards the end of the scene, she permits herself a more directly
satirical comment:

> HERR SCHEINFROMM: Eine Mutter die ihre Kinder liebt: eine Frau,
> die ihrem Manne treu ist, wenn sie es nicht bloß durch die Kraft
> einer übernatürlichen Gnade thut, so sündigt sie.
> CATHRINE: Das ist ja betrübt. So werden wir auf die Art lauter
> Affen und Meerkatzen heyrathen müssen, die wir nur durch eine
> übernatürliche Beihülfe lieben können. (II, 2, 47)

After Scheinfromm's exit, she declares:

> Das ist ein alter Filzhut! Aber zum Schelme bist du mir noch lange
> nicht listig genug. (II, 2, 48)

Never does she oppose him openly.

In *Der junge Gelehrte*, considered by most commentators to represent the highest achievement in comic language in the early and middle
*Aufklärung*,[49] Anton and Lisette occasionally try to manipulate Damis
indirectly by persuasion and apparent agreement, but in general they
practise the politics of confrontation. Where Cathrine smiles quietly up
her sleeve at Herr Scheinfromm, they frequently laugh in Damis's face.
Moreover, Frau Gottsched's dialogue moves slowly. Compare the scene
above with II, 11 of Lessing's play, where Lisette tries to turn Damis
against Juliane by vilifying her, while Anton (who has not yet joined
forces with Lisette) tries to play down her assertions.

> LISETTE:  . . . –Sie ist albern––
> DAMIS: Kleinigkeit!
> ANTON:  Und ich sage: Lügen!
> LISETTE: Sie ist zänkisch––
> DAMIS: Kleinigkeit!
> ANTON: Und ich sage: Lügen!
> LISETTE: Sie ist eitel––
> DAMIS: Kleinigkeit!
> ANTON: Lügen! sag ich.

LISETTE:  Sie ist keine Wirtin—

DAMIS:  Kleinigkeit!

ANTON:  Lügen!

LISETTE:  Sie wird Sie durch übertriebenen Staat, durch beständige Ergötzlichkeiten und Schmausereien, um alle das Ihrige bringen—

DAMIS:  Kleinigkeit!

ANTON:  Lügen!

LISETTE:  Sie wird Ihnen die Sorge um eine Herde Kinder auf den Hals laden—

DAMIS:  Kleinigkeit!

ANTON:  Das tun die besten Weiber am ersten.

LISETTE:  Aber um kinder, die aus der rechten Quelle nicht geholt sind.

DAMIS:  Kleinigkeit!

ANTON:  Und zwar Kleinigkeit nach der Mode! (II, II, 329)

Not only is the briskness of the dialogue characteristic here — Lessing frequently makes effective use of stichomythia — but the fact that Lisette's contentions are pushed to ridiculous lengths, and in the last line quoted Anton abandons his prescribed part in the exchanges and makes a comment for purely satiric effect, shows that Lessing is above all concerned with making the scene funny.[50] Elsewhere in *Der junge Gelehrte*, often in *Der Schatz* (scene 9, for instance), and not infrequently in the other plays, we find scenes where the author's main aim is to bring out the comedy of a particular situation, perhaps to "teach" indirectly through wit (for Lessing by no means discards the *Vernunftprinzip* of the Saxon comedy), rather than subordinating everything in an obvious way to the overall theme or to the development of the plot.[51]

In this preoccupation with laughter for its own sake, the servants are the main vehicle, as they are in general for Lessing's witty dialogue, skilfully taking up a word used by another character, adding an ironic twist or double meaning, and engaging in quick-as-lightning repartee, in short, the sheer joy of words.[52] In his early comedies, Lessing puts the servants through their paces — and lets them find their tongues! Visual comedy, too, the comedy of gesture or physical action, rare in the *Aufklärung* till now (and theoretically rejected), comes into its own again in Lessing's servants, as for instance when in *Der junge Gelehrte*, III, 14, Lisette imitates Damis behind his back. Lisette also hides or eavesdrops in two of the plays. In many ways, Lessing exploits the theatricality of the servants.

But the servants are not, with the possible exception of Lisette in *Die alte Jungfer*, crucial to the dénouement. A characteristic traditional in the comic soubrette is that she believes people's behaviour to be utterly predictable, shaped according to set patterns. It is the basis of her power that she knows, in her worldly wisdom from empirical observation, what those patterns are. When the main characters become a little more individual, which here means a little more sentimental, they become for her less predictable. The Lisette of *Damon* is non-plussed by Damon and Leander's gentlemanly behaviour — as rivals they should surely be fighting tooth and claw! And she has no conception whatever of her mistress's inner feelings, for she automatically assumes them to be governed by practicality and adherence to the time-honoured "way of the world." Juliane's scruples in *Der junge Gelehrte* are, to her Lisette, "eine wunderbare Moral!" (II, 1, 306), and when the mistress rejects her scheming out of hand, the maid can hardly contain herself: "Gift und Galle möchte ich speien, so toll bin ich! . . . Mein guter Rat hat ein Ende. Ich will mich bald wieder in so etwas mengen!" (III, 11, 355–56). Whereas in *Der Mißtrauische*, Philipp and Lisette identify themselves with the noble, though foolish, renunciation of Climene and Damon, in Lessing's play, Lisette and Anton retain a highly critical attitude,though they are powerless in the face of Juliane's honesty.

Again except for *Die alte Jungfer*, a deepening of the comic element and a movement from satire to humour emerges from these plays.[53] Some of the main characters reveal a development beyond their counterparts in the Saxon comedy. In *Der Misogyn* this simply means that the young couple take it on themselves, by means of a plot, to persuade Wumshäter to accept their wishes even though they cannot cure his misogyny. In the other plays the change reaches further: *Der junge Gelehrte* and *Damon* bring noble selflessness into play, and in *Damon,* and to a greater extent in *Der Freigeist*, the resolution of the conflict depends on a change of heart, a spiritual development, in one of the main figures. One might say also that in *Die Juden*, to a limited extent, greater human insight is achieved, though here, because of society's prejudices, it cannot be translated into practical terms and bring about the conventional happy ending. The main characters sometimes operate therefore on a new plane, where servants' intrigues are no longer entirely appropriate. Masters or mistresses and servants thus belong to slightly different moral worlds, for the servants themselves, though their roles are sharpened, though they are funnier and far more effective theatrically, have not changed much in nature. Of the six Lisettes in the completed plays, four (from *Die alte Jungfer*, *Damon*, *Der junge Gelehrte*, and *Die Juden*), despite their varying functions, have this in common: they belong to the old world of below-stairs intrigue. Two (from *Der Misogyn* and *Der Freigeist*) have become milder, less unscrupulous, but without acquiring any outstanding new characteristic.[54] The Lisette or similar figure in European comedy usually seems to be consciously playing a part (so that, paradoxically, she can rarely be "herself"), constantly adjusting her attitude and speech to a particular person according to the purpose she has in mind and employing a deliberate tone ranging from the bantering to the openly ironical. Her very words are consciously manipulative. On the whole this is still true of the six Lisettes here. Very occasionally a straightforward human character breaks through the Lisette veneer, as in *Der Misogyn*, when Wumshäter declares that women love only themselves and Lisette erupts in simple spontaneous indignation:

> Nein, mein Herr, das ist zu toll! Ihre Jungfer Tochter hat zwar Unrecht, daß sie den Mann von Ihrer Hand nicht annehmen will, aber müssen Sie deswegen das ganze Geschlecht lästern? (III, 2, 461)

These early comedies of Lessing show that some development in the direction and purpose of the genre is taking place, though it is certainly no very consistent or systematic change, but nevertheless perceptibly a movement towards the "serious" comedy, with its more individualized and more active main characters. The context in which the servants appear is changing, but they themselves are so far basically unaltered. Their greater articulateness, their heightened comic purpose are not lost later, but they have to become more human. When this happens, Lisette becomes Franziska.

# V

# *Minna von Barnhelm*
# and
# *Die Matrone von Ephesus*

In *Minna von Barnhelm*, the comedy of Lessing's maturity, there is at one point a precise echo of his early play, *Der junge Gelehrte*:

DAMIS: [to Anton]:  Kerl, du bist toll! (II, 4, 319)
TELLHEIM [to Just]:  Kerl, du bist toll! (I, 8, 617)[1]

Damis's exclamation interrupts a speech in which his servant Anton, ostensibly impressed by his master's exposition of certain philosophical and legalistic niceties, in fact makes fun of this pedantry by an outrageous application of Damis's explanations to an everyday situation. The satire is lost on Damis, who takes the speech for a further example of Anton's uneducated, muddled thinking. Tellheim's use of the same phrase comes at the end of his reading aloud of Just's "bill": he has asked his servant to calculate the wages owing to him so that he may pay and dismiss him, being no longer able to keep a servant, but Just, while indicating a trifling sum in back wages, has on the other side of the paper listed a series of payments and favours he and his family have received from his master. The result, according to Just, is that *he* is in Tellheim's debt and ought to be allowed to continue serving him. That each master reacts to his servant with the same exclamatory phrase is coincidence. But that the same words have such widely different meanings in the two cases, and must indeed be spoken in differing tones, is significant. It is not merely a difference in dramatic situation and character—the self-deluding pseudo-scholar Damis despising the down-to-earth Anton and the upright, obstinate Tellheim taken aback, but also moved by the loyalty of his rough diamond Just—more than that, these passages, almost twenty years apart, tell us something of the development of German comedy between the mid-1740s and the mid-1760s.

In his *Pro comoedia commovente* Gellert had spoken of non-heroic love, of friendship, constancy, and a grateful heart as suitable themes for comedy.[2] Though *Minna von Barnhelm* is certainly not a *weinerliches Lustspiel* on the Gellertian pattern, it is an outstanding example of the incorporation of these qualities, and the servants, though their function is still to provoke the most spontaneous and the merriest laughter, embody them, too.[3]

In the Preface to the second edition of the translation of Diderot's plays, 1781, Lessing describes how, by the 1750s, the German comic theatre had become overpopulated with stereotype figures:

> Wir ... hatten es längst satt, nichts als einen alten Laffen im kurzen Mantel, und einen jungen Geck in bebänderten Hosen, unter ein Halbdutzend alltäglichen Personen, auf der Bühne herumtoben zu sehen; wir sehnten uns längst nach etwas bessern, ohne zu wissen, wo dieses Bessere herkommen sollte: als der *Hausvater* erschien.[4]

Since 1758, Lessing continues, empty laughter has been less frequently heard in the theatre, for "das wahre Lächerliche ist nicht, was am lautesten lachen macht; und Ungereimtheiten sollen nicht bloß unsere Lunge in Bewegung setzen." In the *Hamburgische Dramaturgie* also, Lessing makes a clear distinction between "Lachen" and "Verlachen" and questions the established practice of pointing up, in order to correct, ridiculous foibles or vices. "Lachen" presumes sympathy with its object. Comedy's real value lies "in dem Lachen selbst; in der Übung unserer

Fähigkeit, das Lächerliche zu bemerken," [5] and this is indeed the lesson Minna teaches: life viewed with a smile is life viewed objectively, laughter enables us to see straight. [6] Tellheim's sense of honour is not a "verbesserliche Untugend," but a virtue that has got out of hand, that has led its bearer to regard the world with gloomy resentment, to lose his good judgement—and his sense of humour. All this has mainly to do with the leading characters, Tellheim and Minna, but the servants are also to some extent involved in this new conception of the purpose of comedy. [7] For example, in III, 7, after Tellheim's laborious explanations as to why it would be wrong for him to borrow money from his former Sergeant, Werner counters with an ironic

> So, so! Sie wollen es versparen, bis auf beßre Zeiten; Sie wollen ein andermal Geld von mir borgen, wenn Sie keines brauchen. . . . (III, 7, 655–56)

Franziska provides us with another instance in III, 10, when she meets Tellheim's asseverations of the seriousness of his purpose in avoiding another meeting with Minna with a series of light-hearted rejoinders:

> . . . wir können Geschriebenes nicht gut lesen. . . . wir denken, daß das Briefeschreiben für die nicht erfunden ist, die sich mündlich miteinander unterhalten können. . . . (III, 10, 659)

and wins him over—and lightens his mood—in the end by her refusal to take no for an answer:

> Wir wollen [den Brief] auch nicht lesen, denn der Schreiber kömmt selbst. Kommen Sie ja; und wissen Sie was, Herr Major? Kommen Sie nicht so, wie Sie da sind; in Stiefeln, kaum frisiert . . . Kommen Sie in Schuhen, und lassen Sie sich frisch frisieren. —So sehen Sie mir gar zu brav, gar zu preußisch aus! (III, 10, 661)

This even elicits a spontaneous "Ich danke dir, Franziska," revealing a certain inconsistency in Tellheim between purpose and will. In neither scene, however, is there any suggestion that the servant is ridiculing the master. Mutual respect and affection prevail. Tellheim's first words to Franziska in III, 10, for instance, are warm: "Liebe Franziska, ich habe dich noch nicht willkommen heißen können" (III, 10, 658), the sort of thing one says to someone who is very much part of the family. In a very general way in the earlier satiric comedy (with Lessing's own *Die Juden* and *Der Freigeist* marking partial exceptions) dramatist, audience, and other characters are grouped on one side pointing the finger of scorn at the satirized character, who stands aloof from them all. In *Minna von Barnhelm,* dramatist, audience, and almost all other characters, including the servants, stand close to Tellheim and identify with him. In his bitterness he constantly tries to break away from his fellow human beings and they just as constantly reach out to him and pull him back into the social fold.[8]

That another kind of servant exists is brought out both in III, 2, where Just recounts to Franziska the fate of Wilhelm, Philipp, Martin, and Fritz, and in I, 9 by the "Bediente" who changes masters every six weeks. Moreover, that Tellheim is not every servant's ideal is made clear by that same "Bediente" in his parting words to Just: "Kamerad, das wäre kein Herr für mich!" (I, 9, 619). But for all master-servant relationships actually depicted in the play, the appreciation behind Tellheim's "Kerl, du bist toll!" holds good.[9] Tellheim understands Just, even though his rough and quarrelsome nature causes problems — Damis does not understand Anton, nor think it of any consequence that he should. The Tellheim/Just ménage must be the exception that proves the rule expressed in the proverb: "No man is a hero to his own valet."

"Servant" must in the case of *Minna von Barnhelm* be interpreted liberally and that in itself is an indication that the play marks a distinct development. Just is the only one who is a servant in the narrow sense, and, as groom turned valet due to the fall in his master's fortunes, he belongs rather to the pre-valet stage tradition, for there is a good deal of the rough humour of the popular slapstick comedy about him, and he is intended to be quite a coarse character. He can produce a telling argument or retort on occasion, but he is not at all witty. And yet, this is an advance, too: like Tellheim, Lessing has bid adieu to the Wilhelm-Philipp-Martin-Fritz figures of the German comedy convention (all names used for servants in earlier Enlightenment comedy) and is making

do with Just, atypical in name and unfashionable in character. In being
"reduced" to Just as his only servant, Tellheim is "reduced" in human
terms to simple faithfulness.[10] It is true that his attitude to him is just a
trifle lofty—"Nein, es gibt keine völlige Unmenschen!" (I, 8, 618)—but
it must be admitted that Just's mental horizons are limited, and even the
good-natured Werner remarks: ". . . freilich ist an Justen auch nicht viel
Besonders" (III, 4, 469).[11] As for Franziska, it has become almost com-
monplace in commentaries on the play to point to the significance of her
not being just one more Lisette, but even more important than her German name, for, after all, earlier Enlightenment comedy had its Sophies
and Cathrines, is the fact that she has Christian name *and* surname and as
detailed a background as Minna herself (*see* her account to the landlord in
II, 2). Franziska is somewhere between maid and sister to Minna, of the
same age, whereas the soubrette is usually at least a year or two older
than her mistress. Unlike many of her predecessors, she is, as Schreiber
says, "comic without being coarse."[12] The Tellheim-Werner friendship
offers even more new elements, retaining a basic master-servant founda-
tion from their former officer-N.C.O. connection, but thriving essentially on mutual respect. Werner "serves" Tellheim now because he
chooses to, and he has a life of his own apart from Tellheim's affairs. By
marrying him, Franziska will also lead her own life apart from Minna.[13]

Franziska appears in more scenes than any other character (thirty-
five out of fifty-six) and has the third-largest speaking part, after Tellheim
and Minna. Werner and Just are roughly equal in number of speeches and
appearances (sixteen for Werner, seventeen for Just), but Just is particularly prominent in the first act (nine out of twelve scenes) and Werner
in the third (eight out of twelve). While having relatively little to say in
the final act, they contribute to the drama of the situation, Just by his surprise revelation that Minna has the ring that Tellheim pawned with the
landlord, and Werner with his joyful agreement to Tellheim's request for
a loan, which quickly turns to astonishment and hurt when he brings the
money only to be coldly rebuffed. In act III, which is a breathing space
between the dramatic close to act II and Minna's initiation of her "Spiel"
in act IV, the servants dominate. In addition to these three, there are
several anonymous "Bediente," who have brief appearances in a single
scene each.

There are still considerable traces of the traditional servant roles. Werner and Franziska's courtship parallels and contrasts with Tellheim and Minna's, so that the happy resolution of the one is accompanied by the happy ending of the other. Just's dream and his awakening open the play[14] and the proposal of marriage by Franziska to Werner ends it, making a comic frame for an action that often touches on the sad and serious (in fact, Franziska's proposal dries Werner's tears of affection for Tellheim). Franziska's sharp wit, which is too quick for the duller Werner, produces something of the typical relationship of the servant pair. In basic outline Franziska is a direct descendant of Lisette, when we look at some of her functions in the play, but the fleshing out of her character has made her rather different. And the Franziska-Werner relationship will not on closer scrutiny bear comparison to that, say, of Lisette and Anton in *Der junge Gelehrte.* There the materialistic Lisette, because the opportunity offers and she has hopes of a good dowry, will take Anton and probably dominate him for the rest of their lives.[15] With Werner and Franziska the question of a dowry never comes up and the subject of marriage is not broached until the very last scene. Franziska is, atypically in the soubrette, utterly unmercenary and reluctant to accept the money her mistress proffers in the fullness of her heart—"Ich stehle es Ihnen, Fräulein" (II, 3, 633). In Werner and Franziska's lightning courtship, spontaneous, flirtatious, and rather sensual attraction dominates, but there is a more serious element too: whereas in the earlier comedy she would have been paired off with a Wilhelm, Philipp, Martin, or Fritz, here she proposes to Werner because he is "ein gar zu guter Mann" (V, 15, 704), thus paralleling on a simpler level her mistress, who loved Tellheim for his noble qualities before she had even set eyes on him (IV, 6, 678-79).[16] Though Franziska will always be the more voluble and vivacious partner, she will be loyal and devoted. And who, in any case, could conceive of a Lisette thanking Just, as Franziska does, for teaching her the value of honesty? (III, 3, 646) Then, too, Franziska's more traditional repartee is kept largely for her interchanges with Werner or her encounters with the landlord, and toward Minna she often speaks with direct simple feeling. True, she is a foil for Minna's moments of sentimentality (as in II, 3) and for her vanity—"O, Sie kennen sich, mein Fräulein" (II, 7, 637)—but Minna herself is a foil for Franziska's extreme common sense, for instance in the aftermath to the Riccaut scene, when she admonishes her maid:

> Mädchen, du verstehst dich so trefflich auf die guten Menschen: aber, wenn willst du die schlechten ertragen lernen?–Und sie sind doch auch Menschen. (IV, 3, 671)

In one all-important matter, the Minna-Franziska relationship is a reversal of the Juliane-Lisette one in *Der junge Gelehrte,* namely in that Minna, not her maid, is the intriguer, and Franziska an only half-willing co-conspirator (though to her falls the role of telling the bare-faced lie about the disinheritance in IV, 7). How can Minna torment such a good man? "Ich rate nichts," she says when appealed to by Minna at the point where the latter proposes to put her plot in motion (IV, 6, 681). In scenes 3 and 5 of act V she is on tenterhooks, willing Tellheim to notice at last which ring it is that Minna has returned to him, and almost unable to contain her anxiety:

> FRANZISKA(*herausplatzend*): Bald wäre der Spaß auch zu weit gegangen–
> DAS FRAULEIN (*gebieterisch*): Ohne dich in unser Spiel zu mengen, Franziska, wenn ich bitten darf!–
> FRANZISKA (*bei Seite und betroffen*): Noch nicht genug? (V, 5, 689)

At the beginning of scene 9, she begs: " . . . lassen Sie es mit dem armen Major gut sein" (V, 9, 693). Looking back on these scenes when the intrigue is over, she declares:

> Nein, wahrhaftig; ich bin zur Komödiantin verdorben. Ich habe gezittert und gebebt, und mir mit der Hand das Maul zuhalten müssen. (V, 9, 701)

What a contrast to the Lisettes, whose most consistent trait is their unshatterable self-assurance! For his part, Werner is too clumsy and honest to be an intriguer. His one attempt to "correct" Tellheim's fortune at his own expense, by giving him money he pretends is rightfully the Major's

(III, 7), is a transparent fib and ends in discovery. And Just's fidelity would express itself, if allowed, in waylaying and beating up the landlord and seducing the latter's daughter. Intrigue and manipulation as a way of life for the servant figures have disappeared. But they have not simply been transferred to the protagonists. Minna's is an intrigue with a new angle: she is not trying to outwit an elderly antagonist and deprive him of some advantage, but rather to provoke her sweetheart into revealing his true self. That she cannot repent of her intrigue (even though it got out of hand and gave her some moments of real unease) does not put her in the same category as the unprincipled Lisettes, for the reason is different: "Nein," she says toward the end of the play, "ich kann es nicht bereuen, mir den Anblick Ihres ganzen Herzens verschafft zu haben!– Ah, was sind Sie für ein Mann!" (V, 12, 700–701). This is intrigue that is effectually the opposite of deception; this is intrigue humanized.[17]

That there is no elderly intolerant father or guardian, no rival suitor blocking the young couple's happiness, except insofar as Minna fictitiously casts her uncle in the spoilsport's role in the story told to Tellheim, is in itself a development, and it profoundly affects the roles of the servants.[18] The obstacles in this case are provided first by the authorities, against whom Just, Werner, and Franziska are powerless (all they can do is to try to mitigate the consequences in various ways), and second, more importantly, by one of the young pair, Tellheim himself. The solution to the first must come from outside, the answer to the second must be worked out between the young people themselves.

No longer do the servants have a near-monopoly of the comic lines, for the protagonists can make fun of one another, or at least Minna of Tellheim. Whereas in *Der junge Gelehrte* it is Anton who ridicules Damis by reading him Damis's own poem and inducing him to criticize it (III, 15), in *Minna von Barnhelm* it is the heroine herself who makes the audience smile, if not Tellheim, by giving him back word for word his own views on the evils of unequal marriage (V, 9). Not that the servants are denied all opportunity of showing up their masters' faults, but there is a world of difference between Anton's laughing behind his hand at Damis's foolishness and Werner's blunt honesty in telling to his face a Tellheim he loves and respects that he should be willing to receive as well as to give (III, 7).[19] In this scene Werner, who after all has only tried to practise on Tellheim the sort of benevolent deception that Tellheim himself used earlier to help the widow Marloff (but to which she responds much more graciously), has to listen not only to Tellheim's arguments against accepting his help, but also to a sermon on his way of life as well. His reaction, after pressing the Major hard with telling arguments, is a good-natured "Sie wissen besser, was sich gehört" (III, 7, 656), and despite further provocation he closes the discussion with a hearty handshake. Werner, unlike Tellheim, does not cultivate his own resentment and anger: after being treated by Tellheim in V, 11 in peremptory and ungrateful fashion, he needs only to hear a few conciliatory words, which, characteristically, contain a mini-sermon—"Ihr seid eine Art Verschwender" (V, 14, 703)—to become completely reconciled to Tellheim, even blaming himself for the whole thing:

> Ich hätte aber doch so ein Tölpel nicht sein sollen. Nun seh ichs wohl. Ich verdiente hundert Fuchtel. . . . nur weiter keinen Groll, lieber Major! (V, 14, 703)

Tellheim's words, "Wer ein besseres Mädchen, und einen redlicheren Freund hat, als ich, den will ich sehen!" (V, 14, 704), point to the new status of the servant. Apart from the words of appreciation accorded Rosel in Fuchs's *Die Klägliche,* we may search in vain for such a tribute to the Lisettes/Antons/Peters/Philipps of earlier eighteenth-century comedy, no matter how hard they have intrigued on their masters' behalf. Just as Minna and Tellheim are no longer comic types, the servants, too, have become fully rounded human beings. Before *Minna* the servants in comedy seem to be conscious of being ciphers, of playing a prescribed role. In Cronegk's *Der Mißtrauische,* Lisette and Philipp comment in several places on the servant status, and when Philipp in one scene outlines a whole social hierarchy of behind-the-back ridicule, he reveals a view of people as social types fitted into rigid slots:

> Das Glück theilet seine Gaben wunderlich aus: nur das ist noch das Beste, daß es den mindern Ständen die Freyheit giebt, sich immer über die größern auf zuhalten. Siehst du es nicht, wie es in deinem Hause zugeht! Das Aufwärtemädchen hält sich über die Jungmagd

auf, die Jungmagd über die Kammerjungfer. *Er macht ihr eine tiefe Verbeugung.* Du, mein liebstes Lisettchen, lachest Dein Fräulein aus! Diese wird eine Gräfin auslachen, die wieder über irgend eine Prinzeßin spotten. . . . (III, 4, 47)

If one is subordinate to another, one compensates by mocking him—and this principle is in fact the guiding one for valet and soubrette in the greater part of Enlightenment comedy. That they may play stereotype roles is attested to by Pasquin in Lessing's fragment, *Die glückliche Erbin,* when he describes how the poets portray servants (though naturally he flatters himself in doing so): the Pasquins are "allezeit treu, verschlagen, hurtig, und die allerergebensten Liebhaber der Lisetten," while the latter are "jung und hübsch . . . dabei verschmitzt, schnippisch und plauderhaft . . . allezeit buhlerisch, unbeständig und treulos" (I, 1).[20] In *Der junge Gelehrte,* Lisette's "Kömmt denn wohl ohn unser einer irgend in einem Hause eine Heirat zu Stande?" assumes a conception of herself as typifying a class. Franziska never speaks or thinks of herself in this way: she is Franziska Willig, individual human being.

*Minna von Barnhelm* is Lessing's best comedy, but not quite his last practical word on this subject, for the first and second extant plans for *Die Matrone von Ephesus* date probably from the Hamburg period and the third and final one from about 1771.[21] Moreover, his preoccupation with this theme goes back to his student days in Leipzig, with possibly a lost fragmentary *Ur-Matrone* (mentioned by Karl Lessing)[22] dating from 1748 or before, and so the various versions, despite their limitations as fragments, provide an example of how Lessing's approach to the comic treatment of one particular theme changed over the years. He begins in the sphere of satire and ends in "wahre Komödie."

In this case Lessing was using material at least some seventeen hundred years old and dramatized again and again by seventeenth- and eighteenth-century European playwrights. This is not the place to measure Lessing against them in detail,[23] but a discussion of the version written by his contemporary, Christian Felix Weiße (1726–1804), as a very young man will serve to put Lessing's wrestlings with the theme in perspective. Weiße's one-act *Die Matrone von Ephesus,* 1743, in verse, is a straightforward treatment, keeping to the main lines already etched by

Petronius in the *Satyricon*. There are nine scenes and three characters: the widow Antiphila, her maid Dorias, and the intrusive soldier Carion. Antiphila and Dorias are on stage in every scene; Dorias exits briefly in scene 7, but has the largest of the three speaking parts. "Die kuppelnde Vermittlerin," as Prang calls her,[24] she is a creature of pragmatic values and purely physical needs—"Man ißt, man trinkt, man liebt, und keines wird man satt," she declares in one scene (2, 223)[25]—a creature committed to life. Antiphila's mournful song opens the play, but the first words of dialogue are Dorias's: "Ich bin des Klagens satt; Sie, liebe Frau, noch nicht?" (1, 212) and she never ceases trying to persuade her mistress to abandon their immolation in the dead master's tomb, interrupting her tearful raptures again and again: "Es ist ein herrlich Ding um das Gefühl! ja ja!" (1, 216). In the first scene one can almost hear the rumblings of her empty stomach as *continuo* to the dialogue, and in the next her explanation to Carion as to why she keeps her mistress company in the mausoleum takes up again the ever-recurring theme of food:

Mein gutes Herz ließ mich den frommen Vorsatz fassen,
Mit ihr zugleich vor Gram und Hunger zu erblassen:
Denn weil ich mich nie krank gefastet, aber eh
Mich krank gegessen, dacht ich: Hunger thut nicht weh.
(2, 222–23)

Her practicality touches on the crude. In scene 1, when Antiphila describes idyllic hours spent in the country with her husband, Dorias readily believes her, adding virtuously, "ob ich gleich aus Schaam nie zugesehn" (1, 217), but in scene 4, when Antiphila muses on union with her loved one in death, she exclaims briskly:

Ah! der Vereiningung der Herzen muß ich lachen!
Was wollen Sie denn todt mit ihrem [sic] Todten machen?
Sie können, glaub ich nicht, mit ihm ins Hölzchen gehn,
Und in der Sommernacht mehr nach den Sternen sehn. (4, 228)

Once Carion—"mein Retter" (4, 226), since he shares his supper with her—has begun to make an impression on the widow, who nevertheless claims to be offended by his attentions, Dorias helps his suit along with encouraging asides to him. Her handling of her mistress is a judicious mixture of support for and scorn of the idea, together with hints at her scepticism about the widow's dedication to her vow of death, all of which confuses the already wavering Antiphila still further. The irony of the situation is underlined in scene 7: Dorias, who has gone outside, interrupts a love scene when she bursts in with her news that riders are approaching the gallows where hangs the corpse that Carion has been ordered to guard: "Ach! zu Hülfe!" (which is what Antiphila should be saying at this moment, if we are to believe her protestations that Carion's attentions are unwelcome). Instead, Antiphila exclaims, "Wie? was giebts?" (7, 251). Weiße's Antiphila is clearly a victim of self-delusion at whom the audience is meant to laugh, for when it is discovered that the corpse has been stolen, she suggests that her husband's body be put in its place. She and Carion immediately approach the coffin to effect the exchange, and the play ends abruptly with a maxim from Dorias's *Weltanschauung:*

> Der Einfall ist geschickt: ich henk ihn mit hinan.
> Ein Mann, der lebt, gilt mehr, als ein gestorbner Mann. (9, 260)

From the beginning, Lessing approaches the theme more subtly, using recent variations that Weiße had ignored, though the earliest version shows some similarities, notably in the maid. Here, the one speech following on the five-scene *Szenar* is a monologue for the unnamed maidservant in scene 1.[26] It suggests a certain measure of callousness in her attitude to her mistress, as well as a preoccupation with her own physical discomfort:

> Sie schläft fest! –Lustig! Nun kann ich meinen letzten Biscuit kauen! –Wer doch eine Närrin wäre, und hungerte und weinte sich mit ihr zu Tode! Zwar versprach ichs ihr; aber wie konnte ich mir träumen lassen, daß sie Ernst daraus machen würde? –Meinetwegen! Knack! –Er ist verzweifelt harte– . . . (546)[27]

The hunger motif occurs also in the second scene of the scenario itself:

"[Der Soldat] hat Essen bei sich. Die Bediente bekömmt Appetit" (545). The maid's major function is indicated in the summary of scene 5, when the soldier has announced that the body of the hanged man has disappeared: "Der Offizier will verzweifeln. Die Bediente kömmt auf den Einfall den todén Mann an die Stelle zu hängen" (545). This is a significant departure (begun by La Fontaine in his verse-tale *La Matrone d'Ephèse*, 1682, and continued by Houdar de la Motte in his comedy with the same title, 1702) from the previous European "Matrone" tradition, followed by Weiße, which had the suggestion come from the widow herself. La Motte had also given the soldier (Lessing's officer) a valet, and in fact, of his seven characters, four were servants. In Lessing's *Szenar* the soldier's chief function is to bring about the situation in which, by agreeing to the substitution, the widow accepts the officer's suit, for he reveals that his report was false and the original body has not disappeared. This last twist is Lessing's contribution to the development of this European theme.[28]

In the second version, the *Entwurf*, in which the characters are given names, the soldier Dromo still has this function, and the dialogue portion of scene 8 develops this a little in that the officer, Philokrates, threatens to kill him for his lie, but is then forced to agree with Dromo's claim that his trick was the only way to make Antiphila admit her love. That the officer-soldier relationship is akin to the traditional master-servant one is evidenced by Dromo's reaction in scene 6 to Philokrates' high-flown declaration that his meeting with Antiphila was foretold by an oracle: "Nun das gesteh ich, mein Herr kann aus dem Stegreife vortrefflich lügen" (548). There is a slight echo of the hunger motif in scene 3, but Mysis, the maid, has undergone some modification. A lack of sympathy with her mistress still emerges from her monologue in scene 1 —"Wo bin ich? –Ah, noch in dem verwünschten Grabe!" (546)—but here a vivid impression is given of her bleak and uncomfortable surroundings and her own plight is underlined: "Aber ich, die ich nicht sterben will ––O eine Sklavin ist wohl sehr unglücklich ––." No indication is given that it is Mysis who suggests the exchange of corpses, since the summary of the beginning of scene 8 simply states: "Verzweiflung des Offiziers. Erklärung der Witwe" (549). What is worked out in detail in scene 8 is a comic exchange between the servants, clearly meant as the ending to the play, which would then close with Dromo's cynical comments on the "fidelity" of women and Mysis's suddenly more serious note:

MYSIS: Mach, mach, daß wir ihnen nachkommen –
DROMO: Und diese heilige Stätte verlassen, wo sich ein Beispiel der ehelichen Liebe ereignet hat, dergleichen, o dergleichen – dergleichen die Welt alle Tage sieht.
MYSIS: Grausames undankbares Geschöpf! Ist es nicht genug, daß ihr uns verführt, müßt ihr uns auch noch verspotten? (8, 550)[29]

This more serious streak in Mysis is developed further in the third draft (seven complete scenes and part of the eighth), while the comic potential of Dromo is exploited more explicitly, for instance in scene 2, where the trembling soldier first takes the maid for a ghost and then becomes bolder when he realizes she is very much flesh and blood:

... Mit Erlaubnis! (*indem er sie mit der flachen Hand hier und da behutsam betastet*) Gewiß, das Ding ist doch ziemlich compact. (*Geht mit der Laterne rund um sie herum, und leuchtet ihr endlich ins Gesicht*) Ei! Ein allerliebstes Gesichtchen! Nein das Gesichtchen gehört wohl keinem Gespenste. Welch ein Paar Augen! Was für ein Mündchen! Was für ein Paar Bäckchen! (*indem er sie in den einen Backen kneift*) (2, 554)

This moment received very brief treatment by Weiße:

CARION: Beym Element! mich schreckt doch kein Gespenst?
DORIAS (*kommt hervor*):          – Nein, nein;
     Ich dächte zum Gespenst sollt ich zu artig seyn! (2, 219)

Much more is made in Lessing's last version of the relationship of the two servants,[30] and the tension between officer and soldier is also stressed, for instance in the following exchange:

DROMO (*im Hereintreten, mit einer brennenden Fackel*): Sehen Sie! Fürchten Sie sich nur nicht, Herr Hauptmann–

PHILOKRATES: O, den tapfern Dromo an seiner Seite, wer sollte sich fürchten? (4, 561)

Indeed, Lessing does give Dromo some traits of the *miles gloriosus*, timid when facing the unknown, and a braggart when he knows there is no danger.

Lessing's first version of the *Matrone* needed but five scenes to complete the action, the second extended to eight, but the third breaks off in the middle of scene 8 before the question of the vanished corpse has arisen. Dromo's role in the action is therefore not developed further here. Lessing now needs more scenes to explore the widow's character and make her more attractive and understandable, while at the same time pointing to the exaggeration of her attitude and to her self-deception, depicting her, not as the ridiculous prey of self-delusion, but as the victim of a virtue that has got out of hand.[31]

In connection with this new purpose, Mysis also gains depth. Her opening monologue is more or less the same as in the *Entwurf*, but from scene 2 onward she speaks with understanding of her mistress and clearly believes her to be sincere, for she defends her hotly against Dromo's cynical insinuations and repudiates bitterly his scornful disbelief in the fidelity of women in general.[32] Her comment "O Gott, über die Weiber, die einen zweiten Mann nehmen können!" (2, 555) sounds in context simply like a rather ironic echo of her mistress's view, but is perhaps meant from another standpoint to imply her own attitude, that is, not "who could be so unfaithful?" but rather "who could be such a fool?" At the beginning of scene 3, she declares of men: "Die meisten sind keine Träne wert; geschweige, daß man mit ihnen sterben wollte" (3, 557). She scarcely deserves Antiphila's reproach that she is but a mercenary slave (3, 560), nor the later accusation (4, 564) that the intrusion by the military is all her fault. Like Franziska, Mysis does not cry, but shows genuine concern. In scene 3 she tries to combine a sympathetic ear —"Wie jammern Sie mich!" (3, 558), "Die Göttin wird Ihren Schmerz ansehen, und Ihnen verzeihen" (3, 559)— with practical advice: first to return home to mourn, and then, when this is indignantly rejected, to

pretend to be asleep as the best way to avoid contact with the approaching soldiers. In the following scene she does her best to protect Antiphila
from the intrusion, but since she fails, and moreover senses that Antiphila is attracted to Philokrates despite herself—"Fliehen? Ist die Gefahr
so groß?" she asks ambiguously later on (6, 567)—she adapts her counsel
to the change in situation.[33] When Philokrates declares that he was a
friend of Antiphila's husband, quoting names and details, she sees
through the ruse at once (he has simply read off the information carved
on the sarcophagus), but she is ready to back him: "Nur frisch! Das
Eisen glüht; folgen Sie ihr –" (7, 570). At the end of the scene she uses a
clever bit of reverse psychology, promptly backed up by Philokrates, to
ensure that Antiphila will insist on his staying:

> MYSIS: O, liebste Frau, nun dulden Sie den Herrn ja nicht länger!
> Seine Betrübnis würde der Ihrigen nur mehr Nahrung geben.
> Wir brauchen niemand, der uns noch wehmütiger macht, als
> wir schon sind.
> PHILOKRATES: Woran erinnerst du deine Gebieterin? – Doch ich
> kann dir nicht Unrecht geben. – Ich gehe –
> ANTIPHILA: Ah, mein Herr, entziehen Sie mir den Freund des
> Geliebten meiner Seele nicht so schnell. (7, 571)

Would Mysis have taken her support for Philokrates' courtship to the
point of suggesting the substitution of Cassander's corpse for the one
which has ostensibly disappeared? We cannot be sure, for the fragment
breaks off even before Dromo is sent out on an inspection of the
"schimpflichen Pfählern, an welchen die unglücklichen Kolophonier
hangen," the words which end this version in mid-scene (8, 572).

All but one of Lessing's completed original comedies were written
before he came of age, and his interest in the genre might thus be regarded as belonging to his poetic apprenticeship, for despite the glorious
example of *Minna von Barnhelm*, the mature Lessing tends to be thought
of as the theoretician and exponent of tragedy. But his continued,
though sporadic, work on comic themes in the 1750s and 1760s, as well
as the considerable space devoted to aspects of comedy in the *Hamburgische Dramaturgie* (even though little of it produces firm definitions) show

that comedy was not simply an early love largely discarded later. And though, in very strict terms, the third working of *Die Matrone von Ephesus* is Lessing's last practical word on the genre, one cannot entirely exclude *Nathan der Weise,* that work which, as Friedrich Schlegel wrote, is almost impossible "zu rubriciren und unter Dach und Fach zu bringen."[34] As Lessing himself said, it is " . . . nichts weniger, als ein satirisches Stück,"[35] but it does owe something to comedy, structurally and thematically. For instance, looking at the play from an admittedly restricted angle, one might see it as the comic portrayal of a young man whose not entirely reprehensible impulsiveness leads him astray: the Templar's tendency to act first and think later leads him both to save Recha's life and to endanger Nathan's.[36]

Of course, *Nathan der Weise* is much more than that and most parallels with the eighteenth-century comedy in general and Lessing's comedies in particular eventually peter out. It is interesting, though, that the three characters who are portrayed primarily in the context of a master-employee relationship—Daja, Al-Hafi, and Brother Bonafides—provide the funniest scenes (the last-named, it is true, also contributes to the play's most moving moments in IV, 7). However, none is content with present employment: Al-Hafi runs off to the desert to resume his life as a mendicant dervish, the Klosterbruder has been promised a new hermitage, and Daja lives for the day when, with Recha married to a Christian and restored to the bosom of the True Church, she can return to Europe with the happy couple. Al-Hafi and the Klosterbruder, at any rate, fulfil themselves best when they are in no service but God's; and quite unlike the conventional servants, neither belongs in spirit to the everyday, workaday world with its schemes and intrigues, though the Klosterbruder makes not too bad a job of defusing the plots in which his superior involves him.

Daja, because of her duties in a particular household and her function as *confidante,* is the one closest to the servant-type, though she is no mere domestic, but Recha's nurse and companion, "Die mir eine Mutter/So wenig missen lassen!" (V, 6, 430–31).[37] While her language is not comic as such, on two occasions she ties herself into linguistic knots somewhat reminiscent of the word-play of Raps in *Der Schatz:*

Ihr [Rechas] Glück ist, längst zu sein, was sie zu werden
 Verdorben ist. . . . (III, 10, 824–25)

So kömmt das Mädchen wieder unter Christen,
 Wird wieder was sie ist, ist wieder,
 was Sie ward. . . . (IV, 6, 512–14)

In one respect Daja superficially resembles the soubrette: her goal, with
the father as obstacle, is the happy marriage of her charge, a marriage
that will bring advantage to herself. But there the resemblance ends, for
the young girl in this case will have none of it, and there is perfect
harmony between parent and child. Daja ends act IV with a dramatic
monologue in which she decides to reveal to Recha the secret of her
birth. Crying "Ja, ja! Nur zu! Itzt oder nie! Nur zu!" (IV, 8, 773), she
rushes off, never to appear again. That her revelation, which takes place
off-stage between acts IV and V, fails to convert or subvert Recha is
clear from the latter's account of it to Sittah in V, 6 and her impassioned
pleas to Saladin in V, 7. What remains for the absent Daja as the curtain
falls *"Unter stummer Wiederholung allerseitiger Umarmungen"* (V, 8)? Her
conscience has plagued her for seventeen years, during which she knew
only part of the story—what will it do now? Can she continue, far from
the homeland she misses, as companion to a Recha bred in no one faith
and by birth part German and part Kurd, sister to a renegade Templar,
niece to the leader of the Muslims in the Holy Land, and still, with every
ounce of her being, if with no drop of her blood, daughter to a free-
thinking Jew? Of all Lessing's "servants," "die gute, böse Daja" is the
loser, as scheming born of a well-meaning narrow-mindedness is ren-
dered harmless by tolerance and humanity.

# VI

# The Decline of
# Enlightenment Comedy

## Weiße, Iffland, and Hippel

| Männer: | Frauenzimmer: |
|---|---|
| Erster Liebhaber | Erste Liebhabrin [sic] |
| Vater | Soubrette |
| Bediente [sic] | Mutter[1] |
| Zweiter Liebhaber | |
| Oncle | |

The date is 1777 and Maler Müller outlines above, in his *Gedanken über Errichtung eines Deutschen Nationaltheaters,* a basic theatrical ensemble. "Diese Anzahl wäre hinlänglich," he comments, "selbst anzufangen, da man viele gute spielbare Stücke hat, wo die Personen nicht über obige Zahl steigen—und da diese überdies pure Hauptrollen sind, die fast durchgängig in den meisten Stücken vorkommen, hätte man einmal das Notwendigste gewiß. . . . "[2] Nothing would seem to have altered since Gottsched's day, neither the type-casting nor the size of the troupe;[3] Müller's ensemble seems particularly suitable for the bulk of the literary comedies produced on the eighteenth-century German stage up to that point, whether original works, adaptations, or translations. And yet, by

1777, the picture is changing, so that neither the stereotypes he lists nor the number of eight actors, to be expanded for small subordinate roles by the inclusion of young acting apprentices, entirely fit the new developments in the drama. "Bediener" and "Soubrette" in particular can no longer claim a firm place as integral and significant parts of the cast.

Lessing's *Minna von Barnhelm* represents the zenith of *Aufklärung* comedy. Of its kind it has no match; and shortly after its appearance, new approaches to the genre, or even just particular emphases, mean the development of different types of "comic" play (Lenz's dramas, Goethe's *Singspiele* and experiments with literary comedy, and, eventually, the Romantic comedy). But this is not the whole of the story, for although in some literary histories the German Enlightenment seems to drop suddenly from sight at the end of the 1760s, to the general reading public of the last third of the eighteenth century it was still alive as a literary mode, and on the popular theatre-going level, echoes of the comic genre to which the major portion of its dramatic production belonged can be heard until the end of the century.

But first of all, to fill in the picture, we must look in greater detail at a contemporary of Lessing, C.F. Weiße, whose first play, *Die Matrone von Ephesus,* was discussed in the last chapter. Weiße was openly indebted to foreign comic models, notably Holberg and the Italian theatre, and, for the more sentimental plays, to the bourgeois tragedy of the English and of Lessing.[4] Among his considerable output we can find almost every *Aufklärung* comedy type, and the variations in his treatment of the servant figures point to a pragmatic approach. The *Singspiele,* for which he won fame in his own day, lie only at the periphery of our concern, though servants or servantlike characters do appear in them. One of the most successful, *Die verwandelten Weiber, oder der Teufel ist los,* 1766, is based on a French adaptation by M.J. Sedaine of Coffey's play *The Devil to pay or the wives metamorphos'd,* 1728, and its songs, with Weiße's words and J.A. Hiller's music, became hits for a decade and more.[5] It is perhaps a little closer to the comedy proper than other examples of the *Singspiel,* since the "correction" of vices is involved, the cobbler being cured of his unreasonable suspicions of his fun-loving but innocent wife and the noblewoman of her shrewishness. There the resemblance ends, for the cures are effected by magical means, and, as in very many *Singspiele,* the main thrust of the depiction of society is the contrast of negative aspects of the nobility (in other examples, it is urban life) with positive characteristics of simple village folk. The servants of the von Liebreich family are chiefly important as a group, as a background chorus to the major characters. One might be tempted to find traits in Jobsen the cobbler that have been associated with servant-types from the Harlequinade to the Saxon comedy. But in general the servants as this study has viewed them demand to be seen in a servile relationship, that is to say, there must be masters and servants both, whether the connection is one of esteem and affection, indifference, manipulation, or fear. In Weiße's *Singspiele* this relationship is lacking; in most cases the focus is on one village couple, neither masters nor servants in the usual sense.[6] In a negative way, however, the *Singspiel* as a genre is relevant to our study, for in the decade 1766–76, near the beginning of which stands *Minna von Barnhelm,* high point of Enlightenment comedy, these musical plays dominated the stage, affecting adversely the popularity of most other dramatic forms, but particularly the comic.[7] They broke with the regular structure of the literary drama, and after 1770 were even seen by many as characteristically German at a time when the demand for a national content came to the fore.

Weiße's comic production stretched over thirty years, and a selection of his comedies will suffice to show the range of his presentation of the servants. Roughly contemporary with Lessing's early plays, the literary satire *Die Poeten nach der Mode,* 1751, portrays the servant Johann as a valuable aide to Palmer and Henriette in their courtship involving the discomfiture of the poetasters. He has the second-largest number of appearances of any character, but stands only fifth out of seven in size of speaking part. Thus, though in time-honoured tradition ready for anything,

> Wenn niemand mit Gifte zu vergeben ist, so bin ich auch dabey: nur vor dem Galgen habe ich einen natürlichen Abscheu (II, 9),[8]

he remains subordinate, supporting rather than initiating, and has a role as commentator (he is given a great many asides). There is no soubrette, for Henriette, self-assured and humorous, needs no such prop.

In two plays within the next decade, however, Johann is partnered by the soubrette Christiane (these are Weiße's favourite names for his servants): *Alter hilft für Thorheit nicht, oder die Haushälterin,* 1758, and *Ehrlich währt am längsten oder der Mißtrauische gegen sich selbst,* 1761. In the former, Christiane presages the title of the latter when she declares fervently at one point: "Ehrlich währt am längsten" (IV, 7, 388),[9] but in fact she plays a double role, dealing unashamedly in all the devices of pretence, including crocodile tears (IV, 5). She hates her mistress Cleonte, the housekeeper of the title (partly because she is an upstart, a former common serving-woman giving herself airs), but pretends to support her, although she ridicules the master of the house, Geronte, to his face (III, 5 and IV, 5). Toward the sweethearts Valer and Clarisse she is favourably disposed, though as Clarisse does not approve of her tone and methods, she feels constrained to defend herself:

> Christiane weiß alles, ihr Herz ist aber nicht so verderbt, daß sie sich nicht lieber auf die Seite der Tugend und der Gerechtigkeit schlagen sollte – (V, 5, 409)

In Weiße's satiric comedies, the young lovers, particularly the men, scheme cleverly on their own behalf, and so Christiane is not the kingpin of the plot, which is directed by Valer.[10] Though she is much in evidence, being the second most frequently appearing character, her speaking role places her fifth in a cast of seven. Johann, Valer's valet for the last nine years, has the smallest role of all, but is visibly busy and quite a colourful character, bringing news, taking messages, interrupting conversations, entering "in vollem Laufe" so that once, like Harlequin or Hans Wurst, he falls over himself (V, 2). He paints himself as a gay fellow who has led an adventurous life, but he is easily manipulated by Christiane, whom he admires: when at the end of II, 5 Cleonte gives her maid some coins to hand to Johann, Christiane declares at the start of the following scene, "Einer wird doch genug seyn," and pockets the rest (II, 6, 310). In general, while certainly quite attractive figures, Christiane and Johann exhibit the conventional "moralische Indifferenz": the principals stoop with reluctance to deceit as the only means to achieve their just ends, but the two servants positively revel in it.

In *Der Mißtrauische,* however, which, like Schlegel's *Der Geheimnis-*

*volle* and Lessing's *Minna von Barnhelm,* portrays a weakness (here, lack of self-confidence) not in itself a vice, Weiße presents in the single servant Philipp a different type. "Der Teufel, Philipp, Du redest ja, wie ein Sokrates!" complains his rascally master Cleanth (I, 1, 253)[11] when Philipp remonstrates with him. This is probably a trait taken over from the servant of sentimental tragedy (compare Norton's attitude to Mellefont in *Miß Sara Sampson*). Philipp, who has delved with profit into his former master's library, is a moralist. The young people—Cleanth, Arist, Juliane—have the largest roles in the play, while the other three characters—Geronte, Melusine, Philipp—have only about half as much to say. Philipp plays a small role in bringing about the happy ending, the engagement of Juliane to the worthy though tongue-tied and diffident Arist rather than to the braggart fortune-hunter Cleanth, but on the whole simply tries to do as little as possible and not involve himself. In the second-last speech of the play, he sums up its moral and his own attitude, here typical of the servants' way of thinking, that whatever is good must also be useful:

> Itzt sehe ich doch, daß die Ehrlichkeit belohnet wird! wahrhaftig! es verlohnt sich schon der Mühe, ein rechstschaffener Kerl zu seyn! (III, 10, 356)

A spate of plays flowed from Weiße's pen between 1764 and 1769, some highly sentimental pieces, others (like the two just discussed) a combination of satiric comedy and *pièce d'intrigue.*[12] A few have no servants, or at least no comic servants in the usual sense. In the case of *Die Freundschaft auf der Probe,* 1767, and *Walder,* 1769, this is due to their origins as adaptations of pieces by Marmontel.[13] But the original play *Amalia,* 1765, also introduces no servants, perhaps because of its strongly sentimental tone and its treatment of love as an absolute passion rather than as a rational inclination, but more probably because it was first conceived and first performed as a tragedy, then later recast as a comedy. The innkeeper and his wife are "niedrige Figuren," but not conventional servants and in any case not comic types. However, another sentimental play, *Großmuth für Großmuth,* 1768, counts two servants among its five characters, and welcome indeed is their liveliness and down-to-earth attitude amidst all the noble self-sacrificing and lofty sentiment. The two ladies, Mariane and Frau Solms, have the largest parts, followed by medium-sized roles for Mariane's maid Hannchen and the suitor Treuwerth, and a small one for Anton, Frau Solms's grumbling old retainer. Hannchen is not the *meneur de jeu* and her appearances are scattered. Mainly she functions as foil to sentimentality. In the first scene, Mariane excuses Treuwerth for having unwittingly caused her pain:

> HANNCHEN: Mit oder ohne Schuld! Eine Wunde bleibt Wunde: der Schmerz ist immer derselbe. (1, 137)[14]

Hannchen's reaction to Mariane's fine words of renunciation is: don't give up hope yet! Noble thoughts irritate her: "Bersten möchte ich vor Verdruß," she declares (12, 182) over Treuwerth's words, which sound beautiful but still mean that her mistress is to be the loser. Shortly afterward her irritation produces a striking image when she learns of Frau Solms's apparent desire that Mariane be present at her marriage to Mariane's own beloved Treuwerth as proof of her friendship: "Eine lustige Freundschaft, wenn ich in den Himmel sehen, und in der Hölle sitzen soll" (14, 185), she bursts out to Frau Solms and exits. "Ich werde noch toll," is all she can say in the next scene when it turns out that Frau Solms meant Mariane and Treuwerth to marry all along, and her earthy comments provide a needed contrast to the exaggerated unselfishness of the main figures: "Der Henker! Ich schlage mich aufs Maul. Das laß ich Großmuth seyn." (15, 189) Anton, meanwhile, is concerned that, with the change in plans, he will lose certain perquisites, but Hannchen promises him a present from Mariane: "Nur unter der Bedingung," he rejoins in the last words of the play, "lasse ich mir ein bischen Großmuth gefallen" (16, 192). Mistress and servant thus present a contrast, completely divorced in their view of the world. The servants are ready to some extent to admire unselfishness, but they remain with their feet firmly planted on the ground and their eye straying frequently to the main chance.

In the one-act *Die unerwartete Zukunft oder der Naturaliensammler*, 1764, apart from two male servants with brief appearances, there is another Hannchen, this time fully in sympathy with her mistress, speaking out freely to von Busch and offering practical help by hiding her mistress's suitor. But she has the smallest part of the five main characters, and the words with which she closes the play in scene 17 reinforce her subordinate position: "An meine Vergeltung denkt Niemand. Undank bleibt wohl der Welt Lohn."[15]

In *List über List* and *Weibergeklatsche*, both 1767, there is the conventional valet/soubrette pair, though Johann and Hannchen in the latter play appear only very briefly at the beginning. *List über List*, called by Steinmetz "die komplizierteste Intrigenkomödie der Aufklärung überhaupt,"[16] gives Christiane the third-largest and Johann the fourth-largest part among eight characters. Christiane is maid to Madam Rabin, the comic mother who has the main role, but is devoted to the ingénue Karoline, ready to take her part and convinced, as we see from her speech opening the play, that it is she herself who runs the household. She shrewdly assesses situations, does what she can, and lends a sympathetic ear to her mistress's feelings: in IV, 3, Karoline calls her her only friend, and Christiane, normally addressing her respectfully as "Mamsell," responds with an affectionate "gutes Karolinchen" (IV, 3, 290).[17] Johann is an amiable rascal, articulate in his witty exchanges with his master. For instance, when the latter is about to pretend stupidity in order to insinuate himself into Madam Rabin's good graces, Johann reflects:

> Nun, mein Herr? dieß ist der Schauplatz Ihrer Dummheit, oder vielmehr Ihrer Klugheit! denn meinem Bedünken nach gehört mehr Kunst dazu, wenn sich ein Kluger dumm stellen soll, als wenn ein Narr klug seyn will. Dumm genug, mit aller Ehrfurcht gesprochen, sehen Sie aus. (II, 1, 223)

He has a role in the plotting, and is much taken by the "verdammter kleiner listiger Teufel," Christiane (II, 7, 255). But she will have none of him, and in the closing exchanges of the play, skilfully links her refusal to its main theme:

> JOHANN: Nun! was meynt Sie? Wenn alle Dummheiten so glücklich ablaufen, so wäre es wohl der Mühe werth, daß wir zusammen einen dummen Streich machten?

CHRISTIANE: Ich dächte, nein: denn wenn man den Vorsatz hat, eine Dummheit zu begehen, so glaubt man am ersten recht klug zu seyn; und eine eingebildete Klugheit ist in meinen Augen die größte Dummheit. (V, 11, 335–36)

In *Der Projektmacher,* 1766, another variation presents itself. Here there are five servant characters with speaking parts: two valets, one maid, one elderly servant, and a washerwoman. Hannchen and her mistress tie for the second-largest part; the other servants have relatively small roles, localized in particular parts of the play. The washerwoman and one of the valets, for instance, have at one point an important function in the plot hatched by two of the bourgeois characters at the beginning of the comedy. Hannchen supports Isabelle, but is a little too frank in speech for Isabelle's taste, and an expectation of tips plays a large part in her agreement to abet the plotters. Isabelle is by no means unable to speak out for herself—that Hannchen is given a lot to say is due to Weiße's use of her as comic foil whose pithy comments have a psychological effect on Isabelle, who in the latter half of the play is trying to follow a noble, self-sacrificing course against all her natural instincts. The plot misfires; all ends well, but not due directly to the servants' efforts.

Summing up, one can say that Weiße's servants appear, on the one hand, in supportive or reinforcing roles towards the young sweethearts, and on the other, enliven the plays with their sprightly language or physical action. Except possibly for Christiane in *List über List* (and it is a slight exception), Weiße does not, unlike Lessing, attempt to round out and humanize them. Their tone—pert, common-sensical, sometimes even impudent—belongs to an older convention. Weiße adapts the convention with technical skill, but produces no development; rather, he reveals a tendency to tailor the servants to the particular plot in hand. This breadth of variation, but lack of development or deepening, is characteristic of his approach to the comedy in general.[18] Especially the maids offer for the most part a complete contrast to their mistresses, for Weiße's bourgeois sweethearts are often as virtuous, sentimental, and high-minded as Gellert's main figures, though, unlike the latter, they frequently intrigue in order to achieve their happy union, and their

mutual love is portrayed more realistically than in the Gottschedian satiric comedy and given greater stress than in Gellert or even in the later
plays of Schlegel. It would be an exaggeration to see any direct link between Weiße and the popular dramas of the latter part of the eighteenth
century, but the fact that he "sentimentalizes" his virtuous figures, even
in the most satirical of his plays, points perhaps to the growing importance of an element which Iffland, Schröder, and Kotzebue will then
firmly incorporate into their dramas.

Weiße belonged to the generation that still made a distinction between tragedy and comedy, even though in the 1750s and 1760s both
genres had been modified, each absorbing some feature of the other. The
servants in the context in which this study has examined them flourish in
a comedy thus clearly defined as at least partly satirical. The *Sturm und
Drang*, however, deliberately broke down the barriers between the
dramatic genres ("Schauspiel ist — Schauspiel und damit gut!" declared
Bürger),[19] developed tragi-comedy, and accepted a whole range of possibilities in which heroic tragedy and farce still provided the outer limits,
but where the dramatic forms in between, with mixes of the constituent
elements, offered the greatest interest. The non-tragic play was no longer
straightforwardly comic and thus a large part of the servants' function
was precluded. In the *Sturm und Drang* there was also a breakdown of the
strictly classical form, a rejection of the unities, and along with this in
most types of drama an increase, more or less a doubling, of the *dramatis
personae*. The popular light drama of the latter part of the century grafted
in an often superficial way these advances of the *Geniezeit* onto the
*Aufklärung*.[20] When several servants — and often several masters — are
present, the clear-cut role of the servants as one of the three constituent
parts of the *dramatis personae* breaks down. As such they thrived in simple
plots with one central problem, and especially in scenes with one dialogue partner only (servant-young master, servant-elderly foolish figure,
valet-soubrette), in the sort of play, in short, produced by strict
adherence to classical rules.[21] Now there was often not one, but a
number of different conflicts between the main characters, and, moreover, there were frequently both aristocratic and middle-class figures (as,
on a higher literary level, in the plays of Lenz), generating a particular
kind of tension. While forced marriages and unsympathetic parents still

often provided the plot outline, other social factors were involved as well. The basic opposition between old and young may still be there, but it is presented in a more complicated action, in a more diffuse way, and on several social levels.

*Der Hofmeister und die Gouvernante*, probably written in the early 1790s, is a good example. The most frequently appearing of the many servants are: Rossignol, the Count's rascally French valet; Yuri, Negro servant of the Count's bastard son and incarnation of selfless loyalty; and, less important, Zacharias, honest retainer of the foolish *nouveau noble* von Schuhheim (born plain Schuster). They fulfil variously the functions of foil and contrast, whether comic or serious, and of commentator, whether satiric or moralistic. Rossignol, the villain of the piece, is the prime mover in the main intrigue, the Count's abduction of Augusta, but it is an intrigue born of wickedness and he is routed at the end. The other servants have some part in the foiling of bad or foolish schemes, but in this they are aiding others, not acting on their own initiative. Yuri, for instance, reacts to and comments on rather than originates the action. The very number of servants prevents a dominant servant function: besides the three mentioned, and various briefly appearing figures, there are three more house-servants listed in the *dramatis personae* — two male servants, with minor, but specific roles, and a Lisette who appears in one scene only and speaks a few short lines!

*Der Hofmeister und die Gouvernante* has little literary merit, and in that it is typical of the period between *Minna* and Romanticism as far as the comedy is concerned, a period dominated by the productions of the "Routiniere des Lustspielgenres," to borrow Arntzen's phrase, or the "Mitläufer der Klassiker," to use Holl's.[22] The popular comedy writers of the 1760s–90s — among them Löwen, Romanus, Petrasch, Ayrenhoff, Stephanie der Jüngere — tended to combine laughter and tears to produce *Rührstücke* with happy endings. Representative of this mixture on the popular stage, as opposed to the literary comedy, are the works of August Wilhelm Iffland (1759–1815), heir to both Enlightenment theatrical convention and *Sturm und Drang* fashions. His servants show, not an onward development, but a somewhat diffuse exploitation of the various existing possibilities and combinations, using the same basic range of character types provided by the Enlightenment comic repertoire.[23]

Only eight when *Minna von Barnhelm* was first performed, Iffland thus adopts various motifs, functions, and traits in a very pragmatic fashion. Some plays have many servants, because there are several main characters of aristocratic or middle-class rank, each of whom has at least one person to wait on him, or because households are presented in greater detail, with various types of servant, not just valet and soubrette. Sometimes, however, this traditional couple is introduced: in *Scheinverdienst, Die Hagestolzen, Der Mann von Wort*, for instance—and there is even a Lisette in *Die Mündel*. But they are no longer exploited dramatically in the same way as in the *Aufklärung*. Johann and Henriette in *Der Mann von Wort* have the conventional prominent role of voluble commentators—for the first two scenes only. After providing the exposition (frequently the function of servants in Iffland's plays),[24] they have scarcely any further significance in the action. Iffland's servants often have roles concentrated on one spot in the action, or on the other hand, sparse appearances scattered unevenly throughout, and thus in either case only peripheral importance. Sometimes there are no servants at all: in *Dienstpflicht, Der Komet, Die Aussteuer*, for instance. The faithful old retainer-type appears in Jakob of *Der Spieler* and Christian of *Verbrechen aus Ehrsucht*, the latter treated badly by his ne'er-do-well master. Even a young servant often reveals a sentimental streak, for example Christian in *Bewußtsein*.[25] There is one out-and-out rascal: in *Die Hagestolzen* Valentin has got above himself, runs a pawn business on the side with his mistress, tyrannizes the household, threatens his master, and is eventually kicked out. But in general the servants have little part in the action and little practical function in matchmaking. They announce arrivals, carry messages, and in these "family portraits" of Iffland's retain mostly the passive part of their traditional role, that of commentators, usually shaking their heads over the state to which their particular family has sunk, for the plays present general family fortunes rather than a problem caused by one unreasonable member. The focus of the servants' satire has gone, and thus with it the distinct, often tense master-servant relationship that even Weiße had sometimes preserved.

When we come to August von Kotzebue (1761–1819) and thus to the furthest limits of the immediate legacy of Enlightenment literary comedy to the popular drama of the two generations that followed it, we find only here and there a servant with anything to say; given the many characters in his plays, whether they be of the petty bourgeoisie or the aristocracy, servants as an integral part of the action are superfluous.

We have now penetrated some decades into the future and by far overstepped the bounds of what may legitimately be called Enlightenment comic theatre. Let us end, not with this fade-out, but with two examples from a contemporary of Lessing, whose plays fall into Lessing's category of "Versuche junger Leute" and who is thus often omitted completely from the history of German comedy, Th.G. Hippel (1741–96), better known for his novels of the late 1770s to 1790s. Yet his one-act *Der Mann nach der Uhr*, 1765, "reich an drolligen Einfällen,"[26] was a hit in its day. In it, Lisette has the most appearances of any character (thirteen out of eighteen scenes) and the second-largest speaking part, while Johann's more moderate role at least equals that of the suitor Valer. However, in this play the problem is revealed and the stage set before the servants put in an appearance, Lisette in the fourth and Johann in the fifth scene.

The soubrette is the champion of the young couple, but only partly out of sensible concern for a mistress under the domination of a father who regulates his days by the clock and his weeks and months by meaningless anniversaries. Well to the fore in her motivation are hopes of tips and of marriage to Johann with a good dowry, a factor which also dominates Johann's actions. Their marriage is a frequent topic in the dialogue and the dowry a clear condition for their help. Their self-centred attitude is constant: when in scene 4 the pensive Wilhelmine, torn between love and filial duty, wonders if her Valer might not after all have some faults of character, Lisette briskly replies:

> Was für Fehler kann wohl ein junger Herr haben, der Mademoiselle Wilhelmine liebt, der treugehorsamen Lisette manchen gehörnten Siegfried in die Hand drückt, und seinen Bedienten verheirathen will? (4, 380)[27]

Johann reveals certain farcical elements, while Lisette's flippancy serves as contrast to Wilhelmine's tragic moments. Much of the amusement the servants provide stems from the way in which they react verbally to situations, for instance the episode where Johann pokes fun at the "new" time-conscious Valer, playing a part to satisfy the whims of his beloved's father:

> ORBIL: . . . Jetzt bitte ich zu sitzen.
> VALER: Um Vergebung, Herr Orbil. Ich darf mich nicht eher niederlassen, als bis es 5 Uhr schlägt;–ich habe gewisse Stunden festgesetzt, da ich stehe;–gewisse Stunden, da ich sitze;–gewisse Stunden, da ich gehe–
> JOHANN (*Vor sich*): Gewisse Stunden, da ich dem Orbil eine Nase drehe; gewisse Stunden, da ich meinen Johann durchprügle, und was das Beste ist, gewisse Stunden, da ich mich von ihm betrügen lasse.–(15, 406)

There is no evidence, however, that Valer mistreats Johann or that Johann deceives Valer. Like much in the servants' parts, this is padding to extend the comic effect, which in any case is often rather predictable. That the humour was somewhat obvious struck Lessing when he reviewed the play in the 22nd number of the *Hamburgische Dramaturgie*; moreover he found the perspective too narrow, the milieu too localized.[28] The servants' patter is often slick rather than witty. Each has the trick of taking up words uttered by another character, the anadiplotic device Lessing honed to comic perfection, but with Hippel the effect is often a meaningless echo.

Lisette and Johann are supposed to solve the young people's problem, but in fact the unwanted suitor, the Magister, ruins his prospects himself in scene 11 and all Lisette needs to do is to tell Valer to play his part and strike while the iron is hot. In the last scene, with all characters on stage, Lisette is silent and Johann has only a couple of asides early in the scene.

The three-act *Die ungewöhnlichen Nebenbuhler*, 1768, presents a servant in an unusual situation, as the rival in love of his young master, though in his own estimation only, for Clärchen, working in the Dorton household as housekeeper, but in reality a bourgeoise by birth and kinswoman of the Dortons, cannot stand the somewhat foppish and highly conceited valet. Jacob has the largest number of appearances (in twenty-one out of thirty-three scenes) and the largest speaking part. Yet, strangely, he does not dominate the play nor direct the dénouement. His aspirations provide only one part of the plot, the other stemming from the miserly Dorton's schemes for marrying off his children to financial advantage. And the solution is provided in the end by Clärchen's timely revelation of her real identity and her tactful generosity with regard to her new-found fortune.

Nevertheless, Jacob is much in evidence. The play begins with a scene between him and his master, young Dorton, providing exposition of character and situation, and it is followed by a two-and-a-half-page monologue by Jacob, in which he rehearses his anticipated amorous encounter with Clärchen, rolling off his tongue such Baroque phrases as "Blitz, Donner, Hagel und Ungewitter, als die gerechten Werkzeuge des erzürnten Himmels, mögen einzeugen, daß ich (*leise*) Sie liebe–" (I, 2, 290).[29] When he actually uses these words to Clärchen in the next scene, she is simply convinced that he is mad. A later monologue has Jacob again rehearsing what he thinks will happen. His daydreams are significant, for in this play it is the servant who is the dupe of his own nature, and often helpless. He is no *meneur de jeu*. He would like to be, but Clärchen is always one jump ahead of him; despite an active curiosity, he is never quite sure what is going on and is constantly outwitted. The other ridiculous character, the elder Dorton, is better off in the end. True, he makes himself propose to the unattractive stereotype spinster Ehrenpreiß, but the financial gain he had promised himself from marriages forced on his children is his even though they are able to follow their own hearts in the end.

Jacob is not quite consistent. Sometimes he reacts to the foolishness of the bourgeois character in the satirical commonsensical way we have come to expect from his predecessors, for instance, as in the conversation with the elder Dorton when the latter tells him that he intends to marry off his daughter:

DORTON:  . . . meiner Tochter Bräutigam ist kein Geheimniss mehr.

JACOB:  Darf ich ihn also wissen?

DORTON:  Herr Brummer.

JACOB: Sie belieben zu scherzen.–

DORTON: Zu scherzen, warum das?

JACOB: Weil er alt ist–

DORTON: Desto besser, Verstand kommt nicht vor Jahren.

JACOB: Mit dem linken Auge schielt–

DORTON: Vortrefflich, dann wird er mit ihm nicht bei andern Mädchen zu Gaste gehen, sondern fein zu Hause bleiben.

JACOB: Mit dem rechten Fuße hinket–

DORTON: Schön, darum wird er keinen Ball geben.

JACOB: Klein und unansehnlich–

DORTON: Unvergleichlich, so braucht er ja eine Elle Tuch weniger zum Kleide.

JACOB: Und überhaupt wenig Verstand zu haben scheint. (II, 8, 332)

And in his monologue in the next scene, Jacob plays almost a "normal" part in his speculations on the kind of bride old Dorton probably has in mind for his son, expressing conventional pity for the latter, at the mercy of so foolish a parent. Yet sometimes it is old Dorton himself who gives practical advice to Jacob: earlier in II, 8 he heartens Jacob, puzzled by Clärchen's coldness towards himself, by telling him: "Als wenn die Mädchen Ja sagen könnten! . . . Wenn ein Frauenzimmer nicht Nein spricht, so glaubt man, sie habe Ja gesagt" (II, 8, 330–31). Dorton is ridiculous, a miser, and worse, for he has treated Clärchen's family very callously, but he has a clever turn of phrase:

Jacob! Wo sich der Schlingel herumtreibt.–Es geht mir mit dem Schurken eben so, wie mit einer falschen Münze, die man bloß sucht, wenn sie nicht zu haben ist. (II, 3, 314–15)

Jacob, on the other hand, is often very naïve. He assures Dorton that he has no doubts about his paternity:

JACOB: Auf meinen Vater laß ich nichts kommen, lieber Herr Dorton. Man hätte müssen blind seyn, wenn man nicht die

Aehnlichkeit unter uns hätte bemerken sollen. Wir waren Beide pockengrübig.–

DORTON: Pockengrübig?–Ha, ha, ha! (III, 4, 349)

We have in this exchange a reversal of the conventional roles, for old Dorton's satiric laughter belongs properly to a servant.

As Harlequin often was in the improvised comedy, Jacob is a loser, but unlike Harlequin, he is not lovably naïve. He is a rather unattractive character whose constant curiosity strikes one as prying rather than as the legitimate attitude of the manipulative servant; his main talent seems to lie in dressing hair, and he is mean-spirited, for having passionately urged his suit on Clärchen, he makes it clear that he intends to become a petty household tyrant after the wedding (II, 6, 327–28).

Jacob has the last word in the play, a somewhat trite moral spoken directly to the audience:

So geht es gemeiniglich in der Welt–wir erhalten selten, was wir gewünscht haben, allein wir erhalten oft etwas Besseres. (III, 11, 370)

But despite the fact that he has just been given a little money and promised a wife (identity unspecified), in terms of the action of the play itself Jacob is unsuccessful. He is not a very good servant, but neither can he climb higher up the social ladder like Figaro. And the beginning of the last scene may serve in a symbolic way to show how, at the same time as Lessing was providing the best example of the exploitation of the servant role within the framework of Enlightenment comedy, that role had played itself out. Weiße, Iffland, and others found no specific new function for the servant (as Beaumarchais did for Figaro), but simply produced different combinations of elements that had become conventional. Jacob joins the others on stage at the end of the play and is seen to be carrying a bag:

DER JUNGE DORTON: Was ist das für ein Auftritt?
JACOB: Der letzte.

DER JUNGE DORTON: Der letzte?

JACOB: Ja, mein Herr, denn ich bitte um meinen Abschied.

DER JUNGE DORTON: So? Und warum das?

JACOB: Weil ich ihn auch ungebeten erhalten hätte. (III, 11, 370)

The promise of help that follows makes little difference, but simply serves to give the play a neat ending. As we have seen, the servant characters turn up sporadically later for special duty, but in the late 1760s, with their main work done, they hang up their livery and exit.

# TRANSLATIONS

p. 5      ...JA ES GLAÜBTS ...:... I'm sure no one will believe what a hard time we poor messengers have, and the pay is very very bad. Now here I've covered fifty leagues in the last week so that I've got blisters as big as chickens' eggs on the soles of my feet. And if I treat myself to a good meal, then I've swallowed in one day the messenger's pay it took me a week to earn. If only my strength holds out. What's the use? We can't all be noblemen.

p. 6      WEIL DEMNACH...: Because hereafter honest Schlampampe rests in peace, go quietly home again, good people. And when death puts out our life's lamp, then it will be all over with us, as with this play.

p. 6      ...ES [IST] NICHT GEBRAUCH...:... it is not our custom to put a gentleman on the stage without a servant; because we would lose too many opportunities for making jokes.

p. 7     ...DIE ENTSCHEIDENDEN...:... the decisive consequences of that tradition of the *commedia dell'arte* affect German comedy too: the play of pure intrigue, surprise and mistaken identity is permeated with satiric elements, with the goals of satire on classes, manners, fashion (women), and other topical matters.

p. 8     EINE COMÖDIE... : A comedy and a satiric poem are children of the same mother. If they do not portray vices in lively colours and ugly clothing, then both taste as flat as unsalted herrings.

p. 8     ...ALSO MUß AUCH...:... thus a moralist too must offer his bitter pills with a laugh and a pleasant joke. Thus the clown is an indispensable figure in a comedy because through his mediation the satiric truths are less dry, and also less painful.

p. 9     LIEßGEN: Pst! Monsieur Donat, is that you?
         HARL.: I'm not called Monsieur Donat, but where there's a feed to be had, I'll answer to any name.

p. 9     (NACH DIESEN REDEN...: (*After these speeches, Harlequin takes a pipe from the side-table, and with a paper in his hand, signs secretly to Ließgen that she should light it for him, which she refuses with a very cross look; finally Harlequin takes his tinderbox and sponge from his pocket, lights his pipe himself, goes aside and smokes like a trooper:*)

p. 11    WENN ICH ABER... : But if I were in your place, I wouldn't think it a disgrace, but rather an honour, to be of lowly birth, but noble in virtue and other good qualities.

p. 11    (...KRAZEN SICH...: (*... scratch their heads and slowly exit. When they are gone, Harlequin creeps after them, scratches his head too and says:*)

Yes! Yes! That's what comes of
the way we go on. It the same
old humdrum story.

p. 12     MISCHMASCH: Rule: If you cross a chambermaid's palm with silver, you can enjoy all her virtues.

p. 13     ALLE IHRE . . . : All their pieces are full of new elements, improvement, shrewd expressions, delicate satire, and constantly varying hidden moral teachings, every scene is artistically linked to the next by a skilful connection of situation and plot. There is nothing vulgar in their use of double meaning, and no joke is flat or out of place.

p. 14     EY JUNGFER . . . : Hey, Miss, that's not the usual way; other young ladies keep their maids for the very reason why you want to send yours away. Don't be so peculiar!

p. 14     OHNESORGE: Oh! unlooked-for happiness!
SITTSAM: Oh! unexpected ending!
VALENTIN: Oh! brand-new bride! . . .
BEDACHTSAM: Away! to the marriage!
OHNESORGE: Away! to the wedding!
VALENTIN: Away! to bed!

p. 17     MAN KANNTE . . . : Our theatre knew nothing about rules and did not trouble itself about models. Our heroic historical plays were full of nonsense, bombast, smut and vulgar humour. Our comedies consisted in disguise and magic transformations; their wittiest notion was to have one character beat another.

p. 19     DIE KOMÖDIE . . . : Comedy is nothing else than an imitation of an action involving vice, which because of its ridiculous nature can entertain the spectator, but at the same time edify him.

p. 19     KOMÖDIEN SIND ... : Comedies often offer better reasons to persuade someone to abstain from evil than the best rational arguments of ethics. To be sure the plays must be written with this in mind. Virtue must always be portrayed as rewarded, vice as punished.

p. 22     HANSWURST ... : Hanswurst, as an allegorical figure, is immortal, and however certainly he appears to have been buried, he nevertheless unexpectedly makes his appearance again, in some ceremonious costume or other.

p. 25     IN DEN ... : The servant scenes even introduce, though within narrow limits, local colour. Occasionally the servants really speak in an authentically "German" way, and act as uneducated Germans would, according to the views of the time. The main characters remain ... "international."

p. 25     (ER SUCHET ... : (He looks for it for a long time, and since he cannot find it, he unpacks his knapsack, in which he has all sorts of old rags and scatters them across the whole stage....)

p. 26     JOHANN ... : Johann in boots and a hood, a large knapsack on his back; in the dagger-belt strapped over his coat there is a large piece of paper.

p. 28     DIESE ... : This *distancing* allows them to mount satiric attacks, while at the same time their *integration* is the reason why they use means to do this which uphold and defend the new middle-class system: those of reason in the service of virtue.

p. 32   DAß NOCH ... : that in most places in our country, instead of truth, the lewd mouthings of Harlequin, the deceptions and intrigues of Scapin still prevail, if not completely, then at least in part.

p. 34   BESINNE ... : Just remember how close Leander and I were to you. Have you not always been our Privy Councillor?

p. 36   WER SICH ... : He who good-humouredly lets his wife give orders and always does what she wants does not deserve to live.

p. 36   ICH SCHLAG ... : I attack at once: I see, I speak, I love: hesitation gradually cools down ardour.

p. 39   JA, NUN ... : Yes, well, where would we poor people be? if there were no fools among rich people who employ more of us than they need ... thus many a one gets his living; and I myself too.

p. 40   GEHEN SIE! ... : Go! Go! I beg you for Heaven's sake. Don't start acting strange again ... now that the young lady has injected a little sense into your head.

p. 40   DER FRANZOS ... : The Frenchman is entertained by the chatter of a maid and a lackey, who in some of his plays are the cleverest characters. The Englishman only rarely descends to such petty devices and he understands the follies of the characters represented without needing the servants' comments to help him.

p. 45   O JA ... : O yes, I'd ten times rather do that than marry you, for all you're a clergyman. You turned me down first, and I'm turning you down now. But if you want to make someone happy, then let it be Peter.

p. 46    BRIGITTE: So his whole household consists of only three people?
PETER: No, of four. I am one person, my master is also one, but
for certain reasons I have to count Cathrine as two people.

p. 47    ...ABER ICH BIN...: ...but I care more for my honour than
for money; I don't want her, even though I'm a poor peasant.

p. 47    ...UND ICH GLAUBE...: ...and I believe it, because in every
ten words our master speaks there are often nine which no one
can make head or tail of.

p. 47    ICH HABE...: All my life I have been servant to farmers and inn-
keepers, but in no house have I heard so much quarrelling as here.
Even our drunken farm-hands play cards more peacefully than
when two or three clergymen meet at my master's house. One
could swear they had been appointed to office in order to spend
their lives picking quarrels. Whenever there are clergymen in our
house, there is an equal number of heretics, for each accuses the
other of being so.

p. 51    *MAROTTIN...: Meanwhile, by all sorts of mimicry, Marottin expresses
his joy at what took place with Florine.... Marottin continues with his
gestures as though he wanted to tell the Prince what happened.*

p. 55    AMALIA: My heart.
CATHRINE: Oh, the poor heart. Tell it that I don't know a better-
hearted nor also a weaker guarantor, and that its guarantee
might be found very much wanting.
AMALIA: My heart can err in a thousand other matters, but not in
this.
CATHRINE: Always in those matters first, where it believes itself
most certain.

p. 56    SCHLANGENDORF: How can you assert, Cathrine, that he knows
         nothing?
         CATHRINE: Because he has told me nothing, and I believe I know
         how to extract the truth.

p. 57    AMALIA: ... He was modest, he was respectful, and say what
         you will! he was certainly sensible and serious.
         CATHRINE: He had eyes, as fiery as six pairs of others; the sweet-
         est broad shoulders, and small hands, one could have kissed
         them.
         AMALIA: I was sure that he sincerely loved me.
         CATHRINE: And I would wager my honour that you were his
         first love.

p. 57    ... ABER SIND WIR ...: ... But aren't we strange creatures, to
         cry and torture ourselves with his memory, since we shall perhaps
         never see him again?

p. 58    ... IHR HERREN ...: ... You husbands, you can be as wild or as
         dissolute as you like. A good woman will always find means to
         bring you to order.

p. 59    SOLLTEN EINIGE ...: If some should find fault with the *Bet-
         schwester,* the *Loose in der Lotterie,* and the *Zärtlichen Schwestern* for
         arousing sympathetic tears rather than joyful laughter, then I
         thank them in advance for such a beautiful reproof.

p. 62    PFUI ...: Fie, shame on you for speaking so ill of your master!
         My dear mistress is peculiar enough too sometimes! Now she's
         head over heels in love with Damon, I've wormed that out of
         her: and yet she intends to obey her silly father and marry your
         silly master. She must have lost her senses: but you see, I keep
         silence; I don't speak ill of my mistress behind her back.

p. 63     PHILIPP *runs after him and says to him:* He loves her, upon my word. Act as if he had admitted everything.

p. 63     NUN, DAS HEIßT . . . : Well, that's what I call making one's fortune through stupidity. My master gets Climene! Foolish people are always the luckiest.

p. 64     WAS DA NICHT . . . : What patience is needed to cope with such a master! I'm too honest for him; he doesn't deserve a good servant. A person who is too suspicious deserves to be deceived.

p. 64     ICH THÄTE . . . : I should like to do it: but I almost don't have the heart. If you promise to treat me differently, then I'll follow you everywhere, even if it should be to war! I'm fond of you, though I sometimes have a loose tongue. I'll be your companion whatever befalls you.

p. 67     DIE COMOEDIEN . . . : The comedies came first to my hand. Unbelievable as it may seem to some people, they did me great service. From them I learned the difference between courteous and forced, coarse and natural behaviour. I got to know true and false virtues from them, and learned to avoid vices as much for their ridiculous side as for the disgrace in them. If I have practised all this only very inadequately, that is surely due to other circumstances and not to a lack of will on my part. But I almost forgot the chief sphere in which the comedies proved useful to me. I learned to know myself, and since that time I have certainly laughed and mocked at no one more than at myself.

p. 68     WAS IST ABER . . . : But what is the purpose of the comedy? To form and to improve the manners of the spectators. The means it uses for this are to present vice as hateful and virtue as attractive. But because many are too completely corrupt for this method to have any effect on them, it has one which is even more powerful, namely that at the end it always makes vice unhappy and virtue happy: ... It is true that most comedy writers have usually applied only the first means; however, that is also the reason why their plays are more entertaining than effective. Plautus realized this, and thus in the *Captives* he strove to produce a play, *ubi boni meliores fiant,* since he could recommend his other pieces to the spectators only with a *ridicula res est.*

p. 69     LIEBE . . . : Love is love. A Queen does not love more nobly than a beggar woman, nor a bluestocking more nobly than a stupid peasant woman. They're all sisters under the skin.

p. 72     LISETTE: And when it comes down to it, maybe you're a Jew too, whatever you pretend?

CHRISTOPH: That's a much too inquisitive a question for a young lady! Come along!

p. 73     MEINE LEUTE . . . : My people tell me nothing. And what is the cause? Heaven has punished me with a houseful of female servants, and if for once I manage to take a decent fellow into my service, not a month passes before that damned girl, Lisette, has him in her clutches.

p. 73     MARTIN: You must think I'm very stupid. Your master an atheist? . . . But he looks like me and you . . . and you say he is an atheist?

JOHANN: Well? aren't atheists human beings?

MARTIN: Human beings? Ha! ha! ha! Now I hear that you don't know yourself what an atheist is. . . . An atheist is—a spawn of hell . . . a cunning fox . . . a donkey . . . a devourer of human souls. . . .

JOHANN: Do you find anything frightening, anything abominable in me? Am I not a human being like you? Did you ever find that I was a fox, a donkey, or a cannibal?

MARTIN: Why do you ask that?

JOHANN: Because I myself am an atheist; that is, a mighty thinker, as now every honourable fellow must be who follows the fashion.

p. 76 MASKARILL: When I came to announce your happy arrival to Lelio, I found him in his chair, leaning on his arm—

ANSELMO: And drawing his last breath perhaps?—

MASKARILL: Yes, drawing his last mouthfuls from a bottle of Hungarian wine.... He jumped up, ran to the window which overlooks the canal, pulled it open—

ANSELMO: And flung himself out?

MASKARILL: And saw what the weather was like.... He took [his dagger], and—

ANSELMO: Did himself an injury?

MASKARILL: And—

ANSELMO: Alas! unhappy father that I am!

*Scene Eighteen*

MASKARILL: And put it in his belt... He rushed downstairs... and threw himself not far from here (*while Maskarill says this, and Anselmo is turned towards him, Lelio falls down at his feet on the other side*) —at his father's feet.

p. 76 DAS IST...: That isn't fair! —but send me away, or keep me, it's all the same to me; only first pay me the sum that I have already lent you for seven years and out of generosity wanted to lend to you for ten years more.

p. 77 DAMIS...: I speak of the Republic of Scholars. What do we scholars care for Saxony, for Germany, for Europe? A scholar like myself is a citizen of the whole world: he is cosmopolitan; he is a sun which must light the whole orb—

ANTON: But it must be somewhere, the Republic of Scholars.

DAMIS: Be somewhere? stupid wretch! the Scholarly Republic is everywhere.

ANTON: Everywhere? and so it is in the same place as the Republic of Fools? That, they tell me, is also everywhere.

p. 78    VALER...: On his account I would avoid this house, worse than a madhouse, if it were not for a more pleasant object—

LISETTE: Then go, and don't keep the more pleasant object waiting for you any longer.

p. 80    ICH WEIß...: I simply do not know from where so many comic poets derived the rule that the bad character must necessarily at the end of the play either be punished or reform. This rule would be more suitable for tragedy; it can reconcile us to fate and turn grumbling to pity. But in comedy, I think it not only does not help, but rather is very destructive. At any rate it always twists the ending and makes it cold and monotonous.

p. 82    ES LIEGT...: It is a matter of honour with Lisette to fulfil what she promises.

p. 83    SEIN SIE...: Be whom you like, so long as you are not he whom I don't want you to be. Why weren't you at the beginnning the person you are now. And why do you now want to be the person you were not?

p. 83    HERR SCHEINFROMM: So you share my opinion?

CATHRINE: O, to be sure!

HERR SCHEINFROMM: Well, then I'll reveal something to you: I myself till now kept Frau Glaubeleichtin from marrying off her daughter.

CATHRINE: Well, well! who would have thought that?...

HERR SCHEINFROMM: I'm not doing all that from self-interest; I have long been freed of this vice by the grace of God. No, I do it out of sheer zeal for Jungfer Luischen's eternal salvation.

CATHRINE: Oh, that's very evident.

HERR SCHEINFROMM: If a mother loves her children, if a wife is faithful to her husband, and does not do it simply through the power of a supernatural grace, then she sins.

CATHRINE: Well, that's depressing. If that's true, we shall have to marry nothing but monkeys and apes, whom we can only love with supernatural aid.

p. 84    DAS IST . . . : He's an old skinflint! But rogue as you are, you are not nearly cunning enough to get the better of me.

p. 84    LISETTE: She is stupid—

DAMIS: A trifling detail!

ANTON: And I say: lies!

LISETTE: She is quarrelsome—

DAMIS: Trifling detail!

ANTON: And I say: lies!

LISETTE: She is vain—

DAMIS: Trifling detail!

ANTON: Lies, I say!

LISETTE: She's no housekeeper—

DAMIS: Trifling detail!

ANTON: Lies!

LISETTE: She'll spend all your money on exaggerated finery, on entertainments and on parties—

DAMIS: Trifling detail!

ANTON: Lies!

LIESETTE: She'll saddle you with the care of a herd of children—

DAMIS: Trifling detail!

ANTON: That's the first thing the best wives do.

LISETTE: But of children who were not got from the proper source.

DAMIS: Trifling detail!

ANTON: And what's more, a detail that's all the fashion!

p. 87    NEIN . . . : No, sir, you go too far! It's true that your daughter is wrong not to accept the husband you've chosen, but must you vilify our whole sex because of that?

p. 88    DAMIS [to Anton]: Fellow, you're mad!
TELLHEIM [to Just]: Fellow, you're mad!

p. 89    WIR...HATTEN...: We...were long tired of seeing nothing but an old fop in a short coat, and a young coxcomb in beribboned hose blustering around the stage among a half-dozen workaday characters; we had long yearned for something better, without knowing where this better thing should come from, when *Le Père de Famille* appeared.

p. 90    SO, SO!...: I see! You want to save it for better times; you will borrow money from me another time, when you don't need any....

p. 90    ...WIR KÖNNEN...:...we can't read handwriting very well. ... we think that letter-writing wasn't invented for those who can converse with each other face to face.

p. 90    WIR WOLLEN...: We don't want to read [the letter], for the writer is coming to see us himself. Do come; and do you know what, Major? Don't come dressed as you are now; in boots, with your hair untidy.... Put on shoes, and have your hair dressed. —At the moment you look far too like a good Prussian soldier!

p. 94    MÄDCHEN...: My dear girl, you understand good people so very well: but when are you going to learn to bear with the bad ones? —and they are human beings too, after all.

p. 94    FRANZISKA (*bursting out*): Soon the joke will have gone too far—

DAS FRÄULEIN (*imperiously*): Don't interfere in our game, Franziska, if you please! —

FRANZISKA (*aside, taken aback*): Not satisfied yet?

p. 94    NEIN... : No, truly, I am no good as an actress. I trembled and shook, and had to clap my hand over my mouth.

p. 96    ICH HÄTTE... : But I shouldn't have been such a blockhead. I see it clearly now. I deserved a hundred strokes.... just don't be angry any more, dear Major!

p. 96    DAS GLÜCK... : Fortune distributes its gifts in a strange way: and the strangest thing of all is that it gives the lower classes the freedom always to find fault with the upper. Don't you see what the situation is in your house? The serving-maid criticizes· the housemaid, the housemaid the lady's maid. *He makes her a deep bow.* You, my dearest Lisettchen, make fun of your young lady! She will make fun of a countess, and the countess in turn mock at some princess or other....

p. 98    MEIN GUTES HERZ... : My good heart led me to the pious decision to pine away with her from grief and hunger. For since I had never made myself ill by fasting, but rather by over-eating, I thought: being hungry won't hurt.

p. 98    AH!... : Ah! I can't help laughing at this idea of a union of hearts! What are you going to do with your dead husband when you're dead too? You won't, I believe, be able to slip into the woods with him, nor watch the stars together on a summer night.

p. 99    DER EINFALL... : That's a clever idea: I'll help to hang him up. A living man is worth more than a dead one.

p. 99    SIE SCHLÄFT . . . : She's sleeping soundly! — That's good! Now I can chew on my last rusk! — Who could be such a fool, to starve and cry herself to death with her! It's true I promised her I'd do it; but how could I dream that she would be serious about it? — What do I care! Crunch! — [This rusk's] damned hard — . . .

p. 101    MYSIS: Come along, let's follow them —

DROMO: And leave this sacred place where an example of conjugal love has been shown, the like of which, O the like of which — the like of which the world sees every day.

MYSIS: Cruel ungrateful creature! Is it not enough that you lead us astray, must you also mock us into the bargain?

p. 101    . . . MIT ERLAUBNIS . . . : . . . Permit me! (*He touches her cautiously here and there with the palm of his hand*) The creature is certainly pretty well in one piece. (*Walks around her with his lantern and finally shines it into her face*) Look there! A very sweet little face! No, this little face surely doesn't belong to a ghost. What eyes! What a sweet mouth! What cheeks! (*He pinches one of her cheeks*)

p. 101    CARION: Great heavens! This isn't a ghost come to frighten me?

DORIAS (*emerges*): No, no: I should have thought I'm too pretty to be a ghost!

p. 102    DROMO (*entering, with a burning torch*): You see! Don't be afraid, captain —

PHILOKRATES: O, who could be afraid with brave Dromo at his side?

p. 103    MYSIS: O, dearest lady, now don't let the gentleman stay any longer. His grief will only add to yours. We don't need anyone to make us even more melancholy than we already are.

PHILOKRATES: Why do you remind your mistress of her sorrow? But I can't say that you are wrong. — I am going —

ANTIPHILA: Ah, sir, do not deprive me so soon of one who was friend to the beloved of my soul.

p. 105     IHR [RECHAS] GLÜCK . . . : Her [Recha's] good fortune is that she has long since been what she is prevented from becoming now . . . .

p. 105     SO KÖMMT . . . : Thus the girl will come among Christians again, will again become what she is, will be what she became. . . .

p. 106     MÄNNER: Men:                      Women:

| Men: | Women: |
|------|--------|
| First Lover | Ingénue |
| Father | Maid |
| Servant | Mother |
| Second Lover | |
| Uncle | |

p. 108     WENN NIEMAND . . . : As long as it's not a question of poisoning anybody, I'm ready to help; it's only that I have a natural horror of the gallows.

p. 109     CHRISTIANE . . . : Christiane knows everything, but her heart is not so depraved that she wouldn't rather join the side of virtue and justice.

p. 110     ITZT . . . : Now I see that honesty gets its reward after all! truly! It's worth the trouble to be an honest fellow!

p. 111     HANNCHEN: What does it matter whether it's his fault or not. A wound is a wound: the pain is the same in either case.

p. 112     NUN . . . : Well, sir? This is the scene of your stupidity or rather of your cleverness! For to my way of thinking there's greater art in a clever man acting stupid than in a fool pretending to be clever. You look stupid enough, with all due respect.

p. 112     JOHANN: Well! What do you think? If all follies end so happily, then it would probably be worth our while to get up to some nonsense together?

              CHRISTIANE: I should think not: for when a person intends to do something stupid, it's then he starts thinking he's really clever; and imagined cleverness is in my eyes the greatest stupidity of all.

p. 117     WAS FÜR...: Now what kind of faults can a young gentleman have, who loves Miss Wilhelmine, slips many a golden penny into the hand of faithful, obedient Lisette and wants to marry off his servant to her?

p. 118     ORBIL: ... I beg you to sit down now.

              VALER: Forgive me, Herr Orbil. I may not sit down until the clock strikes five; — I have fixed certain hours for standing; — certain hours for sitting; — certain hours for walking —

              JOHANN (*sotto voce*): Certain hours when I make a fool of Orbil; certain hours when I give my Johann a thrashing, and best of all, certain hours when I let myself be deceived by him.

p. 119     DORTON: ... It's no secret any more who my daughter's bridegroom is to be.

              JACOB: Then may I know him?

              DORTON: Herr Brummer.

              JACOB: It pleases you to joke. —

              DORTON: To joke, why do you say that?

              JACOB: Because he's old —

              DORTON: All the better, sense comes with age.

              JACOB: Squints with his left eye —

DORTON: Excellent, that way he won't go visiting other girls, but stay home as he should.

JACOB: Limps with his right foot—

DORTON: Good, then he won't be giving any balls.

JACOB: Small and insignificant—

DORTON: Perfect, then he needs one yard less cloth for his suit.

JACOB: And in general seems to have little common sense.

p. 120    JACOB! . . . : Jacob! I wonder where the rogue has got to—It's the same with the villain as with a false coin, which you only look for when it's not to be had.

p. 120    JACOB: I won't have anything said against my father, dear Herr Dorton. A person would have had to be blind not to see how like each other we were. We were both pock-marked.

DORTON: Pock-marked?—Ha, ha, ha!

p. 121    SO GEHT . . . : That's the way things generally go in the world —we seldom get what we wished for, but we often get something better.

p. 121    YOUNG DORTON: What kind of an entrance is this?

JACOB: My last.

YOUNG DORTON: Your last?

JACOB: Yes, sir, for I'm asking you to discharge me.

YOUNG DORTON: So? And why?

JACOB: Because you would have done it even if I hadn't asked.

# NOTES

## PREFACE

1. J.M. Barrie, *The Plays,* ed. A.E. Wilson (London: Hodder and Stoughton, 1948), p. 354. The butler Crichton is speaking in the first act of the comedy.

2. W.H. Auden, "Balaam and the Ass: the Master-Servant Relationship in Literature," *Thought,* 29 (Summer 1954) : 240.

3. Elisabeth Frenzel, *Motive der Weltliteratur* (Stuttgart: Kröner, 1976), p. 39.

4. *See* Helmut Arntzen, "Komödie und Episches Theater," in *Wesen und Formen des Komischen im Drama,* ed. Reinhold Grimm and Klaus L. Berghahn (Darmstadt: Wissenschaftliche Buchgesellschaft, 1975), p. 454. In further references this collection will be cited as *Wesen und Formen.*

5. *See* Max Kommerell, "Betrachtung über die Commedia dell'arte," in his *Dichterische Welterfahrung: Essays,* ed. Hans-Georg Gadamer (Frankfurt am Main: Klostermann, 1952), pp. 169–70, on this essential element of the *commedia dell'arte.*

6. *See* Walter Hinck, *Das deutsche Lustspiel des 17. und 18. Jahrhunderts und die italienische Komödie* (Stuttgart: Metzler, 1965), pp. 213 ff., and Horst Steinmetz, *Die Komödie der Aufklärung* (Stuttgart: Metzler, 1966), p. 8 (hereafter cited as Steinmetz, *Komödie*). Character in Enlightenment comedy means, with rare exceptions, not individual character but character stereotype, "moralischer Charakter" (p. 2).

7. E.J.H. Greene, "Vieux, Jeunes et Valets dans la Comédie de Marivaux," *Cahiers de l'Association Internationale des Etudes Françaises,* 25 (May 1973) : 177 (hereafter cited as Greene, "Vieux, Jeunes et Valets"). Greene develops this thesis further in *Menander to Marivaux: The History of a Comic Structure* (Edmonton: The University of Alberta Press, 1977), hereafter cited as Greene, *Menander to Marivaux.*

8. When Dorine complains in Molière's *Tartuffe,* II, 3 that her mistress Mariane is too passive and will not assert her own wishes in opposition to her foolish father, she is advocating a change in Mariane that would deprive herself of a theatrical raison d'être (Molière, *Le Tartuffe ou L'Imposteur* [Paris: Editions du Seuil, 1953, p. 104).

9. Monique F. Conn, "Les Valets au théâtre entre 1740 et 1760" (M.A. thesis, University of Alberta, 1972); Peter Wolf, *Die Dramen J.E. Schlegels: Ein Beitrag zur Geschichte des Dramas im 18. Jahrhundert* (Zürich: Atlantis, 1964).

10. As well as numerous articles and the titles mentioned in note 6 above, the following book-length studies have appeared: Helmut Arntzen, *Die ernste Komödie: Das deutsche Lustspiel von Lessing bis Kleist* (Munich: Nymphenburger Verlagsanstalt, 1968); Diethelm Brüggemann, *Die sächsische Komödie: Studien zum Sprachstil* (Cologne and Vienna: Böhlau, 1970); Eckehard Catholy, *Das deutsche Lustspiel,* vol. I: *Vom Mittelalter bis zum Ende der Barockzeit* (Stuttgart: Kohlhammer, 1969), hereafter cited as Catholy, *Lustspiel;* Karl S. Guthke, *Geschichte und Poetik der deutschen Tragikomödie* (Göttingen: Vandenhoeck and Ruprecht, 1961); Paul M. Haberland, *The Development of Comic Theory in Germany During the Eighteenth Century* (Göppingen: Kümmerle, 1971); Michael M. Metzger, *Lessing and the Language of Comedy* (The Hague: Mouton, 1966); Yüksel Pazarkaya, *Die Dramaturgie des Einakters: Der Einakter als eine besondere Erscheinungsform im deutschen Drama des 18. Jahrhunderts* (Göppingen: Kümmerle, 1973); Günter Wicke, *Die Struktur des deutschen Lustspiels der Aufklärung: Versuch einer Typologie* (Bonn: Bouvier, 1965). An older study which includes mention of the servants is Betsy Aikin-Sneath, *Comedy in Germany in the first half of the eighteenth century* (Oxford: The Clarendon Press, 1936).

11. *See* note 6 above.

12. Robert Rentschler, "Lisette, the Laugher," *Lessing Yearbook* 10 (1978) : 46–64.

13. Rüdiger van den Boom, *Die Bedienten und das Herr-Diener Verhältnis in der deutschen Komödie der Aufklärung (1742–1767)* (Frankfurt am Main: Haag & Herchen, 1979).

14. For an excellent short account of Aufklärung comic theory and practice, *see* Steinmetz, *Komödie.*

15. Herbert A. Frenzel, *Geschichte des Theaters: Daten und Dokumente* (Munich: Deutscher Taschenbuch Verlag, 1979), p. 255, mentions, for instance, that in a 48-year career, F.L. Schröder played 584 new dramatic roles and danced in 70 new ballets.

16. Hans Friederici, *Das deutsche bürgerliche Lustspiel der Frühaufklärung (1735–1750) unter besonderer Berücksichtigung seiner Anschauungen von der Gesellschaft* (Halle: Niemeyer, 1957), states that it is difficult to deduce from the stage servants anything about the real condition of the lower classes, since most carry "mehr oder weniger deutlich das Erbteil des Hans Wurst mit sich herum" (p. 45), though in fact his examination of these figures is coloured throughout by a tendency to draw such sociological conclusions. Of some of the one-act plays, Pazarkaya remarks that the emancipated behaviour of the servants provides a contrast to reality, and discerns in general a "Spielstruktur" rather than a "Gesellschafts-struktur" (p. 211). From John W. Van Cleve's study of contemporary journal reviews, *Harlequin Besieged: The Reception of Comedy in German during the Early Enlightenment* (Bern, Frankfurt am Main, Las Vegas: Lang, 1980), it emerges clearly that reviewers almost never discussed lower-class characters, including the servants.

17. Eckehard Catholy, "Die deutsche Komödie vor Lessing," in *Die deutsche Komödie: Vom Mittelalter bis zur Gegenwart,* ed. Walter Hinck (Düsseldorf: Bagel, 1977), p. 177 (hereafter cited as Catholy, "Komödie").


ACKNOWLEDGEMENTS

1. Alison Scott, " 'Kerl, du bist toll!': the Servant in Enlightenment Comedy," *Seminar,* 12 (November 1976) : 199–214.


CHAPTER I

1. Herbert Frenzel, p. 43. In the seventeenth century the English influence gradually gave way to the Italian and French-Italian influence (*see* Hinck, pp. 66–67, 136).

2. For a complete account, *see* Walter Hinck's book and the article by Max Kommerell quoted in the Preface, note 5. Elisabeth Frenzel, p. 43, gives examples of the "überlegene Diener" in Latin comedies in Germany in the fifteenth and sixteenth centuries, for example, Dromo in Reuchlin's *Henno*, 1497, and Syrus in Hegendorff's *De duobus adulescentibus*, 1520.

3. Catholy points out that German seventeenth-century audiences frequently watched plays performed in foreign tongues, thus "der wichtigste und beliebteste Typus war derjenige, der sich am deutlichsten und wirksamsten durch körperliche Komik ausdrücken konnte" and integration of such a figure into an only half-understood plot was not important ("Komödie," p. 41).

4. On the distribution of the *dramatis personae* in the European popular comedy, *see* Greene, *Menander to Marivaux*, pp. 2–3, and Hinck, p. 14: "Das Personal ordnet sich nach wenigen Gruppen: den Vätern, den Liebespaaren, dem Capitano und den Figuren des Dienerstandes, und bewegt sich auf einem bestimmten Grundriß von Konstellationen: die Alten, nicht selten nach der Dienerin begierig, richten mit eigensinnigen Plänen Hindernisse zwischen den Liebenden auf, die durch die Intrigen der Diener überwunden werden; zwischen die Liebespaare tritt der Capitano als Störenfried, wie auch die Liebeshandlung im Dienerstand noch zusätzlich durch einen Nebenbuhler gefährdet wird. Obwohl das Schema mit wechselnden Handlungsfabeln hundertfaltige Variationen erlaubt, weist es allen Figuren typische Funktionen zu und sichert den improvisierenden Darstellern die bestmögliche Ökonomie des Spiels."

5. Hinck, p. 171.

6. Friedrich Michael, *Geschichte des deutschen Theaters* (Stuttgart: Philipp Reclam, Jun., 1969), p. 44.

7. Catholy, *Lustspiel,* p. 166, for example.

8. *See* Holl, p. 101 and Catholy, *Lustspiel,* pp. 161–62.

9. In the 14th *Literaturbrief,* Gotthold Ephraim Lessing, *Werke,* 8 vols., ed. Herbert G. Göpfert (Darmstadt: Wissenschaftliche Buchgesellschaft, 1970–79), V : 60. All further references to this edition will use the abbreviated form *LW*.

10. Werner Rieck, "Die Theorie des deutschen Lustspiels in der Periode von 1688 bis 1736," *Wissenschaftliche Zeitschrift der Pädagogischen Hochschule Potsdam,* 9 (March 1965) : 32, says that Weise freed the *lustige Person* "aus der Tradition einfacher Clownerie." *See also* Steinmetz, *Komödie,* p. 11, Holl, p. 102 (the example of Allegro in the tragedy *Masianello,* 1683), Catholy, *Lustspiel,* p. 163. In an early play, *Die triumphierende Keuschheit,* 1668, the clown figure appears as himself.

11. *See* Catholy, "Komödie," p. 44, and Holl, p. 109.

12. Rieck, pp. 28–29.

13. Norbert Müller, "Die poetische Gerechtigkeit im deutschen Lustspiel der Aufklärung" (Ph.D. dissertation, University of Mainz, 1969), p. 22, sees this particularly in the plays from 1689 onwards.

14. On the origin of the stage-name Lisette, *see* Greene, *Menander to Marivaux*, p. 31.

15. Catholy, *Lustspiel*, p. 171, points to this as an indication that he is simply a disguised Harlequin. *See also* Holl, p. 113.

16. Christian Reuter, *Schlampampe: Komödien*, ed. Rolf Tarot (Stuttgart: Philipp Reclam Jun., 1966). Further references to these plays appear in the text.

17. Several commentators point to Schlampampe as, to quote Catholy, "ein weiblicher Clown" ("Komödie," p. 45), since she uses the time-honoured devices of repetition, exaggeration, and contrast.

18. J.M. Cohen, *A History of Western Literature* (London: Cassell, 1956), p. 218.

19. J.E. Schlegel, *Ästhetische und dramaturgische Schriften*, ed. J. von Antoniewicz (Heilbronn: Henninger, 1887; reprint ed., Darmstadt: Wissenschaftliche Buchgesellschaft, 1970), p. 55. Further references will cite this edition as *Schriften*. The Regnard comedy discussed is *Démocrite*, 1700.

20. Hinck, p. 143; *see also* p. 51.

21. On the influence of Molière on German comedy, *see* Hans Stoffel, "Die Wirkung Molières auf die Entfaltung des deutschen Lustspiels der Aufklärung bis zu Lessings *Minna von Barnhelm*" (Ph.D. dissertation, University of Heidelberg, 1954).

22. *See* Aikin-Sneath, pp. 65–66, for a discussion of lesser known satirical plays with a certain amount of social criticism written early in the century, for instance, the works of C.F. Hunold and F. Callenbach and the anonymous *Der Schlimme Causenmacher*, 1701, with its farcical servants Knapsack and Risibelbusefiz; Aikin-Sneath points out that they rely a great deal on extemporization, are without firm shape, and make little attempt at realistic presentation.

23. *See* Hinck, pp. 68–69, 142–43.

24. Aikin-Sneath, p. 67, remarks that Picander's preface of 1726 "may be ironical, like the 'Dedication to the Fair Sex' which follows, but it is more probable that [he] was trying to steal his opponent's thunder."

25. *See* Hinck, pp. 157–58, 161 for Picander's debt to the *commedia dell'arte* in characters and structure.

26. Brüggemann, p. 39.

27. *Picanders Teutsche Schau-Spiele, bestehend in dem Academischen Schlendrian, Ertzt-Säuffer und der Weiber-Probe, Zur Erbauung und Ergötzung des Gemüths entworffen* (Berlin, Frankfurt, and Hamburg: By the Author, 1726). Further references to these plays appear in the text.

28. Aikin-Sneath shows that Harlekin is often like Stranitzky's Hans Wurst, for instance, where, afraid and stupid, he gives the game away to Vielgeld (p. 68).

29. For comments on the colloquial language of the servants, *see* Brüggemann, pp. 29–30.

30. *See* Brüggemann, p. 36, on a similar parody in *Der Akademische Schlendrian,* and Hinck, p. 158.

31. In the preface to the 1716 edition of his works, after speaking of the good and bad qualities in both ancient and modern poets, and commenting on a possible upsurge in German literature and improvement in literary language, König declares with more enthusiasm than prophetic vision: "So haben ja die sogenannte Sing-Spiele in Teutschland zu unserer Zeit, eine Vollkommenheit erlangt, die ihnen niemand abzustreiten suchen wird. . . . " and calls the opera "das Meisterstück der Dicht-Kunst" (*Theatralische, geistliche, vermischte und galante Gedichte* [Hamburg and Leipzig: Johann von Wiering, 1716], unpaginated preface).

32. After the aria in I, 9 expressing Sybille's longing for a lover, follows this stage-direction: "(*Es kommen/indem sie wegeilet/unter ihrem Rocke ein kleiner* Harlekin *und* Scaramuz *hervor/welche tantzen*)." (*Gedichte*, p. 28).

33. Horst Steinmetz, "Der Harlekin: Seine Rolle in der deutschen Komödientheorie und Dichtung des 18. Jahrhunderts," *Neophilologus* 50 (1966): 103 (hereafter cited as Steinmetz, "Der Harlekin"), points out that König's play is the only Harlequinade to press Harlequin successfully into the service of a didactic message. Scaramuz, Scaramuccia, or Scaramouche has the meaning of Scharmützel. He originated in the Italian theatre in France, where he appeared alongside Harlequin, usually replacing the Capitano. Like the latter, he is a braggart; he imitates the manners of a Spanish nobleman and is beaten for his pains by Harlequin. Marie Ramondt, "Between Language and Humor in the Eighteenth Century," *Neophilologus* 40 (January 1956) : 132, comments on this figure: "At a time when the figures of the *commedia dell'arte* were developing into human beings, Scaramouche, the Italian residing in Paris, developed in the opposite direction from a human being to a stereotyped character; a pale man clothed in black, a slightly sinister-looking figure with a guitar at his side."

34. J.U. König, *Die verkehrte Welt: Ein Lustspiel* (Hamburg, 1749), p. 39.

35. J.U. König, *Der Dreßdner Frauen Schlendrian.* (Hamburg: n.p. 1742). All references to this play appear in the text.

36. *See* Rieck, pp. 29-30.

## CHAPTER II

1. Reinhold Grimm and Klaus L. Berghahn, Foreword to *Wesen und Formen*, p. VII, point out that whereas in European literature from classical times to the present more theory has been written about tragedy than actual examples of the genre, in comedy the opposite is true.

2. References to the *Critische Dichtkunst*, except for that in note 29 below, are to Johann Christoph Gottsched, *Ausgewählte Werke*, ed. Joachim Birke and Brigitte Birke, vol. VI, pt. 2 (Berlin, New York: de Gruyter, 1973); they are cited in the abbreviated form *CD* in the text and the notes following. In the last volume of Gottsched's *Deutsche Schaubühne* there are two tragedies but four comedies. *See also* Michael, p. 61, on the dominance of the comedy in the eighteenth-century repertoire. Allardyce Nicoll, *A History of English Drama*, vol. II (Cambridge University Press, 1952), p. 125, shows that in England, too, from 1700 to 1750, comedy was much more popular than tragedy; there were at least three or four comedies produced each year for every tragedy. In the 1770s, Goldsmith commented that tragedy was no longer "the reigning form of entertainment" it had been, but was displaced by "that natural portrait of Human Folly and Frailty, of which all are judges, because all have sat for the picture" (Oliver Goldsmith, *Collected Works*, ed. Arthur Friedman, vol. III [Oxford: Clarendon Press, 1966], pp. 209-10).

3. Horace Walpole to the Countess of Upper Ossory, 16 August 1776 (*Oxford Dictionary of Quotations*, 2nd edition [London/New York/Toronto: Oxford University Press, 1953], p. 558, item 27).

4. On the incompatibility of the tragic mode with the *Weltanschauung* of the *Aufklärung*, see Horst Steinmetz, Postscriptum to *Die deutsche Schaubühne nach den Regeln und Mustern der Alten*, 6 vols. (Leipzig: Breitkopf, 1741-45; reprint ed., Stuttgart: Metzler, 1973) VI: 15*. Further references to the *Deutsche Schaubühne* use the abbreviated form *DS* and are placed in the text where appropriate.

5. *See* Kurt Wölfel, "Moralische Anstalt. Zur Dramaturgie von Gottsched bis Lessing," in *Deutsche Dramentheorien*, ed. Reinhold Grimm, vol. I (Frankfurt am Main: Athenäum, 1971), pp. 68-69.

6. 17th *Literaturbrief*, *LW* V: 71.

7. Of the thirteen roles from which David Garrick played excerpts at his farewell

performance in 1776, ten came from plays written before 1730 (Kálmán G. Ruttkay, "The crisis of English comedy in the early eighteenth century," in *Studies in Eighteenth Century Literature*, ed. M.J. Szenczi and Laszló Ferenczi [Budapest: Academy of Sciences, 1974], p. 83).

8. *See also* Gottsched's preface, *DS* IV: 4.

9. *See* Ruttkay, pp. 86ff. Fritz Schalk, "Zur französischen Komödie der Aufklärung," in *Europäische Aufklärung*, ed. Hugo Friedrich and Fritz Schalk (Munich: Fink, 1967), p. 247, quotes Bossuet's *Maximes et Reflections*, 1694, which rejected the theatre and laughter on the authority of Christ, who never laughed, "n'en a pas voulu prendre le ris et la joie qui ont trop d'affinité avec la déception et l'erreur." Luther had taken a broader view: "Und Christen sollen Comedien nicht gantz und gar fliehen/ Drumb/ das bisweilen grobe Zoten und Bulerey darinnen seien/ Da man doch umb derselben willen auch die Bibel nicht dürffte lesen" (Martin Luther, *Tischreden oder Colloquia* [Eisleben: Urban Gaubisch, 1566; reprint ed., Konstanz: Bahn, 1967], p. 598 [misprint for p. 584]).

10. The phrase is Caroline Neuber's. In the opening scene of *Ein deutsches Vorspiel*, 1734, a one-act play mirroring the controversy between the Müller and Neuber troupes, Thalia complains about the theatrical reforms proposed by Melpomene: "In jedem Schauspiel soll kein leerer Possen stehn,/ Und auch kein Zötgen nicht; der Harlekin soll schweigen" (Friederica Karolina Neuberin, *Ein deutsches Vorspiel*, ed. Arthur Richter [Leipzig: Göschen, 1897], p. 6).

11. Catholy, "Komödie," p. 45. *See also* Brüggemann, pp. 6–8.

12. *See* Steinmetz, *Komödie*, p. 20.

13. *See* Holl, p. 120. On the abbreviation *DS*, *see* note 4 above.

14. Kommerell, pp. 164–65, declares that dramatists of all periods can be divided into two groups: "je nachdem sie sich der Verlockung durch den Mimus öffnen oder verschließen, und man kann sich streiten darüber, ob der Unverführbare dem Verführten hier vorzuziehen ist."

15. *The Works of Henry Fielding, Esq.*, ed. Leslie Stephen, vol. IX (Dramatic Works II) (London: Smith, Elder, and Co., 1882), p. 74.

16. Frau Neuber's *Bittgesuche*, which were prompted by her controversy with Hofcomödiant Müller, are reprinted in F.J. Freiherr von Reden-Esbeck, *Caroline Neuber und ihre Zeitgenossen* (Leipzig: Göschen, 1881), pp. 147–52.

17. *See* Holl. p. 126.

18. Quoted in Mary Beare, "Die Theorie der Komödie von Gottsched bis Jean Paul" (Ph.D. dissertation, University of Bonn, 1927), p. 14.

19. *See* Rieck, p. 31.

20. Hinck, pp. 174–75.

21. Beare, p. 5.

22. Aikin-Sneath, p. 18.

23. Steinmetz, "Der Harlekin," p. 98; *see also DS* VI, Postscriptum, p. 17*. A similar point is made by Catholy, "Komödie," p. 44.

24. Otto Rommel draws attention to Thomas Hobbes's explanation for our pleasure in the comic: we feel a personal superiority when we suddenly become aware of the inferiority of a fellow human being ("Die wissenschaftlichen Bemühungen um die Analysen des Komischen," in *Wesen und Formen*, p. 4).

25. Quoted by Norbert Müller, pp. 28–29.

26. Steinmetz says: "Schließlich ist . . . Gottscheds Auswahl der nichtdeutschen Komödien zugleich wohlerwogen und inkonsequent" (*DS* VI, Postscriptum, p. 12*). Interestingly, Greene says of Destouches's plays that they "appear to be groping towards something else. Others will learn something from these plays, but apparently not Destouches" (*Menander to Marivaux*, p. 112).

27. Hinck, pp. 175, 214–15, shows how the *Dottore* and *Pantalone* are adapted, and how the lasciviousness of the roles is toned down to produce the *Familienvater*; *see also* Brüggemann, pp. 151–53. Catholy, "Komödie," p. 46, points out how the comic function in eighteenth-century comedy is divided among several figures.

28. *See* Wicke, pp. 17–18 and Holl, p. 122.

29. *Ausgewählte Werke*, vol. VI, pt. 1, pp. 217–18. *See* Hinck, pp. 176–77, for an analysis of this plot outline, which contains parts for hired thugs, but none for servants.

30. Aikin-Sneath, p. 63.

31. Brüggemann, p. 221.

32. August Wilhelm von Schlegel, *Vorlesungen über dramatische Kunst und Literatur*, ed. G.V. Amoretti, vol. II (Bonn and Leipzig: Schroeder, 1923), p. 288. Ramondt, commenting on the interest in *commedia dell'arte* characters in the twentieth century, concludes: "The primitive comic figures lead a charmed life" (p. 138).

33. Hinck, p. 16.

34. *See* Herbert Frenzel, pp. 139, 245, and Michael, pp. 50–51.

35. Quoted in Richard Daunicht, comp., *Lessing im Gespräch* (Munich: Fink, 1971), p.203.

36. Brüggemann, pp. 10–11.

37. Steinmetz, "Der Harlekin," p. 105.

38. H.P. Sturz, "Vom Theater und den Schauspielern," in *Kleine Schriften*, ed. F. Blei (Leipzig: Insel Verlag, 1904), p. 84.

39. Hinck, pp. 284–85.

40. Holl, p. 126 (*see also* p. 127).

41. Hans-Ulrich Lappert, *G.E.Lessings Jugendlustspiele und die Komödientheorie der frühen Aufklärung* (Zürich: Juris, 1968), p. 72. _

42. On Frau Gottsched's translating techniques, *see* V.C. Richel, *Luise Gottsched: A Reconsideration* (Bern and Frankfurt: Lang, 1973), p. 72.

43. *Oeuvres de Molière,* Nouvelle Edition, vol. III (Paris: Ant.-Fr. Jolly, 1734), p. 422.

44. Richel, pp. 70–71. The addition is also noted by Hinck (p.220), among examples showing that in their original plays too the Saxon dramatists by no means eschewed buffonesque elements.

45. Green, *Menander to Marivaux*, p. 105. Frau Gottsched does not, however, attempt to render Michel's speeches in dialect, as Lucas's are in the original.

46. On Holberg, *see* Steinmetz, *DS* VI, Postscriptum, p. 13*.

47. Saint-Evremond does not qualify the statement: "Cette Perrette, qui gouverne la maison" (*Oeuvres*, ed. René de Panthol, vol. II [Paris: A la Cité des Livres, 1927], p. 198).

48. Edward Gibbon, *Autobiography*, ed. M.M. Reese (London: Routledge and Kegan Paul, 1970), p. 55.

49. *See* Norbert Müller, pp. 123–24.

50. Brüggemann, pp. 50–51.

51. In Quistorp's *Der Bock im Prozesse*, the servants get "Hochzeit-und Bräutigamsgeschenke" (I, 7: *DS* V: 266); *see also* by the same author *Der Hypochondrist*, I, 4 (*DS* VI: 301–2). In Krüger's *Der glückliche Banquerotierer*, Lisette refers to her perquisites thus: "es sind so kleine Accidentien, wie wir Kammermägdchen es nennen" (II, 1: *Poetische und Theatralische Schriften,* ed. J.F. Löwen [Leipzig: M.G. Weidmanns Erben und Reich, 1763], p. 490).

52. *Der Bock im Prozesse*, I, 8 (*DS* V: 265).

53. S.E. Schreiber, *The German Woman in the Age of Enlightenment* (New York: King's Crown Press, 1948), p. 42.

54. For an account of the arguments on the question of the "originality" of this play, *see* Michael Waters, "Frau Gottsched's *Die Pietisterey im Fischbein-Rocke*: Original, Adaptation or Translation?" *Forum for Modern Language Studies* II (July 1975): 252–67. Brüggemann summarizes his discussion of the weaknesses of the translated portions by saying that the author "transponiert ein rhetorisch stilisiertes Französisch in eine unstilisierte deutsche Umgangssprache" (p. 219; *see also* pp. 58–60).

55. Steinmetz, *Komödie*, p. 30. "Binomisch" are for Steinmetz all of Frau Gottsched's plays except *Das Testament*, Borkenstein's *Bookesbeutel* comedies and Uhlich's "sequel" to the first of these, Fuchs's *Die Klägliche*, Mylius's *Ärzte*, and Schlegel's fragment, *Die Pracht zu Landheim*. The other Schlegel full-length comedies, Mylius's *Der Unerträgliche*, Quistorp's plays, and Frau Gottsched's *Testament* are "monomisch," that is, the only "vice" portrayed is the social foible concentrated in one individual.

56. On this scene as well-placed interpolation and example of Frau Gottsched's technique of accumulation, *see* Richel, p. 26.

57. On the popular "Deutsch-Franzose" them, *see* Aikin-Sneath, who mentions, among others, the anonymous three-act play, *Die Franzosen in Böhmen*, 1743, and *Der Franzose*, 1745 (pp. 87–88).

58. Friederici, p. 180, nevertheless considers that the servants in this play owe nothing to the Hans Wurst tradition and calls Erhard "eine erstaunlich selbständig erfundene Figur."

59. Steinmetz, *Komödie*, p. 41, says that in general servants have a bigger role in "monomic" than "binomic" comedies, and sees in the "monomic" comedy more of a direct descendant of the *commedia dell'arte*, leading to the rule of thumb that if the servants do not take part in the intrigue, the play is not a satiric comedy. This yardstick, while useful, is not entirely adequate, for to Steinmetz, *Das Testament* is a monomic comedy.

60. In writing of *Die Hausfranzösinn* in No. 26 of the *Hamburgische Dramaturgie*, Lessing comments. " . . . sie ist nicht allein niedrig, und platt, und kalt, sondern noch oben darein schmutzig, ekel, und im höchsten Grade beleidigend" (*LW* IV: 348).

61. *Der Bookesbeutel, Lustspiel von Hinrich Borkenstein*, ed. F.F. Heitmüller (Leipzig: Göschen, 1896), p. 3.

62. Ibid., p.5. Borkenstein might have been less than pleased, could he have foreseen Helmut Prang's description of his play as a "derb-realistische Posse" (*Geschichte des Lustspiels von der Antike bis zur Gegenwart* [Stuttgart: Kröner, 1968], p. 143). Wicke sees the play's strength in its tight construction: "Nirgends gibt es Abschweifungen oder Einlagen, nirgends eine burleske Szene um ihrer selbst willen" (p. 17).

63. Ed. cit., pp. 22–23. *See* Aikin-Sneath, p. 86. Servants appear more frequently on stage in *Bockesbeutel auf dem Lande, oder Der Adeliche Knicker*, 1746, listed as anonymous by most commentators, but ascribed by Steinmetz to Borkenstein (*Komödie*, p. 34).

64. Christlob Mylius, *Vermischte Schriften*, ed. G.E. Lessing (Berlin: Ambr, Haude and Joh. Carl Spener, 1754; reprint ed., Frankfurt am Main: Athenäum, 1971), pp. 473, 481. *Die Schäferinsel* was the only play Lessing included in his edition.

65. In the fifth of the six letters composing the "Vorrede" to his edition of his cousin's works (*LW* III: 541). In the fourth letter he comments: "Denn mit wenigen alles zu sagen, er schilderte seinen Unerträglichen, ich weiß nicht ob so glücklich, oder so unglücklich, daß sein ganzes Stück darüber unerträglich war" (*LW* III: 538). Aikin-Sneath, p. 80, takes *Der Unerträgliche* as clearly reflecting Mylius's estrangement from Gottsched and contemporary critical taste.

66. As Aikin-Sneath does, p. 80.

67. Christlob Mylius, *Der Unerträgliche* (Leipzig, 1746),p. 50.

68. *See* Wicke, p. 44, Aikin-Sneath, p. 80, and Friederici, p. 176.

69. *See* Aikin-Sneath, p. 84, Hinck, p. 220, Friederici, p. 72, and Kommerell, p. 164. Kommerell links the *stupidus* and *irrisor* of ancient mime with the first and second *zanni* of the *commedia dell'arte*.

70. Gottlieb Fuchs, *Die Klägliche* (Hamburg: Johann Adolf Martini, 1747), I, 1, 7. Further references to this play appear in the text. In a review in the *Berlinische Privilegierte Zeitung*, 1755, Lessing quotes Zachariä's account of the shabby treatment of Fuchs by Gottsched, under whose patronage he began to write when a student in Leipzig (*LW* III: 231–32).

71. On Rosel's use of metaphor, often with sexual undertones, *see* Brüggeman, pp. 172–73.

72. For instance, the self-assured Heinrich in *Der Hypochondrist* stumbles, like any of his more naïve colleagues, over Latin words, making "Elleboi" into "Ellenbogen" (V, 2: *DS* VI: 379).

73. Friederici, p. 184; Brüggemann, p. 154.

74. Friederici, p. 166.

75. On other *commedia dell'arte* types in the cast, *see* Hinck, p. 213.

76. Friederici, p. 176 and p. 182, sees Hans Wurst characteristics in Peter and in Heinrich of Quistorp's *Der Hypochondrist.*

77. Hinck, p. 220.

78. J.E. Schlegel, *Schriften,* p. 196.

79. *Schriften,* p. 218.

80. *Literaturbrief* 312, quoted by Lessing in the *Hamburgische Dramaturgie,* no. 52 (*LW* IV: 472–74). However, while saying of the characters: "So denkt, so lebt, so handelt der Mittelstand unter den Deutschen," Mendelssohn adds: "Allein ich gähnte vor Langeweile" (p. 472). Lessing calls Schlegel's play an immature piece (p. 471), but, as Charles Borden has shown, he was to some extent indebted to it: "The Original Model for Lessing's *Der junge Gelehrte,*" *University of California Publications in Modern Philology* 26 (1952): 113–28.

81. Wicke, p. 18, calls it "das gottschedischste aller Lustspiele." On Schlegel's "sudden" devotion to comedy about 1741 and the various influences on his comedy writing, *see* W. Paulsen, *Johann Elias Schlegel und die Komödie* (Bern and Munich: Francke, 1977).

82. J.E. Schlegel, *Die Stumme Schönheit,* ed. Wolfgang Hecht, *Komedia,* vol. I (Berlin: de Gruyter, 1962), p. 41.

83. Fritz Martini also points out how in scene 6 Jacob uses loan-word rhymes to describe the elegant manners of the town: "Provinz/Prinz," "Lackey/Liverey" ("Johann Elias Schlegel: *Die stumme Schönheit*" in *Lustspiele—und das Lustspiel* [Stuttgart: Klett, 1974, p. 60). Modern critics perhaps tend to overpraise this playlet, following Lessing, who gives it pronounced approval *(Hamburgische Dramaturgie,* no. 13: *LW* IV: 291–93). Paulsen, for instance, declares categorically, "daß dem Dichter in diesem einen Fall wirklich die Komödie des achtzehnten Jahrhunderts par excellence gelungen ist" (p. 81).

84. Emil Staiger, "Ein vergessenes Lustspiel," in *Beiträge zum zwanzigjährigen Bestehen der Neuen Schauspiel A.G.* (Zürich, n.d.), p. 67.

85. On the servants' function in the symmetrical structure of *Die stumme Schönheit, see* Pazarkaya, pp. 223–24, and Martini, p. 44.

86. *See* Johann Heinrich Schlegel's remarks on this in his edition of his brother's works: J.E. Schlegel, *Werke,* ed. J.H. Schlegel (Copenhagen and Leipzig: Christian Gottlob Prost und Rothens Erben, 1764–73; reprint ed., Frankfurt

am Main: Athenäum, 1971) III: 526. Further references to this edition will cite it as Schlegel, *Werke*.

87. Schlegel, *Werke*, vol. III: pp. 540, 542.

88. *See* Wicke, p. 75.

89. *See* Hinck, p. 234, and on Krüger and the *commedia dell'arte*, pp. 251–52. In his Postscriptum to the reprint of two Krüger plays, Jürgen Jacobs says that Krüger's *Vorspiele* in particular are Gottschedian (J.C. Krüger, *Die Geistlichen auf dem Lande/Die Candidaten* [Frankfurt and Leipzig: publ., 1743 and 1748; reprint ed., Stuttgart: Metzler, 1970], p. 4*). None of the *Vorspiele* contains any servants.

90. References to *Die Geistlichen auf dem Lande* and *Die Candidaten* are to the edition cited in note 89 above and appear in the text. Since the reprint puts together two originally separate publications in one volume, the plays are paginated individually, not continuously.

91. Brüggemann points out, however, pp. 118–19, that in two places Cathrine is linked to the reasonable characters: in I, 3 she says that she was made "klug" by Wilhelmine (and in fact she does give Muffel very reasoned arguments for her previous belief in the work of the devil), while Muffel in turn claims she has been infected by the "Vernunftsseuche."

92. Friederici finds, p. 47, a lack of understanding and sympathy for Cathrine in the play, despite the exposure and censure of Muffel at the end.

93. In a review of a comedy about lawyers in the *Berliner Privilegierte Zeitung*(*LW* III: 200) and in the fourth part of the preface to Mylius's works (*LW* III: 537), Lessing severely castigates writers who, by satirizing one figure, hold up a whole profession to ridicule, and in each case *Die Geistlichen auf dem Lande* is one of his examples. After all, Johann Gottfried Lessing was "ein Geistlicher auf dem Lande" and the excesses of Muffel and Tempelstolz must have struck an odd note in Gotthold Ephraim, whose father felt deep unease at his contact with the wicked world of the theatre in Leipzig, whose pious sister burned his "godless" poems and whose mother had been indignant and dismayed to learn that he had shared her Christmas *Stollen* with his free-thinking cronies and washed it down with wine! It is clear that Lessing regards the picture Krüger paints of the clergy as pure exaggeration for satiric effect, and of course this picture *is* overdrawn and crude, but one might consider the possibility that the problem lay in the lack of a tradition of serious satire, so that Krüger was forced to use comic form developed to ridicule mere foolishness in order to portray real corruption. Thus exaggeration, which in the former case would heighten comic effect, here leads to uncomfortable disproportion. Lessing faced the same problem in his early comedy, *Die Juden*, though he solved it a little better.

94. Brüggemann, pp. 108–9, points to a mixture of a linguistic kind that is general in the Saxon comedy and in this play affects particularly the servants: namely, that there is one level of speech for pronouncing moral dicta, and another, more colloquial, for reporting on events and for ordinary conversation. Holl finds elements of Harlequin in Peter (p. 143), but Friederici insists on the thoroughgoing realism in his portrayal (p. 54).

95. References to further plays of Krüger discussed in this chapter are to *Poetische und Theatralische Schriften* and appear in the text.

96. *See* Friederici, pp. 45, 177, on clown traits in Peter and Hinck, pp. 234–36 on the Italian comedy elements in the night scenes and so on.

97. Of this aspect Lessing remarks in *Hamburgische Dramaturgie*, no. 83: "Er hatte Talent zum niedrig Komischen, wie seine Kandidaten beweisen. Wo er aber rührend und edel sein will, ist er frostig und affektiert" (*LW* IV: 617).

98. Hinck, p. 243.

99. Wicke calls this play "mehr ein Weihespiel . . . Feier, Erbauung, nicht Lehre" (p. 84). However, Aikin-Sneath points out, pp. 63–64, that despite their settings, *Der blinde Ehemann* and *Der Teufel ein Bärenhäuter* contain allusions to the vices of court life and other social abuses.

100. *See* Hinck, pp. 238, 241.

101. *LW* IV: 617.

102. *See* Hinck, p. 247.


## CHAPTER III

1. *LW* V : 69 (*Literaturbrief* 16).

2. *Schriften*, pp. 209, 213. Wölfel believes that Schlegel's ideas in the *Gedanken* have "fast einen marktanalytischen Charakter," taking current popular taste into account (p. 59).

3. Hinck, pp. 285–87, sees in Schlegel's and Lessing's preference for the female servant a refinement of the Colombina figure, evidence of "einer geistigen und sprachlich-literarischen Verfeinerung der Komödie" (p. 287).

4. References to *Der Geheimnisvolle* and *Der Triumph der guten Frauen* are to *Werke* II and appear in the text.

5. Lessing said of this play in *Hamburgische Dramaturgie,* no. 52, that Schlegel's title figure was not at all like the "homme tout mistere" described in Molière's *Le Misanthrope,* II, 4, on which the playwright avowedly based him, but "ein gutes ehrliches Schaf, das den Fuchs spielen will, um von den Wölfen nicht gefressen zu werden" (*LW* IV : 471). Wicke sees the play as "heiteres, gelöstes, nur sich selbst verantwortliches Spiel" (p. 76), while for Hinck, p. 211, it is "ein bühnengerechteres Verkleidungs– und Verwechslungsspiel" (*see also* p. 223).

6. There is a somewhat similar exchange between Minna and Franziska in *Minna von Barnhelm,* II,1, when Franziska responds to Minna's " . . . mein Herz sagt es mir . . . daß ich ihn finden werde" with "Man traue doch ja seinem Herzen nicht zu viel. Das Herz redet uns gewaltig gern nach dem Maul" (*LW* I: 624–25).

7. Norbert Müller, p. 193, sees Cathrine as representing the *Aufklärung,* hence the contrast Amalia/Cathrine as that of heart/reason.

8. *Schriften,* p. 168.

9. On Johann as "Spiegelfigur," *see* Brüggemann, p. 103.

10. Lessing praised this play highly, calling it in one place in the *Hamburgische Dramaturgie,* no. 52, "unstreitig eines der besten deutschen Originale" (*LW* IV : 471) and in another "die beste deutsche Komödie" (*LW* IV : 474) and quoting extensively from Moses Mendelssohn's enthusiastic remarks on it in the *Literaturbriefe.*

11. Hinck, p. 222, says: "Die Kammerzofe hat den Harlekin ersetzt."

12. *See* Norbert Müller, p. 203.

13. In the *Hamburgische Dramaturgie,* no. 52, Lessing quotes Mendelssohn's remarks on this point (*LW* IV : 474).

14. Paulsen disagrees, calling the maid's wit "abgedroschen" and the play as a whole humourless (p. 79). Hinck, p. 220, remarks that Schlegel keeps clear of the grotesque comedy of the *zanni:* "Ihm gelingen als erstem deutschen Lustspieldichter abgerundete Muster der 'feinkomischen' Darstellung."

15. C.F. Gellert, *Die zärtlichen Schwestern,* ed. H. Steinmetz (Stuttgart: Philipp Reclam, 1965). In this play Cleon weeps at the memory of his long-dead wife, at the sight of his daughters praying, at a piece of good news (II, 20, 54: "Ich habe vor Freuden schon darüber geweint") and Damis speaks in one place of "Tränen der Wollust" (II, 3, 33).

16. *C.F. Gellerts Lustspiele* (Leipzig: Johann Wendler, 1747; reprint ed., Stuttgart: Metzler, 1966), unpaginated.

17. When David Garrick in his Prologue to Goldsmith's *She Stoops to Conquer*, 1773, declares: "The Comic Muse, long sick, is now a'dying" (*Collected Works*, V : 102), the malady in question is irritation of the tear-ducts through over-use. That Goldsmith's comedy promoted a sudden recovery is attested to in a letter to him from James Boswell on 29 March 1773. Boswell congratulates Goldsmith on the success of the play and the revival of the spirit of mirth:

> ... The English nation was just falling into a lethargy. ... their comedies, which should enliven them like sparkling Champagne, were become mere syrup of poppies, gentle, soporifick draughts. ... You must know that my wife was safely delivered of a daughter the very evening that *She Stoops to Conquer* first appeared. I am fond of the coincidence. My little daughter is a fine healthy lively child. ... She has nothing of that wretched whining and crying which we see children so often have; nothing of the *comédie larmoyante*.

(James Boswell, *Letters*, ed. C.B. Tinker [Oxford: Clarendon Press, 1924], I: 192–93.) Goldsmith, using what were for the 1770s somewhat old-fashioned arguments based on Boileau, expressed his own opposition to the prevailing mode in the short essay "Sentimental Comedy," 1773, in which he argued that comedy equalled laughter, a truth founded in nature (*Collected Works*, III : 211), whereas Lessing maintained in the *Theatralische Bibliothek* and the *Hamburgische Dramaturgie* (no. 3, for instance) that a mixture of laughter and tears is the natural human condition. One should not forget, however, that the sentimental comedies in England were by no means all irreproachable presentations of respectable middle-class life like Gellert's plays, but often had immoral plots.

18. There was a limited controversy over the *comédie larmoyante* in the *Critische Beyträge*, as a result of A.D. Richter's article "Regeln und Anmerkungen der lustigen Schaubühne," 1741, which advocated a more serious comedy with virtuous characters drawn only from the upper class, and not portrayed in any case as prey to comic vices. Luigi Riccoboni had put forward in 1737 the idea that the private problems of upper-class figures might be presented in the theatre in a dramatic form lying between tragedy and comedy, and very shortly after Gottsched's concession to the new comedy in 1751, M.C. Curtius was declaring that princes can appear in comedy like anyone else, in his "Abhandlung von den Personen und Vorwürfen der Comödie," Preface to his translation of Aristotle, 1753 (*see* Wölfel, pp. 81–82).

19. Brooke's Prologue to Edward Moore's *The Foundling*, 1747, (quoted by Nicoll, pp. 206–7):

He gives you more of moral than of Sport;
He rather aims to draw the melting Sigh
Or steal the pitying tear from Beauty's Eye;
To Touch the Strings, that humanize our Kind,
Man's sweetest Strain, the Musick of the Mind.

The Gellert quotation is from the Preface to his *Geistliche Oden und Lieder* (C.F. Gellert, *Sämtliche Schriften*, vol. 2 [Leipzig: M.G. Weidmanns Erben und Reich und Caspar Fritsch, 1769; reprint ed., Hildesheim: Olms, 1968], p. 89).

20.  *Hamburgische Dramaturgie*, no. 22, *LW* IV : 330.

21.  *See* Schreiber, pp. 115-16, and Hinck, p. 193.

22.  The faithful retainer turns up occasionally in later comedies (Weiße, Iffland), but probably under the influence of similar figures in the *bürgerliches Trauerspiel*, his true home: for instance, Waitwell in Lessing's *Miß Sara Sampson*, with his noble simplicity, and Truworth in Brawe's *Freigeist*, who tries to save his master's soul.

23.  Greene, *Menander to Marivaux*, p. 153, points out that in French comedy "the exclusion of the comic means in practice the reduction of the servant level to insignificance," in the works of Nivelle de la Chaussée, for instance.

24.  One each for the sisters in *Die zärtlichen Schwestern*, in *Die Betschwester* five for Frau Richardinn and three for Lorchen, and in *Das Loos in der Lotterie* four each for Frau Damon, Frau Orgon, and Carolinchen.

25.  Steinmetz, *Komödie*, p. 55, calls Cronegk a backward step in comparison to Schlegel and Weiße, but for the purpose of our study, his place is here.

26.  J..F. von Cronegk, *Der Mißtrauische: Ein Lustspiel in fünf Aufzügen*, ed. Sabine Roth, Komedia 14, (Berlin: de Gruyter, 1969), p. 11. Further references to this play appear in the text. In general, the soubrette in eighteenth-century European comedy is better educated than the male servant, sometimes even having enjoyed the same education as her mistress.

27.  *Werke*, vol. II: 188.

28.  *LW* IV : 471-72.

## CHAPTER IV

1.  In the Preface to the *Schrifften: 3. Teil* (*LW* III: 525).

2. *Briefe von und an otthold Ephraim Lessing,* ed. F. Muncker, 5 vols. (Leipzig: Göschen, 1904) I : 16 (letter of 28 April 1749).

3. *Briefe* I : 8 (letter of 20 January 1749).

4. Johann Christian Brandes in his *Lebensgeschichte,* 1799, recorded by Daunicht, pp. 182–83. In a letter to G.L. von Hagedorn in 1768, C.F. Weiße called Lessing a great defender of "das Niedrigkomische" (ibid., p. 249).

5. *LW* III : 503–4 (*Beschluß der Critik*). In the *Critik* there is a defence of the frequent coarseness of Plautus's servants, which Lessing sees as realistic, given that they were slaves and barbarians, whereas eighteenth-century servants may— equally realistically—be made more refined (*LW* III : 495).

6. The dates refer to the completion of the plays as given on their title-pages when first published and are not in all cases the same as the actual date of first publication.

7. Hinck, p. 285, sees in the Lisettes an adaptation of the Colombina figure, while Prang, p. 152, speaks of "die unvermeidliche Lisette." In an interesting study Robert Rentschler stresses the continuity she provides, "a 'Leitfaden' that runs through all of the early comedies (save *Der Schatz*), not to mention numerous experimental fragments and the accomplished *Minna.* . . . In tracing Lisette's antics, we simultaneously follow the evolution of her Saxon master in matters comic" (Robert Rentschler, "Lisette, the Laugher," *Lessing Yearbook* X [1978] : 47. All further references to Rentschler, except for that in footnote 39 below, will be to this article). Rentschler divides Lisette's function into three stages: 1. "The abrasive laugher" (*Der junge Gelehrte, Damon*), 2. "The upstaged laugher" (*Die alte Jungfer, Der Misogyn*), 3. "The superfluous laugher" (*Die Juden, Der Freigeist*).

8. *See* Karl S. Guthke's remarks in the introduction to his notes on Lessing's comedies, *LW* II : 631–34. On the influence of the Italian comedy on Lessing via France, *see* Hinck, p. 266. In the *Theatralische Bibliothek* Lessing printed a German translation of Luigi Riccoboni's *Histoire du Théâtre Italien,* 1728 (2. *Stück,* 1754) and twenty-four "Entwürffe ungedruckter Lustspiele des italiänischen Theaters" (4. *Stück,* 1758).

9. *See* Friederici, p. 170; Prang, p. 153; and Wicke, p. 89.

10. Rentschler argues that the close of the play puts Lisette for awhile in grave danger of "being tossed out into the cold" and adds: "Unlike the soubrette of the past, Lisette no longer emerges from intrigues unscathed" (p. 51). True, her mistress seems determined to dismiss her, but it is equally clear that she will be overruled. The motto of the play seems to be: you can't keep a bad Lisette down! Hinck, p. 268, sees in the close of the comedy two characteristics of the

*commedia dell'arte:* the "moralische Indifferenz" in most of the characters and the fact that the final situation could lead to another play.

11. On the language of *Die alte Jungfer* (including a comparison with that of *Der junge Gelehrte* and *Damon*), *see* Metzger, pp. 68–71. He says of the play in general that Lessing never writes like this again "possibly because it moves only to cruel laughter . . . " (p. 68).

12. *See* Schreiber, p. 144, on Lisette as the "typical maid of French comedy."

13. References to *Damon, Die Juden, Der Misogyn, Der Freigeist, Der junge Gelehrte,* and *Der Schatz* are from *LW* II and appear in the text.

14. Metzger, p. 65, points out that if one takes Lisette together with Oronte, also a comic figure, they have between them nearly half the lines of the play and dominate six of the ten scenes, their lively language also a counterbalance to the stiffness and long-windedness of the other characters (p. 58).

15. Rentschler, p. 48: " . . . the servant's thwarted scheme is the rule in Lessing's comedies. Only once — in *Damon* — does one of her designs prove successful."

16. Metzger, p. 90. In the literal sense they did not appear on the stage until 1766 in Nürnberg (Ursula Schulz, *Lessing auf der Bühne: Chronik der Theateraufführungen 1748–1789* [Bremen and Wolfenbüttel: Jacobi, 1977], p. 16). Metzger also points to three levels of language: the rough speech of Stich and Krumm, the witty language of Christoph and Lisette, and the elevated tones of the others (p. 89). As Harvey I. Dunkle notes, the major characters in this play have no individual names, but the servants do, which happens in no other Lessing play ("Lessing's *Die Juden:* An Original Experiment," *Monatschefte* 49 [November 1957] : 326).

17. Metzger notes that there are more images and metaphors in scene 1 than in the entire rest of the play, while in scene 2 Krumm's attempts to imitate polite language produce a comic "archaic pomposity" (p. 92). Stich and Krumm do not in fact speak "die ordentliche hiesige Bauernsprache," as the Traveller describes it (2, 380), but "the common colloquial language associated with the lower social levels in Lessing's plays with a few dialect forms added" (p. 91). Lessing has made valet and soubrette linguistically "almost cosmopolitan in order to distinguish them from Krumm and Stich" (p. 95); they are "more urbane and witty" than the servants in his other early comedies (p. 93), and even use in general the third-person plural to each other (no other of Lessing's servants do this), and the third-person singular in a few places for particular effect (pp. 93–94).

18. Rentschler sees this Lisette as "a shadow of the former sprite, one getting on in years . . . the poltroon Krumm is the only personage this diminished Lisette can master and bandy about" (p. 55).

19. In a modern adaptation of *Die Juden*, consisting of Lessing's play with amendations to the last two scenes, followed by a new second act, Erwin Sylvanus develops Christoph's role so that he shares the lead overall with the Traveller, while Lisette drops behind her mistress into third place along with the other characters. This adaptation, premièred in Wilhelmshaven on 27 October 1979, explores what happens if the Traveller and the girl try to resolve their religious differences and marry. Christoph becomes the active, supportive valet, rescuing his master from a new outrage by Krumm and Stich; Lisette, his future wife, is simply his helper. (Erwin Sylvanus, *Lessings Juden: Ein Lustspiel* [Frankfurt am Main : Suhrkamp, 1979].)

20. Pazarkaya, p. 212. One of the scenes in which the servant speaks thus, scene 8, is reminiscent of I, 9 of Marivaux's *La Seconde Surprise de l'Amour,* where the servant Lubin has packed for departure and his master, the Chevalier, changes his mind (*Théâtre de Marivaux* [Paris: Librairie Garnier Frères, n.d.], I : 171–72). Lubin, however, is comic rather than impertinent.

21. *See* Guthke's note, *LW* II : 634. Hans Mayer, who believes that *Die Juden* "tiefer greift, hellsichtiger argumentiert als das Schauspiel vom weisen Nathan," says that Lessing treats the theme "als handle es sich um ein mentales oder emotionales Außenseitertum im Sinne der französischen Typenkomödie" (*Außenseiter* [Frankfurt am Main: Suhrkamp, 1977], p. 333).

22. Hinck, p. 280: the comment refers also to *Der Freigeist* (*see also* p. 282). Of the plot of *Die Juden*, Dunkle, p. 326, says: "The snuffbox causes the thief to be caught, but, so far as the element of *Tendenz* is concerned, there is no need for the thieves to appear on stage or to be found out." Pazarkaya, p. 115, finds a linguistic split too: whenever the Jewish problem is mentioned, the language becomes "langatmiger . . . relativ umständlich und affektiert."

23. *See* Rentschler, p. 56.

24. Hinck, p. 284: "Der potentielle Harlekin gilt als existent, aber der Autor bedarf seiner nicht."

25. In the original one-act comedy of 1748, Lisette appears in eleven scenes out of seventeen; when Lessing recast it in three acts for publication in 1755, he added six new scenes, but Lisette appears in only one of these.

26. In Molière's *Tartuffe,* II, 2, Orgon repeatedly commands the maid Dorine to be silent, and in V, 5, declares: "Taisez-vous: c'est le mot qu'il vous faut toujours dire" (p. 236).

27. *See* Norbert Müller, p. 184. Rentschler, p. 51, sees Hilaria as playing the role given to Lisette in earlier plays, and remarks of the play's close: "Lisette in essence invites the misogynist back into the united fold" (p. 54).

28. The draft of *Der Freigeist* lists the servants as follows:

> JEAN DE LA FLECHE, sonst *Hans Pfeil.* Bedienter des Adrasts und Affe seines Herrn.
> MARTIN. Bedienter des Theophans; dumm.
> LISETTE. Kammermädchen. (*LW* II : 651)

On their language in the finished play, *see* Metzger, p. 119.

29. In the *Hamburgische Dramaturgie,* no. 14, Lessing explains that Adrast is not the only free-thinker in the play: "Die eitle unbesonnene Henriette, der für Wahrheit und Irrtum gleichgültige Lisidor, der spitzbübische Johann, sind alles Arten von Freigeistern . . . " (*LW* IV : 297).

30. Act II, Scene 5 was perhaps already fully worked out in the draft. Lappert comments that this episode offers "jene handgreifliche Bestrafung eines Freigeistes, die wir in der Haupthandlung vermissen" (p. 39). "Punishment" of Adrast, however, was never Lessing's aim, rather the sympathetic correction of his prejudice against the clergy.

31. Rentschler, p. 57, calls Lisette a mediator rather than initiator, "metaphorically" split between Juliane and Henriette, the latter having something of the role of the Lisettes in the earlier plays.

32. Rentschler, p. 54; *see also* Lappert, p. 72.

33. *See* Hinck, pp. 272–73.

34. Hinck considers this play an example of how Lessing gradually emancipated himself from the Italian-French comedy and sees a strong influence of Holberg, though some elements are still reminiscent of the *commedia dell'arte* (pp. 273–74).

35. Metzger, p. 50, remarks: "In this play, which is otherwise almost totally barren of any images or metaphors, or even of any concretely descriptive adjectives, Anton's dialogue fairly bursts with images and metaphors. His range of images embraces the very folkish and concrete, on one hand, and the rather sophisticated and literary, on the other." Lappert believes that in giving Anton a German name, knowledge of Wendish, and other characteristics Lessing is attempting "wenigstens dem Diener heimische Züge zu leihen, selbst wenn er zwischendurch so witzig spricht wie irgendein französischer Diener" (p. 16). Anton is for Metzger " . . . far more reminiscent of the sly slaves of the Roman comedy than of the Pasquins and Arlecchinos . . . of the *théâtre italien*" (p. 121), a "surrogate Hans Wurst" (p. 50).

36. This is not to say that Anton's and Lisette's attitude to Damis is humane. Some-

times it borders on the callously cruel. Rentschler, pp. 48–49, points to Valer's first speech in III, 9 as a criticism of this cruelty.

37. Compare Brüggemann, p. 155, on this scene as a *commedia dell'arte*-type *lazzo*.

38. *See* Brüggemann, p. 213.

39. *See* Manfred Durzak, "Von der Typenkomödie zum ernsten Lustspiel. Zur Interpretation des 'Jungen Gelehrten'," *Poesie und Ratio: Vier Lessing-Studien* (Bad Homburg: Athenäum, 1970) p. 34. Chrysander is nonetheless presented as a ridiculous figure in the course of the play and Conrad Wiedemann invests him with too much dignity in defining him as "der merkantil denkende Bürger der Zeit," a representative of *Aufklärung* economic man (Conrad Wiedemann, "Polyhistors Glück und Ende: Von D.G. Morhof zum jungen Lessing," *Festschrift Gottfried Weber* [Bad Homburg: Gehlen, 1967], p. 235). The point is that Chrysander is a "gemischter Charakter," as indeed too are Valer and Juliane, who are virtuous and high-principled, but not without their weaknesses (in Juliane's case an unrealistic view of life deriving from an addiction to chivalric romances). On the new "serious" characters in this play, *see* Durzak, pp. 36, 38–40, and Wiedemann, p. 235, and for the view that all characters, including the servants, are "mixed," Robert Rentschler, "Lessings Fragmented Norm: a Reexamination of *Der junge Gelehrte*," *Germanic Review* 50 (May 1975) : 165–81.

40. *LW* IV, 684–85.

41. Some critics have overlooked Juliane's intervention: Lappert ascribes the "Happy-End" entirely to Lisette (pp. 151–52) and similarly overstates the maid's role in *Der Misogyn* (p. 153). Hinck, too, speaks of the servant pair in *Der junge Gelehrte*, "das . . . alle Verwicklungen zu einem glücklichen Ende steuert" (p. 274).

42. On Lessing's particular concern in the fragments with form rather than content and the attention he pays to characterization by language and style, *see* Metzger, p. 120.

43. *LW* II : 370.

44. Heinrich Wilhelm Seyfried reported in 1791, however, that Lessing found the dialogue in many of his plays, from the point of view of stage performance, too "ermüdend" and many scenes too long: "Meinen kleinen Finger gäbe ich, wenn ich den jungen Gelehrten zurück hätte; denn mit diesem Stücke erreichte ich meine Absicht gar nicht" (Daunicht, p. 449).

45. Greene, *Menander to Marivaux*, p. 17, sees *Trinummus* as close to the *comédie larmoyante*; Metzger regards it as "essentially a comedy of situation" (p. 132).

46. *See* Metzger, p. 132. Prang understands the modernization as Lessing's attempt to turn Plautus's comedy of situation into comedy of action (p. 157). Waldemar Oehlke calls it the best of Lessing's early plays (*Lessing und seine Zeit*, vol. I [Munich: Beck, 1919], p. 28); however, Friederici finds it "blaß, unwahrscheinlich, konstruirt" (p. 169).

47. On Plautus's use of puns to differentiate between the speech of slaves and masters, *see* Metzger, pp. 141–43.

48. L.A.V. Gottsched, *Die Pietisterey im Fischbein-Rocke,* ed. W. Martens (Stuttgart: Philipp Reclam Jun., 1968), pp. 44–45. Further references to this play appear in the text.

49. Brüggemann, p. 211, speaks of a "geglückte Synthese von umgangssprachlicher und rhetorischer Stilisierung" (*see also* p. 186). *See also* Lappert, pp. 26–28, and, for a detailed analysis of the various levels of language in the play, Metzger, pp. 35–50.

50. Wicke, p. 41, uses this scene as a contrast example to Schlegel's *Der geschäfftige Müßiggänger* with its "monotone, formlose Aneihung." Hinck, p. 276, links the triadic structure of the dialogue in II, 11 to Bergson's comments on the comic nature of repetition. Lappert, pp. 22–23, comments on II, 11 as provoking laughter at all three characters.

51. Norbert Müller, p. 119: "Bei Lessing übernimmt die witzige Sprache, der pointierte Dialog die Funktion einer mittelbaren Belehrung." Steinmetz, *Komödie*, p. 58, comments that the play consists of a "bunten, teilweise recht losen Folge von Einzelszenen."

52. On anadiplosis, *see* Brüggemann, p. 52, and Metzger, p. 36: "Through this subtle linking, Lessing makes the characters seem closely related, listening and responding to each other within the world of the play." Lappert, p. 26, points out that in 1775 C.H. Schmid already commented on Lessing's contribution to comic language. *See also* Steinmetz, *Komödie,* pp. 43–44, 59.

53. Paul Böckmann traces Lessing's path from "Witz" to "Komik und Humor," showing how witty form acquires ever more significant content, so that "er die witzige Form in die symbolische Form überführt hat und damit die Rokokohaltung überwindet" ("Das Formprinzip des Witzes bei Lessing," *Gotthold Ephraim Lessing*, eds. Gerhard and Sybille Bauer, [Darmstadt: Wissenschaftliche Buchgesellschaft, 1968], p. 176). Böckmann sees this process as beginning in *Der junge Gelehrte,* but becoming more pronounced in *Der Freigeist.*

54. I agree with Rentschler (*see* note 7, above) only insofar as the diminishing role of Lisette in the action of the early comedies is a gauge for Lessing's develop-

ment as a comic writer, from the purely satiric to the more serious. The modifications in her own attitude are too slight to warrant his view that, while upholding the cause of laughter, she shows increasing sympathy and concern for others (p. 47).

## CHAPTER V

1. References to *Minna von Barnhelm* are to *LW* I and appear in the text.

2. *LW* IV : 42 (Lessing's translation of Gellert's lecture in the *Theatralische Bibliothek*, 1754).

3. On the influence of the *comédie larmoyante* and the early eighteenth-century English comedy on *Minna von Barnhelm*, see Hinck, pp. 290–91.

4. *LW* IV : 150.

5. *LW* IV : 363 (no. 29). In 1761 Henry Home had made a similar distinction between the "risible" and the "ridiculous" (*Elements of Criticism*, ed. J.R. Boyd [New York, Cincinnati, Chicago: American Book Company, 1855], chap. VII : 159); *see also* chap. X : 189–90. On Lessing's view of the comic in the *Dramaturgie*, see Norbert Müller, p. 57.

6. If Schröder's rule of thumb holds—an interpretation of *Minna* that stresses comedy and supports Minna herself is pro-*Aufklärung*, while one that sees hidden tragedy and takes Tellheim's part is anti-*Aufklärung*—then I happily admit to the former! (Jürgen Schröder, "Lessing: *Minna von Barnhelm*," *Die deutsche Komödie: Vom Mittelalter bis zur Gegenwart*, ed. Walter Hinck [Düsseldorf: Bagel, 1977], p. 50.)

7. They also show the skill with which Lessing uses natural colloquial speech, while characterizing each linguistically in a distinct way: *see* Metzger, pp. 194, 208–9 on Just's language, pp. 209–10 on Werner's, and pp. 211–13 on Franziska's. Ironically, in the same year in which *Minna* appeared, H.P. Sturz complained of German comedy: "sobald wir aber die komische Sprache verfeinern wollen, so werden wir fade und gekünstelt" (*Kleine Schriften*, p. 84).

8. As Schröder points out, Tellheim "spielt . . . hartnäckig Tragödie, obwohl er sich in dem Spielraum der Komödie bewegt" (p. 57).

9. Bruce Duncan suggests a different reading, however: "Just's *Rechnung* satisfies Tellheim that he owes nothing for past services, while the story of the dog con-

vinces him that he will owe nothing in the future" ("Hand, Heart and Language in *Minna von Barnhelm," Seminar* 8 [March 1972] : 18). Duncan makes the perceptive point that Tellheim keeps his hands clean by letting Just dirty his (p. 17). Staiger reads Tellheim as accepting Just to a limited extent, "though with no joy" (Emil Staiger, "Lessing's *Minna von Barnhelm,"* tr. Sylvia P. Jenkins, *German Life and Letters* 1 [July 1948] : 265).

10. Hinck sees something characteristically German in Just's doggedly faithful, non-intriguing nature, in comparison with the French valet-type culminating in Beaumarchais's Figaro: "Mit Menschen wie Just lassen sich keine Revolutionen machen" (p. 297).

11. Arntzen, p. 27, points out that Just sees the world as a polar confrontation between his wronged master and the rascally landlord. He does not listen to the quite reasonable excuses made by the landlord, but he does "listen" to the liquor! (p. 28).

12. Schreiber, p. 220. In the old Italian theatre the female servant was sometimes of a higher social class than the male, and Colombina often sister or friend of the leading lady (*see* Hinck, p. 299). Arntzen sees the difference between Franziska and Minna as "Bewußtseinsdifferenz": Franziska is reasonable, "nur ist ihre Verständigkeit noch ungebildet, zufällig" (p. 31). Similarly, the social differences between Franziska and Minna, and Werner and Tellheim, are based on "Unterschied von Bewußtseinserhellung, von Aufklärung" (p. 44). Arntzen sees in Werner's closing words a reference to one of the critical questions of the play, reflecting only "ein problematisches Glück" (p. 45.).

13. This prompts the not entirely frivolous question: who will serve Tellheim and Minna then? In the sort of elegant establishment that the Major and his bride will no doubt set up, even though it be in the "stillsten, heitersten, lachendsten Winkel" (V, 9, 694), will Just continue as Tellheim's valet or will he be sent back—the poodle with him—to the stable? And will Minna have her hair dressed and her coffee ordered by a pert Lisette?

14. For this scene Lessing was indebted to an idea he found in Riccoboni's *Le Soupçonneux,* one of the "Entwürffe" printed in the *Theatralische Bibliothek* (*see* Hinck, pp. 263–64).

15. *See* Lappert, p. 16.

16. Duncan argues that the play points up the one-sidedness of Minna's and Tellheim's noble qualities: "The playful reciprocity of Franciska and Werner suggests a more successful approach to life than do the rigid virtues of their masters" (pp. 15, 28).

17. Lukács declares: *"Minna von Barnhelm* ist das Aufklärungs märchen vom not-
    wendigen Endsieg einer zur Anmut gewordenen Vernunft" (Györgi Lukács,
    *Werke,* vol. VII: *Deutsche Literatur in zwei Jahrhunderten* [Neuwied and Berlin:
    Luchterhand, 1964], p. 34). For a different viewpoint in a critique of Minna's
    *Spiel, see* Horst Steinmetz, *"Minna von Barnhelm* oder die Schwierigkeit, ein
    Lustspiel zu verstehen," in *Wissen aus Erfahrungen,* ed. A. von Bormann (Tübin-
    gen: Niemeyer, 1976) pp. 146 ff. Agreeing with remarks made by Eschenburg in
    1767, Steinmetz sees the intrigue as frivolous and irresponsible trickery (p. 146).

18. In a French adaptation of *Minna von Barnhelm,* Rochon de Chabannes's *Les
    Amans généreux,* 1774, the Comte de Bruxhal is the central figure, a loudmouth
    and a gourmand, Minna is a young widow, and the motif of disinheritance is no
    longer mere pretence on Minna's part. After a very successful première on 13
    October 1774 at the Théâtre Français, eleven further performances were given
    and the play was frequently repeated in France. Even French critics who knew
    the German original considered the Chabannes version much more refined!
    (Hans Kinkel, *Lessings Dramen in Frankreich* [Darmstadt: Otto, 1908], pp.
    12–19). This adaptation was performed in Germany at the Berlin French theatre
    in the late 1770s (*see* K.G. Lessing to his brother, 7 November 1778) and in the
    1790s in Hamburg.

19. Both Duncan and Ilse Appelbaum Graham comment extensively on Tellheim's
    inability to accept help (Ilse Appelbaum Graham, "The Currency of Love: A
    Reading of Lessing's *Minna von Barnhelm," German Life and Letters* 18 [July
    1965], 270–78). Graham sees in III, 7 "the sharpest and ugliest verbal duel in
    the drama" (p. 272). *See also* Jürgen Schröder, "Das parabolische Geschehen der
    'Minna von Barnhelm'," *Deutsche Vierteljahresschrift* 43 (August 1969): 240.
    Duncan, p. 19, says that Tellheim "relegates the Wachtmeister to the status of
    the poodle: called upon to show affection and loyalty, but forbidden any con-
    tributing role."

20. *LW* II: 454–55.

21. On the *Entstehungsgeschichte* of Lessing's *Matrone von Ephesus, see* Robert Petsch,
    *"Die Matrone von Ephesus:* Ein dramatisches Bruchstück von Lessing," *Dichtung
    und Volkstum* (*Euphorion,* new series) 41 (1941): 87–90. Petsch sees the first plan
    as contemporaneous with the writing of *Der junge Gelehrte,* as does Theodor van
    Stockum, on the basis that the tone and latent psychology belong to the farce
    ("Lessings Dramenentwurf *Die Matrone von Ephesus," Neophilologus* 46 [January
    1962]: 129). Karl Guthke, however, thinks it most probable that all versions
    were drafted during the Hamburg period, 1767–69 (Postscriptum to G.E.
    Lessing, *D. Faust. Die Matrone von Ephesus* [Stuttgart: Philipp Reclam Jun.,
    1968], p. 76).

22. K.G. Lessing, *Gotthold Ephraim Lessings Leben,* vol. I (Berlin: Voß, 1793), pp. 63–64.

23. On the "Matrone" theme in general, *see* Peter Ure, "The Widow of Ephesus: Reflections on an International Comic Theme," *The Durham University Journal* 49 (December 1956) : 1–9.

24. Prang, p. 163.

25. References to this play are to C.F. Weiße, *Lustspiele,* vol. I (Karlsruhe: Schmieder, 1778) and appear in the text.

26. Although Auden, p. 238, declares "a slave is not a servant because he has no sovereignty whatsoever," Lessing, like other European dramatists who deal with this theme, is clearly using servant/slave interchangeably in this case. In the *Szenar* the widow's companion is referred to as "die Bediente" throughout; in the *Entwurf* she is listed as "Die Magd" and refers to herself as "eine Sklavin"; in the last version she and all other three characters use the term "Sklavin."

27. References to the *Matrone* fragments are to *LW* II and appear in the text.

28. *See* van Stockum, p. 129.

29. Van Stockum calls this: "Ein höchst merkwürdiger, aber wenig würdiger Schluß für diese im Grunde so grimmige Tragikomödie!" (p. 130).

30. Metzger says of the two servants: "More than providing a gratuitous common touch, however, they comment epigrammatically on the central matter of the play. While they distinctly lead their own lives as characters, they are more thoroughly integrated into the structure than most of the servants encountered [before *Minna von Barnhelm*]" (p. 183) and " . . . this dialogue [scene 2] between Mysis and Dromo fairly bubbles with a colloquial common sense which belies the background against which it takes place" (p. 185). On anadiplosis and other techniques in the play and its suppleness of language, *see* Metzger, p. 186, and on the individualization of the language, van Stockum, p. 132.

31. Petsch sees in the widow a "Verkrampftheit" like Tellheim's (p. 90) and in Philokrates' supposed friendship with the dead man a "Kriegslist" similar to Minna's pretence (p. 94). On his difficulty with the material, *see* Lessing's remarks in the *Hamburgische Dramaturgie,* no. 36 (*LW* IV : 395–96.)

32. Dromo's extreme cynicism seems to me to preclude his remarks on Antiphila from arising simply from "humane rationality sense [*sic*]" and reflecting "the attitude of Lessing," as Metzger believes (p. 186). Metzger further states that Mysis really agrees with Dromo, her statements in scene 2 being "quite out of line with her normally skeptical and rational character" (p. 186) and simply an echo of her mistress.

33. Petsch, p. 93, points out that advice, which, like that of Mysis to Antiphila here, produces the opposite of the intended result, is an old comic motif. He comments, pp. 91–92, on Mysis's "eigentümliche Doppelrolle" — she *is* faithful to Antiphila, yet acts to break the tension; while Dromo still belongs to traditional comedy, Antiphila and Mysis reflect a higher level of the genre.

34. Friedrich Schlegel, "Über Lessing" (1801), in *Gotthold Ephraim Lessing,* p. 27.

35. Lessing to his brother Karl, 20 October 1778: "Es wird nichts weniger, als ein satirisches Stück, um den Kampfplatz mit Hohngelächter zu verlassen. Es wird ein so rührendes Stück, als ich nur immer gemacht habe, . . . " (*Briefe* II : 289).

36. On comedy elements in Lessing's non-comic dramas, *see* Robert R. Heitner, "Lessing's Manipulation of a Single Comic Theme," *Modern Language Quarterly* 18 (September 1957) : 183–98, and Klaus-Detleff Müller, "Das Erbe der Komödie im bürgerlichen Trauerspiel: Lessings *Emilia Galotti* und die commedia dell'arte," *Deutsche Vierteljahresschrift* 46 (January 1972) : 28–60. Karl Lessing wrote in the preface to *Der Schlaftrunk* that in a conversation with a group of people including Ramler, in Berlin in 1766, his brother maintained that one could turn any dramatic material into either tragedy or comedy (*Theatralischer Nachlaß* I, 1784, quoted in *LW* II : 785).

37. References to *Nathan der Weise* are taken from *LW* II and appear in the text.

## CHAPTER VI

1. Friedrich ("Maler") Müller, "Gedanken über Errichtung eines Deutschen Nationaltheaters" (1777) in *Sturm und Drang: Kritische Schriften,* eds. E. Loewenthal and L. Schneider (Heidelberg: Lambert Schneider, 1972), p. 774.

2. Ibid., pp. 774–75.

3. From the seventeenth until well into the nineteenth century there was a tendency for actors to be type-cast, particularly in the case of the comic figure. On the usual basic ensemble (five men, three women, and two extra of each), *see* Herbert Frenzel, p. 236, and Michael, p. 59.

4. Hinck, p. 302.

5. Weiße had produced an earlier version in 1752, based on Coffey's play alone, with music by J.C. Standfuß (some of which Hiller used for his score later), but a full libretto is not preserved: *see* H.A. Koch, *Das deutsche Singspiel* (Stuttgart: Metzler, 1974), pp. 44, 46; *see also* Hinck, p. 306.

6.  On this point, *see* Hinck, pp. 312–13.

7.  *See* Koch, pp. 48–49.

8.  C.F. Weiße, *Lustspiele,* 3 vols. (Leipzig: Verlag der Dykischen Buchhandlung, 1783) I : 70. Revisions to the original form of his plays that Weiße made for later collections such as this do not affect the servants' role to an extent that would alter their analysis materially.

9.  References to this play are to C.F. Weiße, *Beyträge zum deutschen Theater,* 5 vols. (Leipzig: Verlag der Dykischen Buchhandlung, 1759 – 68) II and appear in the text. In this edition, speeches in three places are mistakenly attributed to Lisette rather than to Christiane (pp. 310, 311, 314); Lisette is mentioned once in a stage direction (p. 324) and once by another character (p. 236).

10. Steinmetz, *Komödie,* p. 54, sees as Weiße's only innovation in his satirical plays the double function of the intrigue, which serves both to expose the comic vice and to realize the goals of the "normal" characters.

11. References to this play are to *Beyträge,* vol. III and appear in the text. Although no maidservant appears on stage in *Der Mißtrauische,* a Lisette is mentioned once (II, 3, 289).

12. *See* Arntzen, p. 48.

13. One could perhaps count as servant (as Arntzen does, p. 48) the villain Woodbe, "Bettmeister auf dem Gute des Blandford," who is hardly a comic figure. Disliked by the other, all highly noble-minded characters in the play, he is contemptuous of everyone and intrigues for his own advantage. Although he is not the most frequently appearing figure (eleven scenes out of thirty-two), he creates tension whenever he does come on stage and Weiße uses a particular technique to achieve this: in each of the first three acts, Woodbe appears in the last two scenes only, in the penultimate one in a tense dialogue with one, or two other characters, while in the last he delivers a dramatically villainous monologue. He appears twice in act IV, opens act V with a monologue beginning with the complaint "Ah, es ist doch ein verzweifeltes Ding um die liebe Tugend" (*Lustspiele* III : 105), then, after his schemes seem to promise success again, fails and is dramatically dismissed in scene 8: "(*Woodbe geht murmelnd ab*)" (p. 128).

14. References to this play are to *Lustspiele* III and appear in the text.

15. *Lustspiele* II : 202.

16. Steinmetz, *Komödie,* p. 55.

17. References to this play are to *Lustspiele* III and appear in the text.

18. *See* Steinmetz, *Komödie*, p. 54.

19. G.A. Bürger, "Aus Daniel Wunderlichs Buck," 1776, (*Sturm und Drang: Kritische Schriften*, p. 804).

20. On the decline of the comedy as a strictly defined literary genre and the increase of popular productions, *see* Arntzen, pp. 46ff. The popular comedies of the 1750s and 1760s (often anonymous and largely derivative, if not outright adaptations) usually portray the same kinds of servants in the same considerable roles as the literary examples, but in those of the 1770s and 1780s the servants' parts are often insignificant.

21. Greene makes a similar point about the French comedy in "Vieux, Jeunes et Valets," p. 181.

22. Arntzen, p. 50; Holl, p. 200.

23. *See* Michael M. Metzger and Gerard F. Schmidt, Postscriptum to *Der Hofmeister und die Gouvernante* (Berlin: de Gruyter, 1969), p. 95. Prang, p. 192, argues that Iffland's plays are more valuable as documentary material for their time than as contributions to comic literature.

24. *See* Wolfgang Schaer, *Die Gesellschaft im deutschen bürgerlichen Drama des 18. Jahrhunderts* (Bonn: Bouvier, 1963), p. 146.

25. Pazarkaya, pp. 213–14, points out that in the one-act *Rührstücke* the servants frequently become faithful friends of their masters.

26. *LW* IV : 671 (*Hamburgische Dramaturgie*, no. 96) and 332 (no. 22).

27. References to *Der Mann nach der Uhr* and *Die ungewöhnlichen Nebenbuhler* are to Th.G. von Hippel, *Sämtliche Werke*, vol. X (Berlin: Reimer, 1828) and appear in the text.

28. *LW* IV : 332.

29. Compare the opening sentence of *Asiatische Banise*, 1689: "Blitz, Donner und Hagel, als die rächenden Werkzeuge des gerechten Himmels, zerschmettere den Pracht deiner goldbedeckten Türme..." (Heinrich Anshelm von Zigler und Kliphausen, *Asiatische Banise* [Leipzig: Gleditsch, 1689; reprint ed., Munich: Winkler, 1965,] p. 15).

# BIBLIOGRAPHY

PRIMARY SOURCES

*Beyträge zur Critischen Historie der deutschen Sprache, Poesie und Beredsamkeit* [ = *Critische Beyträge*]. Herausgegeben von einigen Liebhabern der deutschen Literatur. 8 vols. Leipzig: Breitkopf, 1732–44.

Borkenstein, Hinrich. *Der Bookesbeutel.* Edited by F.F. Heitmüller. Deutsche Litteraturdenkmale des 18. und 19. Jahrhunderts, vol. 56/57. Leipzig: Göschen, 1896.

Boswell, James. *Letters.* Vol. 1. Edited by C.B. Tinker. Oxford: Clarendon Press, 1924.

Cronegk, Johann Friedrich von. *Der Mißtrauische.* Edited by Sabine Roth. *Komedia: Deutsche Lustspiele vom Barock bis zur Gegenwart,* vol. 14. Berlin: Walter de Gruyter, 1969.

Fielding, Henry. *The Works of Henry Fielding, Esq.* Vol. 9 (*Dramatic Works,* vol. 2). Edited by Leslie Stephen. London: Smith, Elder, and Co., 1882.

Fuchs, Gottlieb. *Die Klägliche.* Hamburg: Johann Adolf Martini, 1747.

Gellert, Christian Fürchtegott. *Lustspiele.* Leipzig: Johann Wendler, 1747; reprint ed., Stuttgart: Metzler, 1968.

————. *Sämtliche Schriften.* Vol. 2. Leipzig: M.G. Weidmanns Erben und Reich und Caspar Fritsch, 1769, reprint ed., (10 vols. in 5). Hildesheim: Olms, 1968.

————. *Die zärtlichen Schwestern.* Edited by Horst Steinmetz. Stuttgart: Philipp Reclam Jun., 1965.

Gibbon, Edward. *Autobiography.* Edited by M.M. Reese. London: Routledge and Kegan Paul, 1970.

Goldsmith, Oliver. *Collected Works.* Vols. 3 and 4. Edited by Arthur Friedman. Oxford: Clarendon Press, 1966.

Gottsched, Johann Christoph. *Ausgewählte Werke.* Vol. 6, parts 1 and 2 ( = *Versuch einer critischen Dichtkunst vor die Deutschen*). Edited by Joachim Birke and Brigitte Birke. Berlin and New York: Walter de Gruyter, 1973.

Gottsched, Johann Christoph, ed. *Die deutsche Schaubühne nach den Regeln und Mustern der Alten.* 6 vols. Leipzig: Breitkopf, 1740–45; reprint ed., with a Postscriptum by Horst Steinmetz, Stuttgart: Metzler, 1973.

Gottsched, Luise Adelgunde Viktorie. *Die Pietisterey im Fischbein-Rocke.* Edited by Wolfgang Martens. Stuttgart: Philipp Reclam Jun., 1968.

————. *Die Hausfranzösinn.* In *Deutsche Schaubühne nach den Regeln und Mustern der Alten.* Vol.5. Edited by J.C. Gottsched. Leipzig: Breitkopf, 1744; reprint ed., Stuttgart: Metzler, 1973.

————. *Das Testament.* In *Deutsche Schaubühne nach den Regeln und Mustern der Alten.* Vol. 6. Edited by J.C. Gottsched. Leipzig: Breitkopf, 1745; reprint ed., Stuttgart: Metzler, 1973.

————. *Die ungleiche Heirath.* In *Deutsche Schaubühne nach den Regeln und Mustern der Alten.* Vol. 4. Edited by J.C. Gottsched. Leipzig: Breitkopf, 1743; reprint ed., Stuttgart: Metzler, 1973.

————. *Der Witzling.* In *Deutsche Schaubühne nach den Regeln und Mustern der Alten.* Vol. 6. Edited by J.C. Gottsched. Leipzig: Breitkopf, 1745; reprint ed., Stuttgart: Metzler, 1973.

Henrici, Christian Friedrich [Picander]. *Picanders Teutsche Schau-Spiele, bestehend in dem Akademischen Schlendrian, Ertzt-Säuffer und der Weiber-Probe, Zur Erbauung und Ergötzung des Gemüths entworffen.* Berlin, Frankfurt, Hamburg: By the Author, 1726.

Hippel, Theodor Gottlieb von. *Sämtliche Werke.* Vol. 10. Berlin: Reimer, 1828.

*Der Hofmeister und die Gouvernante.* Edited by Michael M. Metzger and Gerard F. Schmidt. *Komedia: Deutsche Lustspiele vom Barock bis zur Gegenwart,* vol. 15. Berlin: Walter de Gruyter, 1969.

Home, Henry, Lord Kames. *Elements of Criticism.* Edited by J.R. Boyd. New York, Cincinnati, Chicago: American Book Company, 1855.

Iffland, August Wilhelm. *Theatralische Werke in einer Auswahl.* 6 vols. Leipzig: Göschen, 1858.

König, Johann Ulrich. *Der Dreßdner Frauen Schlendrian.* Hamburg, 1742. Yale German Baroque Literature Microfilm, reel 604, no. 1712.

―――. *Die Verkehrte Welt.* Hamburg, 1749. Yale German Baroque Literature microfilm, reel 604, no. 1711.

―――. *Theatralische, geistliche, vermischte und galante Gedichte, allen Kennern und Liebhabern der edlen Poesie, zur Belustigung ans Licht gestellet.* Hamburg and Leipzig: Johann von Wiering, 1716.

Kotzebue, August von. *Theater.* 40 vols. Leipzig and Vienna, 1840–41.

Krüger, Johann Christian. *Die Geistlichen auf dem Lande/Die Candidaten.* Frankfurt and Leipzig, 1743 and 1748; reprint ed., with a Postscriptum by Jürgen Jacobs, Stuttgart: Metzler, 1970.

―――. *Poetische und Theatralische Schriften.* Edited by J.F. Löwen. Leipzig: M.G. Weidmanns Erben und Reich, 1763.

Lessing, Gotthold Ephraim. *Briefe von und an Gotthold Ephraim Lessing.* 5 vols. Edited by F. Muncker. Leipzig: Göschen, 1904–7. (In *Sämtliche Schriften.* 3d ed. Edited by K. Lachmann, rev. F. Muncker. Vols. 17–21).

―――. *Werke.* 8 vols. Edited by Herbert G. Göpfert. Darmstadt: Wissenschaftliche Buchgesellschaft, 1970–79.

*Lessing im Gespräch: Berichte und Urteile von Freunden und Zeitgenossen.* Compiled and edited by Richard Daunicht. Munich: Fink, 1971.

Luther, Martin. *Tischreden oder Colloquia.* Eisleben: Urban Gaubisch, 1566; reprint ed., Konstanz: Bahn, 1967.

Marivaux, Pierre Carlet de Chamblain de. *La Seconde Surprise de L'Amour.* In *Théâtre de Marivaux.* Vol. 1. Paris: Librairie Garnier Frères, n.d.

Molière, Jean-Baptiste Poquelin, *known as. Le Misanthrope.* In *Oeuvres de Molière.* Vol. 3. Paris: Ant.-Fr. Jolly, 1734.

―――. *Le Tartuffe ou L'Imposteur.* Paris: Editions du Seuil, 1953.

Mylius, Christlob. *Die Ärtzte.* Leipzig, 1745.

―――. *Die Schäferinsel.* In *Vermischte Schriften.* Edited by G.E. Lessing. Berlin: Ambr. Haude and Joh. Carl Spener, 1745; reprint ed., Frankfurt am Main: Athenäum, 1971.

————. *Der Unerträgliche*. Leipzig, 1746.

Neuberin, Friederica Karolina. *Ein deutsches Vorspiel*. Edited by Arthur Richter. Deutsche Litteraturdenkmale des 18. und 19. Jahrhunderts, vol. 63. Leipzig: Göschen, 1897.

Quistorp, Johann Theodor. *Die Austern*. In *Deutsche Schaubühne nach den Regeln und Mustern der Alten*. Vol. 4. Edited by J.C. Gottsched. Leipzig: Breitkopf, 1743; reprint ed., Stuttgart: Metzler, 1973.

————. *Der Bock im Prozesse*. In *Deutsche Schaubühne nach den Regeln und Mustern der Alten*. Vol. 5. Edited by J.C. Gottsched. Leipzig: Breitkopf, 1744; reprint ed., Stuttgart: Metzler, 1973.

————. *Der Hypochondrist*. In *Deutsche Schaubühne nach den Regeln und Mustern der Alten*. Vol. 6. Edited by J.C. Gottsched. Leipzig: Breitkopf, 1745; reprint ed., Stuttgart: Metzler, 1973.

Reuter, Christian. *Schlampampe: Komödien*. Edited by Rolf Tarot. Stuttgart: Philipp Reclam Jun., 1966.

Saint-Evremond, Charles de Marguetel de Saint-Denis de. *Les Opéra*. In *Oeuvres*, vol. 2. Edited by René de Panthol. Paris: A la Cité des Livres, 1927.

Schlegel, Johann Elias. *Ästhetische und dramaturgische Schriften*. Edited by Johann von Antoniewicz. Deutsche Litteraturdenkmale des 18. und 19. Jahrhunderts, vol. 26. Heilbronn: Henninger, 1887; reprint ed., Darmstadt: Wissenschaftliche Buchgesellschaft, 1970.

————. *Der geschäfftige Müßiggänger*. In *Deutsche Schaubühne nach den Regeln und Mustern der Alten*. Vol. 4. Edited by J.C. Gottsched. Leipzig: Breitkopf, 1743; reprint ed., Stuttgart: Metzler, 1973.

————. *Die stumme Schönheit*. Edited by Wolfgang Hecht. *Komedia: Deutsche Lustspiele vom Barock bis zur Gegenwart*, vol. 1. Berlin: Walter de Gruyter, 1962.

————. *Werke*. Vols. 1–3. Edited by Johann Heinrich Schlegel. Copenhagen and Leipzig: Christian Gottlob Prost und Rothens Erben, 1764–73; Reprint ed., Frankfurt am Main: Athenäum, 1971.

Schröder, Friedrich Ludwig. *Dramatische Werke*. 4 vols. Edited by E. von Bülow. Berlin: Reimer, 1831.

*Sturm und Drang: Kritische Schriften*. Edited by Erich Loewenthal and Lambert Schneider. Heidelberg: Schneider, 1972.

Sylvanus, Erwin. *Lessings Juden: Ein Lustspiel*. Frankfurt: Suhrkamp, 1979.

Theophrastus. *The Characters*. Translated by Philip Vellecott. Harmondsworth: Penguin Books, 1973.

Uhlich, Adam Gottfried. *Erste Sammlung neuer Lustspiele, welche theils übersetzt, theils selbst verfertiget hat.* Danzig and Leipzig: Johann Heinrich Rüdiger, 1746.

———. *Zweite Sammlung neuer Lustspiele, welche theils übersetzt, theils selbst verfertiget hat.* Danzig and Leipzig: Johann Heinrich Rüdiger, 1746.

———. *Der Unempfindliche.* In *Deutsche Schaubühne nach den Regeln und Mustern der Alten.* Vol. 6. Edited by J.C. Gottsched. Leipzig: Breitkopf, 1745; reprint ed., Stuttgart: Metzler, 1973.

Weise, Christian. *Bäurischer Machiavellus.* Edited by Werner Schubert. *Komedia: Deutsche Lustspiele vom Barock bis zur Gegenwart,* vol. 10. Berlin: Walter de Gruyter, 1966.

———. *Schauspiel vom Niederländischen Bauer.* Edited by Harald Burger. Stuttgart: Philipp Reclam Jun., 1969.

Weiße, Christian Felix. *Beyträge zum deutschen Theater.* 5 vols. Leipzig: Verlag der Dykischen Buchhandlung, 1759–68.

———. *Lustspiele.* Vol. 1. Karlsruhe: Schmieder, 1778.

———. *Lustspiele.* 3 vols. Leipzig: Verlag der Dykischen Buchhandlung, 1783.

von Zigler und Kliphausen, Heinrich Anshelm. *Die Asiatische Banise: oder Das bluthige — doch muthige Pegu.* Leipzig: Gleditsch, 1689; reprint ed., Munich: Winkler, 1965.

## SECONDARY LITERATURE

Aikin-Sneath, Betsy. *Comedy in Germany in the first half of the eighteenth century.* Oxford: Clarendon Press, 1936.

Appelbaum Graham, Ilse. "The Currency of Love: A Reading of Lessing's *Minna von Barnhelm.*" *German Life and Letters* 18 (1965) : 270–78.

Arntzen, Helmut. *Die ernste Komödie: Das deutsche Lustspiel von Lessing bis Kleist.* Munich: Nymphenburger Verlagsanstalt, 1968.

———. "Komödie und episches Theater." In *Wesen und Formen des Komischen im Drama,* edited by Reinhold Grimm and Klaus L. Berghahn, pp. 441–55. Wege der Forschung, vol. 62. Darmstadt: Wissenschaftliche Buchgesellschaft, 1975.

Auden, W.H. "Balaam and the Ass: The Master-Servant Relationship in Literature." *Thought* 29 (1954) : 237–70.

Beare, Mary. "Die Theorie der Komödie von Gottsched bis Jean Paul." Ph.D. dissertation, University of Bonn, 1927.

Böckmann, Paul. "Das Formprinzip des Witzes bei Lessing." In *Gotthold Ephraim Lessing,* edited by Gerhard and Sybille Bauer, pp. 176–95. Wege der Forschung, vol. 211. Darmstadt: Wissenschaftliche Buchgesellschaft, 1968.

Borden, Charles E. "The Original Model for Lessing's *Der junge Gelehrte.*" *University of California Publications in Modern Philology* 36 (1952) : 113–27.

Brüggemann, Diethelm. *Die sächsische Komödie: Studien zum Sprachstil.* Mitteldeutsche Forschungen, vol. 63. Cologne and Vienna: Böhlau, 1970.

Catholy, Eckehard. *Das deutsche Lustspiel.* Vol. 1: *Vom Mittelalter bis zum Ende der Barockzeit.* Stuttgart: Kohlhammer, 1969.

———. "Die deutsche Komödie vor Lessing." In *Die deutsche Komödie: Vom Mittelalter bis zur Gegenwart,* edited by Walter Hinck, pp. 32–48. Düsseldorf: Bagel, 1977.

Cohen, J.M. *A History of Western Literature.* London: Cassell, 1956.

Conn, Monique F. "Les Valets au théâtre entre 1740 et 1760." M.A. thesis, University of Alberta, 1972.

Conrady, K.O. "Zu den deutschen Plautusübertragungen. Ein Überblick von Albrecht von Eyb bis zu J.M.R. Lenz." *Euphorion* 48 (1954) : 373–96.

Coym, Johannes. *Gellerts Lustspiele: Ein Beitrag zur Entwicklungsgeschichte des deutschen Lustspiels.* Palaestra, vol. 2. Berlin: Mayer and Müller, 1899.

Duncan, Bruce. "Hand, Heart and Language in *Minna von Barnhelm.*" *Seminar* 8 (1972) : 15–30.

———. "The Implied Reader of Lessing's Theory of Comedy." *Lessing Yearbook* 10 (1978) : 35–45.

Dunkle, Harvey I. "Lessing's *Die Juden:* An Original Experiment." *Monatshefte* 49 (1957) : 323–29.

Durzak, Manfred. "Von der Typenkomödie zum ernsten Lustspiel. Zur Interpretation des *Jungen Gelehrten.*" In his *Poesie und Ratio: Vier Lessing-Studien,* pp. 9–43. Schriften zur Literatur, vol. 14. Bad Homburg: Athenäum, 1970.

Eggert, W. *Christian Weise und seine Bühne.* Germanisch und Deutsch, Studien zur Sprache und Kultur, vol. 9. Berlin: Walter de Gruyter, 1935.

Frenzel, Elisabeth. "Der überlegene Diener." In her *Motive der Weltliteratur: Ein Lexikon dichtungsgeschichtlicher Längsschnitte,* pp. 38–50. Stuttgart: Kröner, 1976.

Frenzel, Herbert A. *Geschichte des Theaters, 1470–1840: Daten und Dokumente.* Munich: Deutscher Taschenbuch Verlag, 1979.

Friederici, Hans. *Das deutsche bürgerliche Lustspiel der Frühaufklärung (1735–1750) unter besonderer Berücksichtigung seiner Anschauungen von der Gesellschaft.* Halle: Niemeyer, 1957.

Geißler, Waltraud. "Der Beitrag Johann Elias Schlegels zur Theorie und Praxis des Dramas in der deutschen Aufklärung." Ph. D. dissertation, University of Jena, 1968.

Greene, E.J.H. *Menander to Marivaux: The History of a Comic Structure.* Library of the *Canadian Review of Comparative Literature,* vol. 1. Edmonton: University of Alberta Press, 1977.

————. "Vieux, Jeunes et Valets dans la Comédie de Marivaux." *Cahiers de l'Association Internationale des Etudes Françaises* 25 (1973) : 177–90.

Grimm, Reinhold and Berghahn, Klaus L., eds. Foreword to *Wesen und Formen des Komischen im Drama,* pp. vii–xxx. Wege der Forschung, vol. 62. Darmstadt: Wissenschaftliche Buchgesellschaft, 1975.

Guthke, Karl S. *Geschichte und Poetik der deutschen Tragikomödie.* Göttingen: Vandenhoeck and Ruprecht, 1961.

————. "Lessings Problemkomödie *Die Juden.*" In *Wissen aus Erfahrungen: Festschrift Hermann Meyer,* edited by A. von Bormann, pp. 122–34. Tübingen: Niemeyer, 1976.

————. Postscriptum to *D. Faust. Die Matrone von Ephesus: Fragmente,* by G.E. Lessing, pp. 69–77. Stuttgart. Philipp Reclam Jun., 1968.

Haberland, Paul M. *The Development of Comic Theory in Germany During the Eighteenth Century.* Göppinger Arbeiten zur Germanistik, vol. 37. Göppingen: Kümmerle, 1971.

Hecht, W. *Christian Reuter.* Sammlung Metzler, vol. 46. Stuttgart: Metzler, 1966.

Heitmüller, Friedrich. *Hamburgische Dramatiker zur Zeit Gottscheds und ihre Beziehungen zu ihm.* Dresden: E. Pierson, 1891.

Heitner, Robert R. "Lessing's Manipulation of a Single Comic Theme." *Modern Language Quarterly* 18 (1957) : 183–98.

Hinck, Walter. *Das deutsche Lustspiel des 17. und 18. Jahrhunderts und die italienische Komödie: Commedia dell'arte und théâtre italien.* Germanische Abhandlungen, vol. 8. Stuttgart: Metzler, 1965.

————. "Das deutsche Lustspiel im 18. Jahrhundert." In *Das deutsche Lustspiel,* vol. I, edited by Hans Steffen, pp. 7–26. Kleine Vandenhoeckreihe, vol. 271 (S). Göttingen: Vandenhoeck and Ruprecht, 1968.

Holl, Karl. *Geschichte des deutschen Lustspiels.* Leipzig: J.J. Weber, 1923; reprint ed., Darmstadt: Wissenschaftliche Buchgesellschaft, 1964.

Immerwahr, Raymond. "J.E. Schlegel and Ludvig Holberg as creators and theorists of comedy." *Germanic Review* 13 (1938) : 175–89.

Jacobs, Jürgen. "Gellerts Dichtungstheorie." *Literaturwissenschaftliches Jahrbuch* 10 (1969) : 95–108.

————. Postscriptum to *Die Geistlichen auf dem Lande/Die Candidaten,* by J.C. Krüger, pp. 3*–22*. Frankfurt and Leipzig, 1743 and 1748; reprint ed., Stuttgart: Metzler, 1970.

John, David. "Marivaux' Harlequin: His influence on Johann Christian Krüger and German Comedy." *Seminar* 14 (1978) : 15–30.

————. "Problems of form and content in the comedies of Johann Christian Krüger." Ph.D. dissertation, University of Toronto, 1977.

Kinkel, Hans. *Lessings Dramen in Frankreich.* Darmstadt: Otto, 1908.

Koch, Hans-Albrecht. *Das deutsche Singspiel.* Sammlung Metzler, vol. 133. Stuttgart: Metzler, 1974.

Kommerell, Max. "Betrachtungen über die Commedia dell'arte." In his *Dichterische Welterfahrung: Essays,* edited by Hans-Georg Gadamer, pp. 159–73. Frankfurt am Main: Klostermann, 1952.

Lappert, Hans-Ulrich. *G.E. Lessings Jugendlustspiele und die Komödientheorie der frühen Aufklärung.* Zürich: Juris, 1968.

Lessing, Karl Gotthelf. *Gotthold Ephraim Lessings Leben, nebst seinem noch übrigen litterarischen Nachlaß.* Vol. I. Berlin: Voß, 1793.

Lukács, Györgi. *Sämtliche Werke.* Vol. 7: *Deutsche Literatur in zwei Jahrhunderten.* Neuwied and Berlin: Luchterhand, 1964.

Markwardt, B. *Geschichte der deutschen Poetik.* Vol. 2: *Aufklärung, Rokoko, Sturm und Drang.* Grundriß der Germanischen Philologie, vol. 13/II. Berlin: Walter de Gruyter, 1956.

Martini, Fritz. "Johann Elias Schlegel: *Die stumme Schönheit.*" In his *Lustspiele — und das Lustspiel,* pp. 37–63. Stuttgart: Klett, 1974.

————. "Riccaut, die Sprache und das Spiel in Lessings Lustspiel *Minna von Barn-helm.*" In *Gotthold Ephraim Lessing,* edited by Gerhard and Sybille Bauer, pp. 376–426. Wege der Forschung, vol. 211. Darmstadt: Wissenschaftliche Buch-gesellschaft, 1968.

Martino, A. *Geschichte der dramatischen Theorien in Deutschland im 18. Jahrhundert.* Vol. 1: *Die Dramaturgie der Aufklärung.* Translated by W. Pross. Studien zur deutschen Literatur, vol. 32. Tübingen: Niemeyer, 1972.

Mayer, Hans. *Außenseiter.* Frankfurt am Main: Suhrkamp, 1977.

Metzger, Michael M. *Lessing and the Language of Comedy.* Studies in German Litera-ture, vol. 8. The Hague: Mouton, 1966.

Michael, Friedrich. *Geschichte des deutschen Theaters.* Stuttgart: Reclam, 1969.

Müller, Klaus-Detleff. "Das Erbe der Komödie im bürgerlichen Trauerspiel. Lessings *Emilia Galotti* und die commedia dell'arte." *Deutsche Vierteljahresschrift* 46 (1972): 28–60.

Müller, Norbert. "Die poetische Gerechtigkeit im deutschen Lustspiel der Auf-klärung." Ph.D. dissertation, University of Mainz, 1969.

Nicoll, Allardyce. *A History of English Drama.* Vol. 2: *Early Eighteenth Century Drama.* 3d ed. Cambridge: University Press, 1952.

Oehlke, Waldemar. *Lessing und seine Zeit.* 2 vols. Munich: Beck, 1919.

Paulsen, Wolfgang. *Johann Elias Schlegel und die Komödie.* Bern: Francke, 1977.

Pazarkaya, Yüksel. *Die Dramaturgie des Einakters: Der Einakter als eine besondere Erscheinungsform im deutschen Drama des 18. Jahrhunderts.* Göppinger Arbeiten zur Germanistik, vol. 69. Göppingen: Kümmerle, 1973.

Petsch, Robert. *"Die Matrone von Ephesus.* Ein dramatisches Bruchstück von Les-sing." *Dichtung und Volkstum (Euphorion,* new series) 41 (1941): 87–95.

Potter, Harold. "Johann Friedrich von Cronegk." Ph.D. dissertation, University of Zürich, 1950.

Prang, Helmut. *Geschichte des Lustspiels von der Antike bis zur Gegenwart.* Stuttgart: Kröner, 1968.

Ramondt, Marie. "Between laughter and humour in the eighteenth century." *Neo-philologus* 40 (1956): 128–38.

Reden-Esbek, F.J. Freiherr von. *Caroline Neuber und ihre Zeitgenossen.* Leipzig: Göschen, 1881.

Reichel, Eugen. *Gottsched.* 2 vols. Berlin: Gottsched-Verlag, 1908–12.

Rempel, Hans. *Tragödie und Komödie im dramatischen Schaffen Lessings.* Neue Forschung, vol. 26. Berlin: Junker and Dünnhaupt, 1935.

Rentschler, Robert E. "Lessing's Fragmented Norm: A Reexamination of *Der junge Gelehrte.*" *Germanic Review* 50 (1975) : 165–83.

———. "Lisette, the Laugher." *Lessing Yearbook* 10 (1978) : 46–64.

Richel, Veronica C. *Luise Gottsched: A Reconsideration.* Europäische Hochschulschriften, series I, vol. 75. Bern and Frankfurt am Main: Lang, 1973.

Rieck, Werner. *Johann Christoph Gottsched: Eine kritische Würdigung seines Werkes.* Berlin: Akademie Verlag, 1972.

———. "Die Theorie des deutschen Lustspiels in der Periode von 1688 bis 1736." *Wissenschaftliche Zeitschrift der Pädagogischen Hochschule Potsdam* 9 (1965) : 27–39.

Rommel, Otto. "Die wissenschaftlichen Bemühungen um die Analyse des Komischen." In *Wesen und Formen des Komischen im Drama,* edited by Reinhold Grimm and Klaus L. Berghahn, pp. 1–36. Wege der Forschung, vol. 62. Darmstadt: Wissenschaftliche Buchgesellschaft, 1975.

Runte, Roseann. "The Matron of Ephesus in Eighteenth-Century France: The Lady and the Legend." *Studies in Eighteenth-Century Culture* 6 (1977) : 361–76.

Ruttkay, Kálmán G. "The crisis of English comedy in the early eighteenth century." In *Studies in Eighteenth-Century Literature,* edited by M.J. Szenczi and Laszló Ferenczi, pp. 83–115. Budapest: Academy of Sciences, 1974.

Schaer, Wolfgang. *Die Gesellschaft im deutschen bürgerlichen Drama des 18. Jahrhunderts: Grundlagen und Bedrohung im Spiegel der dramatischen Literatur.* Bonner Arbeiten zur deutschen Literatur, vol. 7. Bonn: Bouvier, 1963.

Schalk, Fritz. "Zur französischen Komödie der Aufklärung." In *Europäische Aufklärung: Festschrift Herbert Dieckmann,* edited by Hugo Friedrich and Fritz Schalk, pp. 247–59. Munich: Fink, 1967.

Scherpe, Klaus R. *Gattungspoetik im 18. Jahrhundert.* Stuttgart: Metzler, 1968.

Schlegel, August Wilhelm von. *Vorlesungen über dramatische Kunst und Literatur.* Edited by G.V. Amoretti. Vol. 2. Bonn and Leipzig: Schröder, 1923.

Schlegel, Friedrich. "Über Lessing" (1797). In *Gotthold Ephraim Lessing,* edited by Gerhard and Sybille Bauer, pp. 8–35. Wege der Forschung, vol. 211. Darmstadt: Wissenschaftliche Buchgesellschaft, 1968.

Schmidt, Erich. *Lessing: Geschichte seines Lebens und seiner Schriften.* 2 vols. Berlin: Weidmann, 1899.

Schreiber, S.E. *The German Woman in the Age of Enlightenment: A Study in the Drama from Gottsched to Lessing.* Columbia German Studies. Morningside Heights, New York: King's Crown Press, 1948.

Schröder, Jürgen. "Lessing: *Minna von Barnhelm.*" In *Die deutsche Komödie: Vom Mittelalter bis zur Gegenwart,* edited by Walter Hinck, pp. 49–65. Düsseldorf: Bagel, 1977.

————. "Das parabolische Geschehen der *Minna von Barnhelm.*" *Deutsche Vierteljahresschrift* 43 (1969) : 222–59.

Schulz, Ursula. *Lessing auf der Bühne: Chronik der Theateraufführungen 1748–1789.* Repertorien zur Erforschung der frühen Neuzeit, vol. 2. Bremen and Wolfenbüttel: Jacobi, 1977.

Staiger, Emil. "Ein vergessenes Lustspiel [J.E. Schlegel: *Die stumme Schönheit*]." In *Beirtäge zum zwanzigjährigen Bestehen der Neuen Schauspiel A.G.,* pp. 67–74. Zürich, n.d.

————. "Lessing's *Minna von Barnhelm.*" Translated by Sylvia P. Jenkins. *German Life and Letters* 1 (1948) : 260–71.

Steffen, Hans. "Die Form des Lustspiels bei Johann Elias Schlegel: Ein Beitrag zur Lustspielform der deutschen Frühaufklärung." *Germanisch-Romanische Monatsschrift* 42 (new series 11) (1961) : 413–31.

Steinmetz, Horst. "Der Harlekin: Seine Rolle in der deutschen Komödientheorie und -dichtung des 18. Jahrhunderts." *Neophilologus* 50 (1966) : 95–106.

————. *Die Komödie der Aufklärung.* Sammlung Metzler, vol. 47. Stuttgart: Metzler, 1966.

————. "*Minna von Barnhelm* oder die Schwierigkeit, ein Lustspiel zu verstehen." In *Wissen aus Erfahrungen: Fest schrift Hermann Meyer,* edited by A. von Bormann, pp. 135–53. Tübingen: Niemeyer, 1976.

————. Postscriptum to *Die deutsche Schaubühne nach den Regeln und Mustern der Alten,* edited by J.C. Gottsched, vol. 6, pp. 1*–20*. Leipzig: Breitkopf, 1740–45; reprint ed., Stuttgart: Metzler, 1973.

Stoffel, Hans. "Die Wirkung Molières auf die Entfaltung des deutschen Lustspiels der Aufklärung bis zu Lessings *Minna von Barnhelm.*" Ph.D. dissertation, University of Heidelberg, 1954.

Strohschneider-Kohrs, Ingrid. "Die überwundene Komödiantin in Lessings Lustspiel." *Wolfenbütteler Studien zur Aufklärung* 2 (1975) : 182–99.

Sturz, Helferich Peter. "Vom Theater und den Schauspielern" (1767). In *Kleine Schriften*, edited by F. Blei, pp. 84–92. Leipzig: Insel Verlag, 1904.

Tisch, J.H. *J.C. Gottsched (1700–1766): seine dramatische Theorie und Praxis zwischen Barock und Aufklärung.* Hobart: University of Tasmania Press, 1966.

Torbrügge, Marylin. *J.C. Gottsched.* Sammlung Metzler, vol. 125. Stuttgart: Metzler, 1974.

Ure, Peter. "The Widow of Ephesus: Reflections on an International Comic Theme." *The Durham University Journal* 49 (1956) : 1–9.

Van Cleve, John Walter. *Harlequin Besieged: The Reception of Comedy in Germany during the Early Enlightenment.* New York University Ottendorfer Series, new series, vol. 13. Bern, Frankfurt am Main, Las Vegas: Lang, 1980.

Van den Boom, Rüdiger. *Die Bedienten und das Herr–Diener Verhältnis in der deutschen Komödie der Aufklärung (1742–1767).* Frankfurt am Main: Haag & Herchen, 1979.

Van Stockum, Theodor C. "Lessings Dramenentwurf *Die Matrone von Ephesus.*" *Neophilologus* 46 (1962) : 125–34.

Waters, Michael. "Frau Gottsched's *Die Pietisterey im Fischbein-Rocke:* Original, adaptation or translation?" *Forum for Modern Language Studies* 11 (1975) : 252–67.

Wicke, Günter. *Die Struktur des deutschen Lustspiels der Aufklärung: Versuch einer Typologie.* Abhandlungen zur Kunst-, Musik- und Literaturwissenschaft, vol. 26. Bonn: Bouvier, 1965.

Wiedemann, Conrad. "Polyhistors Glück und Ende. Von Daniel Georg Morhof zum jungen Lessing." In *Festschrift Gottfried Weber*, edited by H.O. Burger and K. von See, vol. 1, pp. 215–35. Frankfurter Beiträge zur Germanistik, vol. 1. Bad Homburg: Gehlen, 1967.

Wilkinson, Elizabeth M. *J.E. Schlegel: A German Pioneer in Aesthetics.* Oxford: University Press, 1945.

Wolf, Peter. *Die Dramen J.E. Schlegels: Ein Beitrag zur Geschichte des Dramas im achtzehnten Jahrhundert.* Züricher Beiträge zur deutschen Literatur und Geistesgeschichte, vol. 22. Zürich: Atlantis, 1964.

Wölfel, Kurt. "Moralische Anstalt. Zur Dramaturgie von Gottsched bis Lessing." In *Deutsche Dramentheorien*, edited by Reinhold Grimm, vol. 1, pp. 45–122. Frankfurt am Main: Athenäum, 1971.

Zander, C.G. "Christian Felix Weiße und die Bühne: Ein Beitrag zur Theatergeschichte des 18. Jahrhunderts." Ph.D. dissertation, University of Mainz, 1949.

# INDEX